MISSION
and
SPIRITUALITY

CREATIVE WAYS
OF BEING CHURCH

Papers read at the biennial conference of the
British and Irish Association for Mission Studies
at the University of Cardiff,
June 2001

Editors
Howard Mellor & Timothy Yates

**CLIFF COLLEGE
PUBLISHING**

ISBN 1 898362 28 9
© 2002 Cliff College Publishing

British Library Cataloguing in Publication Data.
A catalogue record for this book is available
from the British Library.

**Cliff College Publishing,
Calver, Hope Valley, Nr Sheffield S32 3XG**

Printed by:

MOORLEY'S Print & Publishing

23 Park Rd., Ilkeston, Derbys DE7 5DA
Tel/Fax: (0115) 932 0643

from data supplied on disk

CONTENTS

The British and Irish Association for Mission Studies is an inter-confessional body founded in 1990 as a forum for both academic teachers and missionary practitioners and others interested in mission.

It publishes a twice-yearly newsletter and holds day conferences and biennial residential conferences.

Details of membership can be obtained from the Secretary,
C/o The Henry Martyn Centre,
Westminster College,
Cambridge CB3 OAA
or from the website
http://www.martynmission.cam.ac.uk/BIAMSConf.htm

CONTRIBUTORS

John Burgess is a minister of the United Reform Church, working in the Bloomsbury Mission Project in Birmingham

Michael Crowley had served with the South American Mission Society in Chile before becoming Development Officer of the Centre for Anglican Communion Studies in the University of Birmingham and a lecturer in the Selly Oak Colleges.

Saunders Davies is Bishop of Bangor in the Church of Wales. He has written a Welsh commentary on St Luke's gospel *Y Daith Anorfod* (1993).

Craig Gardiner is engaged in doctoral studies at the University of Cardiff, where he is a part-time teacher in the department of Religious Studies, having trained for Baptist ministry at South Wales Baptist College.

David Hay is a retired zoology lecturer from the University of Nottingham with a special interest in religious and spiritual experience, who is based at the Centre for the Study of Religions of the university.

Robert Kaggwa is a Ugandan Roman Catholic theologian who teaches at the Missionary Institute in North London. He has studied at the Gregorian University in Rome, at Tübingen and Toulouse.

Laurenti Magesa is a Tanzanian Roman Catholic theologian, who has been appointed William Paton Research Fellow in the University of Birmingham.

Brian Stanley is a Fellow of St Edmund's College, Cambridge and Director of the Henry Martyn Centre. He has acted as Director of the Currents in World Christianity project in the Faculty of Divinity. His publications include the *History of the Baptist Missionary Society* (1992) and he has co-edited *The Church Mission Society and World Christianity 1799-1999* (2000).

Esther de Waal is a recognised Anglican authority on Benedictine and Celtic spirituality. Her works include *A life giving way: commentary on the Rule of St. Benedict* (1995) and *The Celtic Way of Prayer* (1996).

Pete Ward is a lecturer in Youth Ministry and Theological Education at King's College, London and has acted as Archbishop of Canterbury's adviser on youth ministry. He is author of *God at the Mall* (1999).

FOREWORD

We were jointly responsible for the production of *Mission – an invitation to God's future* (2000), in which the main papers were given by Professors Jürgen Moltmann, Theo Sundermeier and Anton Wessels. The book, which originated in a BIAMS conference, was well received. It was listed by *Missiology* in their 'essential' purchases for libraries specialising in mission publications, and the review in the *Expository Times* called much of the content 'very good indeed' and 'exactly the kind of theological writing which can inspire the ministerial general practitioner', certainly part of the motive in its production. We have agreed happily to produce a further book of this kind.

Between the conference which resulted in the first book and its successor, a day consultation was mounted in Birmingham to consider 'The Spirituality of the Unchurched'. Dr David Hay has kindly agreed to his paper at that meeting being included here and it provides an essential background to *Mission and Spirituality – Creative Ways of Being Church.* The result of his extensive research, with his co-worker Kate Hunt, as also of the work of Sir Alister Hardy to which he refers, is to suggest that human beings are 'hard-wired' to be religious. Dr Hay wants to turn Feuerbach's questions back on the philosopher, as a result of what he found empirically through many discussions with individuals, who have beliefs and often pray but outside the churches: far from God being a projection of human needs, it is part of the nature of human beings to reach out to some kind of beyond, an implanted and inescapable characteristic.

Colin Greene, invited as a respondent from the Bible Society, confirmed this from personal experience, when he told us of his meetings with a divorced ex Roman Catholic whose spiritual quest was second only to his ten year old son in order of priority. Here was a man who had outgrown the Christian story as learned from his days as an altar boy who, without overt reference to Nietzsche, saw himself as 'beyond good and evil' and 'part of a vast spiritual quest that involved the pedagogy of the whole human race by some unknown force we called God'. Religion, in such circles, is out, with its outmoded meta-narratives, according to current perception: spirituality is in, because (Greene) 'it pertains to the individual and hence private quest for some sense of meaning and purpose to life'.

Under these conditions, religion 'means a sort of private, inchoate vocabulary, whereby mainly inarticulate individuals struggle to make sense of highly complex phenomena called spirituality'.

It was against this background that the present set of papers was planned. In Greene's terms again, the Church of inherited Christendom faces 'a deepening cycle of decline' but the issue to be faced is 'the challenging and exciting process of simply re-inventing the church'. The title of this book, *Mission and Spirituality – Creative Ways of Being Church*, had a considered background: the recognition that for many modern seekers, strongly affirming the spiritual, what Pete Ward calls here 'heavy church' with its traditional approach does not connect with felt needs and (Greene) 'will remain largely an irrelevance to their spiritual quest and aspirations unless there is a radical ground breaking change in every aspect of institutional life'.

The association (BIAMS) was invited to the University of Cardiff by Professor Paul Ballard in summer 2001. Here Saunders Davies, Bishop of Bangor in the Church of Wales, linked his opening address to Jürgen Moltmann's emphasis on life in the previous book. The Welsh people, a people of long-standing spirituality which went back to their Celtic saints, though historically an oppressed people by the dominant English, had retained a spirituality shaped by Trinitarian belief and strong values, expressed in community as a reflection of Trinitarian life. Welsh poets expressed these realities: 'we fought and were always in retreat' (R.S. Thomas) but, equally, 'look for the diamonds in débris. Thank God for all his mystery and live!' (Gwyneth Lewis).

Two African theologians added a welcome emphasis on *oikoumene*: Robert Kaggwa from Uganda gave a lively and vital systematic theologian's approach to 'Mission and the Spirit'. He was, as in his sub-title, 'searching for a theology of the Spirit' and so 'leading us to respond actively and as a community in contemporary Britain and Ireland'. His introduction recalled the Canberra meeting of the WCC in 1991, and the attempt there to relate Australian aboriginal spirituality to the Spirit by way of Korean *shamanism*, with a prayer from the Korean theologian, Chung Hyung Kyung, on 'letting ourselves go' towards 'the rhythm of life', matters which had deeply offended the participants from the Orthodox Church. This presentation raised the crucial question of *discernment*, in New Testament terms, the need to 'test the spirits, whether they are of God' (1 John 4:1). Dr Kaggwa, who noticed in passing Kirsteen Kim's paper in the earlier book on David Bosch's approach to the Holy Spirit, helped participants to understand the context of post-modernity and fragmentation within pluralism, while also describing what he termed 'trajectories of the Spirit', which could be discerned from Scripture and contemporary Christian thought, what he called communities of 'relational knowing' and forms of modern creativity: 'discernment will be necessary ... but let us not be cautious ... in such a way that we stifle the Spirit of God'.

Laurenti Magesa found that, in Tanzania, it was just this caution which was stifling life. The Small Church Communities (SCC's) were seen as threatening by ecclesiastical authority. Once again, discernment was needed. The frightening example of Credonia Mwerinde and the Movement for the Restoration of the Ten Commandments in Uganda, which ended with the sect being burned alive in March 2000, showed how easily a movement from below could result in tragedy. Despite such aberrations, Dr Magesa saw the need for making space for SCC's, AIC's and other groups towards the inculturation of the gospel in Tanzania and elsewhere.

These two African contributions provided an example of the two basic themes of the present book. 'Mission and Spirituality' has led within it to very different approaches to the spiritual. The necessary undergirding of a theology of the Holy Spirit, the Celtic way in the Welsh tradition (Saunders Davies) and at large (Esther de Waal, John Burgess); Benedictine spirituality, as practised in South Africa; a spirituality of missionary activism in the great pioneer William Carey in India (Brian Stanley); the kind of neo-monasticism pre-figured in Dietrich Bonhoeffer's writings about Finkelwalde and the contemporary experience at the Iona community (Craig Gardner); the community under Methodist auspices of the Amelia Farm Trust, where young offenders are rehabilitated and given hard manual work to do in a rural setting, whose farming director and Methodist minister provided a fascinating case study and told us that 'theologically I feel close to 'Creation Theology' and a style of church working that talks and preaches less but listens more' (John Stacy Marks).

Fundamental to the book's intention has been the question of the re-shaping of the church's life in response to the modern predicament, here handled most radically and in a highly stimulating form by Pete Ward in 'Liquid Church': but also by reference to the SCC's in Tanzania and the base communities (CEB's) of Latin America, described by the late Michael Crowley in his substantial treatment of both Roman Catholic and Pentecostal ecclesial realities. It is interesting that, as with the opening paper on the Welsh tradition, it was to the Trinitarian model that Dr Crowley returned, both as a 'critical principle' against which to measure Christian community and its institutional formation and as the theological core to understanding mission to a whole society, in which 'churches as communion possess a high vocational mission', confronted however with great obstacles. This last comment provided a common description of the churches in Wales, East Africa, Latin America and Western Europe generally.

We hope that this collection of reflections from very different perspectives, by thinkers and practitioners in widely different settings, will form a contribution toward shaping the mind of the Church towards the future of its mission in a new century and new millennium.

Howard Mellor

Timothy Yates

Editors' Note: Since this conference in June 2001, the Revd Dr Michael Crowley has been tragically drowned when on holiday in the Canary Islands. We express our deep sympathy to Mrs Crowley and his family in their loss and our gratitude for the high quality of Dr Crowley's contribution to this collection.

Acknowledgements: The editors acknowledge with gratitude permission to reproduce Welsh poetry given by Professor Norma Rinsler of *Modern Poetry in Translation* (King's College, London) and by the Gomer Press.

PART I

MISSION AND SPIRITUALITY

THE SPIRITUALITY OF THE UNCHURCHED
David Hay

Some statistics

Philip Richter and Leslie Francis have shown us in their book *Gone but not Forgotten* (Richter & Francis, 1998), that it is not quite accurate to say of most people in Britain that they are entirely 'unchurched'. However, it cannot be denied that an increasing number, especially in the under-forty age group, are very remote indeed from the Christian institutions. Others are detaching themselves from the mainstream churches at an alarming rate. The UK Christian Handbook *Religious Trends 1999/2000* notes that regular Church attendance in Britain fell from 4.74 million in 1989 to 3.71 million in 1998; a drop of more than 20% in ten years. Rather less than 8% of the population are likely to be in church on an average Sunday.

The figures I have just quoted are well known to you. Here are some less well-known statistics concerning report of religious or spiritual experience. They cover approximately the same period as the data I quoted for declining church attendance. In 1987 Gordon Heald (at that time director of Gallup Poll in this country) and I published the results of a survey of reports of such experience in

Britain. They showed that 48% of the national sample felt they were personally aware of this kind of experience in their lives. Just thirteen years later, in June of this year, we obtained the results of a repeat survey, which we did in conjunction with the BBC's recent *Soul of Britain* series. These suggest that more than 76% of the national population would admit to having had a spiritual or religious experience. That is to say, in not much more than a decade there has been almost a 60% rise in the positive response rate to questions about this subject. The great majority of these people are of course not regular churchgoers.

The commonest kind of experience reported in Britain is the recognition of a transcendent providence: a patterning of events in a person's life that convinces them that in some strange way those events were meant to happen. In our recent survey 55% of the national sample recognised this in their own lives. That is a 90% rise compared to the response when the question was asked in 1987. Many people feel they have been aware of the presence of God. We know from our research that this can often be when they are deeply distressed. They tell us that the experience of God's presence helps them to bear their suffering. At the other end of the scale, people talk of being aware of God when they are very happy. In the latest poll, 38% of the sample said they had personal awareness of such a divine presence - a 41% rise on thirteen years ago. In great unhappiness or fear many people, including those who are uncertain about God's existence, turn for help to prayer. A total of 37% of those recently questioned feel they have received such help - a 40% increase on 1987.

Another commonly reported experience is an awareness of a sacred presence in nature, rather like William Wordsworth's description of a presence that "rolls through all things" in his lines written above Tintern Abbey. A total of 29% of the sample felt that they had had this kind of experience - an 81% rise since 1987. A surprisingly large number of people, 25% of the national sample, feel they have been in touch with someone who has died - this is a 38% rise since 1987. More ominously, a quarter of all the people interviewed feel they have been aware of an evil presence - a rise of over 100%. The dramatic increase in positive response rates to all these questions since 1987 took us by surprise. The figures are startling if only because our lengthy research experience tells us that people are very shy about admitting to spiritual experience. This makes it even more remarkable that the responses were obtained in the relatively uncongenial circumstances of a national telephone poll.

Spirituality as a human phenomenon

My guess is that in reality there has been no great change over the past few years in the frequency with which people encounter the spiritual dimension of their lives. What is probably changing is people's sense of the degree of social permission for such experience. Somehow or other (perhaps through the influence of postmodernism) there is a growing feeling that it is acceptable to admit to such awareness, though it is still something most people feel quite deeply embarrassed about.

I am myself a zoologist by training and my opinions are based on a theoretical perspective on human spirituality drawn from the work of the zoologist Alister Hardy (1966). Hardy believed that what he called "religious experience" is biologically natural to us and has evolved through the process of natural selection because it has survival value. To those of us who have religious belief, and I count myself in that group, I need to make a comment here about perspective. I am talking about a naturalistic basis for spirituality and you may feel that I am taking up a rather familiar reductionist sociobiological stance. In his book *Theology and Social Theory*, John Milbank (1993) mounts a strong attack on the submissiveness of theologians to what he calls 'secular reason' in the study of religion. "The pathos of modern theology", says Milbank,

> ...is its false humility. For theology this must be a fatal disease, because once theology surrenders its claim to be a metadiscourse, it cannot any longer articulate the word of the creator God, but is bound to turn into the oracular voice of some finite idol, such as historical scholarship, humanist psychology, or transcendental philosophy [or he might have added, "evolutionary biology"] (Milbank, p.1)

I think Milbank is right in so far as scholarship is used in an arrogant way to dismiss religion. But Hardy was not a dismissive critic of religion. He was, if you like, inside the camp, concerned with what it is about our human nature that enables us to be religious or spiritual in the first place. In fact the perspective he adopted can be seen as protecting religion since if he is right it is not possible to dismiss spirituality as "nothing but" cultural construction. If Hardy is right, spirituality has its roots in what we are as biological organisms.

Research so far shows that Hardy's hypothesis is highly resilient when tested against other reductionist naturalistic accounts such as those of Marx, Freud and Durkheim (Hay, 1994). I need to add however that the hypothesis amounts to a claim that religious awareness is "hard-wired" into the human organism. Hence, it cannot be limited to members of any particular religion or indeed religious people in general. Everybody, including people who hold no religious beliefs whatsoever, must be at least potentially in possession of such awareness. There is such a thing as secular spirituality. I therefore propose to replace Hardy's term with "spiritual awareness" to cover all these cases, whilst recognizing that from a religious perspective it is this natural awareness that makes religious experience possible in the first place. I would add from my Christian point of view that another way of putting this is to say that God the Holy Spirit communicates with all of Creation. From this perspective one might see the mission of the Church as to be alert to - and be in tune with - the ways in which God is already in touch with everybody, inside or outside the Church.

Researching spirituality outside the Church

The statistics I quoted at the beginning of this talk were gathered as part of a programme of research designed to try to understand the spiritual life of people who never go to church. Two years ago my colleague Kate Hunt and I started conversing with some of them about their spirituality and how it relates to their understanding of the religious institutions. The way we did this was to employ the services of a London based polling organisation, the *Opinion Research Business* (ORB), founded by Gordon Heald. ORB identified a sample of Nottingham people who fitted two criteria (a) they never went to Church (b) they felt that in some way they were nevertheless spiritual or religious. We divided these people into four focus groups each containing eight people, structured according to our preconceptions about likely differences between different social groups. Thus, one focus group was made up of people less than 40 years of age, another of people who were over forty. This was because of an intuition we had that this age marks a kind of cultural watershed between a time when most people had at least a minimal religious education and today, when most people probably have very little knowledge of religion. One of the remaining focus groups was made up of women, the other of men; again, on the assumption that there might be gender differences on matters of spiritual and religious belief.

We filmed and audio-taped the conversations with each of the focus groups and followed that up with tape-recorded private conversations with each of the individuals in the groups. Since then we have been immersing ourselves in the data. The essence of qualitative research is the way it reveals subtle and complex phenomena in relation to the individuality of those people being studied. In a short talk I cannot go into that satisfactorily. Nevertheless, I want to try to share some 'headlines' with you, emphasising in particular what people had to say about their personal faith and about the Church.

Some aspects of personal faith

Timidity

People are very timid when it comes to talking about religion. Nevertheless, we feel now that we were too conservative in insisting that those we spoke with ought at least to claim to be either spiritual or religious. Almost anybody who didn't go to church would have been suitable. All those we spoke to, without exception, had an easily recognizable personal faith, though it was characteristic of most research conversations that this only became clear towards the end, when it was felt safe to do so. Quite often as the person sensed that the conversation was coming to a close, they would ask us about our own beliefs and experience. By this point it had become sufficiently obvious that we were not intending either to criticise or to convert them. A simple and honest response in terms of our personal religious life often led to a further and vivid account of experience on the part of those with whom we were in conversation. But the necessary precursor for this was absolute clarity that we were researchers, *not* evangelists.

Individuals, in Quest Mode

There are two important riders to add. Firstly, there is the overwhelming evidence that everybody's spirituality is unique, relating as it does to the highly individual life histories, personalities and cultural contexts in which they grew to maturity. Any effort at classification, (and of course that is necessary if one is to attempt to make general statements), has to be in the light of this individuality. Secondly, the way many conversations developed suggested that most people's spirituality is in what

Daniel Batson (1993) calls the 'Quest Mode'. People sometimes said explicitly that they were on a journey following a route that was not clear, or as on person put it 'It is like a foggy day.' Their search was dynamic. Even as each conversation developed it was often obvious that a rethinking was going on. It is important to add that of course this was a two way process. We ourselves were constantly changing our understanding as we listened to what people were saying to us. There is no other way for open-minded research to proceed, or, I would add, for us as researchers to be open to the working of the Holy Spirit.

The Christian God and the Generic God

Having emphasised the quest, I also need to say that the parameters within which people expressed their spirituality were broadly speaking those of the Christian metanarrative with varying proportions of ideas drawn from other sources (e.g. Eastern religions, spiritualism, paganism, science fiction etc.). Some people, particularly those in the older age group, spoke in a consciously Christian manner about their spirituality. Their statements of belief were doctrinally no different from those of the average churchgoer, and in some cases, more sophisticated. For this small group the only recognizable feature that differentiated them was their choice to be absent from the pews on a Sunday. Behind this refusal there was often a history of painful mistreatment by one or other of the religious institutions.

On the other hand when most people said they believed in God, this was a 'generic' God rather than the Trinitarian God of Christianity. References to Jesus tended to come only from people who had had a childhood background in Christianity, but even they were unsure of their doctrine as the following quotation from 'Emma' illustrates: [talking about believing in Jesus]

"Yes, yeh, um, I think that's quite a difficult really, yes, he does, yeh, I mean because I believe in the um, you know, in Jesus as such, he came down and, I don't necessarily understand it, but I, you know, believe it to have happened as such. I wouldn't be able to pinpoint a role for him at the moment you know, I don't quite know what he's doing now, what he's got on his c.v. as such, but yes I do.

The confusion and evident embarrassment, covered over by humour, is very characteristic and suggests the strength of the taboo on talking about religion in contemporary culture.

'Something There'

Another much larger group offered the commonest response of all, in that they were uneasy about saying anything positive about their spiritual experience, beyond the conviction that there is 'something there', and sometimes adding that it matters very much that it is there. In fact 'something there' was so commonly used that we are thinking of drawing on it as the title of the book we are writing about our research. At one level this refusal suggests a widespread suspicion about the adequacy of traditional theological language to describe our experience of God, perhaps not surprising after 300 years of sustained critique of religion within European culture.

Sophisticated religious people might be inclined to dismiss such vague talk, but another way of looking at it is to see it as falling into the apophatic tradition, seeking to approach God through refusing to make positive statements about the divine. There is a good deal of evidence that behind this approach lies not only a suspicion or resentment of religious doctrine in general, but annoyance about cut and dried answers which seem to deny the mysteriousness of life. This came out particularly in 'James' who spoke of that which he encounters as 'deeper than God' and of his communion with this as 'more profound than prayer'. James had gone up to university to study theology but given up in disgust at what he saw as the hypocrisy of his fellow students (and perhaps the staff). He is not the first person to do this. He reminded me of William James' father, Henry James the elder, who quit his studies at Princeton Theological Seminary during the mid-Nineteenth Century, because it wasn't religious enough.

Self constructed theologies

Another kind of response comes particularly from people in the under forty age group who have grown up isolated from direct contact with the religious institution. They construct a theology of their own, quite often using fragments of the Christian metanarrative that are available to them. 'Stephanie' is an example. She had discovered New Age teachings during her search for meaning and she spoke with strong conviction of the importance of meditation and of being in connection with the 'Universal Consciousness'. Her beliefs had remarkable similarities to traditional Christian beliefs and practices but they were expressed in different language. For example Stephanie's concept of Universal Consciousness seemed to be similar to the Christian understanding of the Holy Spirit; a presence that connected everyone and everything in the universe:

> I have experienced vast chasms of empty loneliness ... and getting in touch with the universal consciousness is like being in touch with everyone else who's out there. Um and it's like filling yourself up with that, um, to take that feeling away.

Later on in the conversation, Stephanie spoke about the importance of forgiveness in her own life:

> And I think one of the hardest things was learning to send my love and forgiveness to people who had done things that had caused me pain. ... What you put out you'll get back tenfold. The universe will look after me. The universe will look after them. If they've done something bad to me, the universe will take care of them, not me, it's not my place. I mean your God as you call him, like vengeance is mine, sayeth the Lord, well it's that theory, but in my words, is the universe will take care of it, I don't.

Theodicy

Traditionally, God is seen as almighty, omnipotent, omniscient. God is also seen as male and, especially amongst men, punitive. He is the transcendent God who saves and redeems his people, but also condemns. This idea of God poses grave difficulties for people on the periphery or outside of the Christian faith. The issue appears to be primarily to do with theodicy. One of the questions in our recent national survey was put in the following way: "Some people don't think there is a God. Why do you think this is?" The largest single group by quite a long way, 41% of the national sample, agreed with the alternative which stated "There is too much suffering, poverty and injustice in the world for God to exist". It is often thought that the advent of the scientific attitude is the major stumbling block to religious faith. But the number of people concerned about theodicy was almost double the size of the group suggesting that loss of belief was because 'science has explained the mysteries of life'.

The figures for the national sample are fully supported by the content of our research conversations. Traditional monotheism is still the natural religious assumption for the ordinary person in the street, but the idea has been watered down to mean not much more than that God will intervene if my relatives or I get into difficulty. People speak of God helping their families at the same time as having difficulty in believing in God because of all the disasters in the world. Here is 'Steven' (whose wife is a practising Catholic) talking about homeless people:

> ... this is, this is somewhere where um, God could do more if he could. If there was somebody um, he'd look after everybody in the world. But, um, if he's that good, then why is there so much suffering? [Does that make it hard for you to believe in God?] Yeah, I think it does. Um, I suppose I believe in him in a, in a small sort of way whereas um, like he's looking after my children and the children's schools and sort of, um, all the Catholic friends what, you know, um that we have, that we know. But then again, like I say, there's that much suffering and pain in the world that, maybe, you know, there isn't, there isn't a God.

So God has shrunk down to become a 'household god', looking after an individual's family, but not able to intervene in a wider context. In some cases there is the suggestion that this household god is different from the remote and frightening creator God.

The Church and Churchgoers

Criticism of the religious institution is the 'default mode' in public discourse. This was very clear in the focus groups when people were asked for their opinion of the Church. In fact the references to hypocrisy, bigotry, being out of touch and other critical clichés were boring in their repetitiousness. In private, where the social pressure to conform to stereotypical opinions was reduced, the negative critique was on the whole not so severe. Where it carried particular weight was when it came from someone who was personally devout but had ceased to attend church. Thus Mary, whose devotional life was thoroughly Christian (she spoke of her daily prayer, and how through prayer she had learned of the compassion of God, 'God is not a snooper') enumerated the defects of the Church as (a) obsession with control, (the church should be a servant), (b) living in the past (God is a God of the living, not the dead), (c) failure to be concerned with humanity as a whole - political commitment to the poor (collections for the poor of the world are mere tokenism!). Mary angrily pointed out that stopping going to church has nothing to do with losing faith; 'we need more religion now, not less'.

Inauthenticity was frequently cited as offputting. Sometimes this meant citing double standards on the part of churchgoers, expressed as a cloying 'niceness' (one man called it 'humble arrogance') in the context of the church, allied to doubtful behaviour in personal and professional life outside the church.

Remoteness from the institution combined with curiosity can lead to toe-curling embarrassment. 'Sharon' remembered one occasion when she did venture into the local parish church and felt terribly uncomfortable:

> But I think they ought to do like a church for beginners really, because if you're not used to going, because they always have communion here. [she goes on to explain how she was encouraged to go forward for Communion] It was a really awkward situation, do you know what I mean? And he was giving us the sip of the wine, and the um, and he beckoned us to bring the children up as well, and they give you, whatever it is they give you to eat. Is it rice paper?

There seemed to be no place for the 'beginner' and equally as serious, no place for the honest searcher. One of the most moving occasions during our research conversations was when people, usually towards the end of the chat, spoke of their personal search, and many of them were on the search. 'Colin' was burned up with anger at the institutional church, yet later on spoke wistfully of his longing for a plausible basis for belief. Another man explained sadly that he had been unable to find a church open enough to accept him as a searcher. One woman spoke for many when she said 'I think about it (the meaning of life) all the time', yet admitted that she talked about it to nobody else.

Two major dissuasives were operating. Firstly there was a general fear that opening a conversation with a member of the clergy would invite an embarrassing attempt to guide them into accepting Christian beliefs about which they were at best doubtful. People in general were put off by their perception of religious orthodoxy as requiring them to sign up to a list of beliefs. This came to a head on those occasions where contact with the church was sought, for example because of a desire to have an infant baptized. The ritual itself was acceptable, even strongly desired, but not the doctrinal accompaniment, at least when handed to them without discussion. The second dissuasive was fear of being laughed at by friends and colleagues. One woman cringed as she imagined the mockery, 'She's seen the light, haven't you Evelyn?' Amongst the men the fear was stronger still 'If my mates in the football club knew I was talking like this they'd think I was crazy.'

The social construction of masculinity certainly plays an important part here. Spirituality is for women, or if it is spoken about at all by men it happens only late at night, after having had too much to drink. 'Sean' spoke proudly of being too insensitive to get in touch with his spirituality, 'probably my brain cells have rotted from too much alcohol'.

Some reflections on mission

I take it that the audience I am addressing is made up largely of people who have had a theological education and who are professionally concerned with mission. I am by training an empirical scientist and my professional life has been spent almost entirely in universities. It follows that these reflections on the task of mission are offered from that limited outsider's perspective.

Reflecting on our images of God and the Church

A central theme for reflection on the part of those concerned with mission must be a detailed exploration of the nature of contemporary images of God and the Church. Almost all of those we spoke with are perfectly aware that anthropomorphic ideas of an old man in the sky are inadequate. I mentioned earlier that in general, people do not want to be explicit about God, sometimes for perfectly good 'apophatic' reasons. Nevertheless there is a strong undertow of doctrinal assumption in much of what people say, and some of these assumptions are problematic. Thus, for many of those we talked to, the immanence of God is more acceptable than God's transcendence. Sometimes of course this is a matter of 'taming' God, holding to a sentimental and cosy picture that is reassuring when existential panic sets in. This is tied in with an understanding of the function of the Church as over-whelmingly to offer comfort to people who are inadequate in some way, and to soothe the elderly as they face death. In fact this keys in to the 'deprivation' theory of religion (Beit-Hallahmi & Argyle, 1997); that people are religious because they are personally lacking in some way (poverty, loneliness, ill-health, social repression etc.). That in itself is a turn off.

The notion that religion could be challenging did not appear very often in our conversations. When it did, it was sometimes in the context of a maturing and growing beyond conventional faith. Thus people spoke to us about their spiritual life as going beyond God, and their communion with the sacred as being deeper than prayer. This suggests to me that the religious institution, in so far as it has reached them, has failed to offer a profound enough, serious enough understanding of the nature of the religious search. In particular I want to emphasise the question of theodicy which often seems to have been sidestepped. Yet as I mentioned earlier, it figures more heavily in people's minds as a dissuasive than any other factor.

Secularity as a social construction.

A major issue that has to be faced is the nature of social construction. My work in the field of religious and spiritual experience has brought me to the opinion that the standard Feuerbachian inversion, i.e. that human beings have constructed God (with all the subsequent consequences for current sociological and psychological explanations of religion) is itself a culturally constructed mistake. I say that we need to make a second inversion and assert that European Enlightenment ideas have constructed a secular world-view in such a way that wherever that culture has come to dominate, it has obscured the natural spirituality of the human species. Seen in that light, the postmodern movement is actually of considerable help to Christian mission, because of course it suggests that it is possible to deconstruct secularism in exactly the same way that secular theorists have tried to deconstruct religion.

Individualism versus Relational Consciousness

I have discussed this in some detail in *The Spirit of the Child*. Here I would like to refer very briefly to a point that I did not go into deeply in that book. One of the most powerfully constructed strands in European modernity is individualism, multitudinous in its origins (Lukes, 1973) but in its severest form typically traced back, in England at least, to the 17th Century materialism of Thomas Hobbes. His interpretation of human nature led him to the view that in the state of nature life is a warfare of all against all. For Hobbes, if we co-operate with other people it is only because we see these interactions as in our interest. His assumption that each of us is in a struggle for power against everyone else is based on a materialist metaphysics that states that "minds never meet, that ideas are never really shared and that each of us is always and finally isolated from every other individual" (Hampton, 1986). This extreme individualism (or political atomism) was attacked in Hobbes' own day. One critical contemporary of Hobbes said that he, "... might as well tell us in plain termes, the all the obligation which a child hath to a parent, is because he did not take him by

22

the heels and knock out his braines against the walls, so soon as he was born".

Though he was writing in the 17th century, Hobbes is anything but out-of-date. C.B. MacPherson (1962), one of the most influential modern interpreters of the 17th Century English Revolution, charges Hobbes with creating the doctrine on which bourgeois liberal society still operates, or as he calls it "the theory of possessive individualism". Marx identified this individualism in full flood in the masters of Nineteenth Century Europe, when he depicted the typical capitalist entrepreneur as unencumbered by any social ties," ... that is, an individual separated from the community, withdrawn into himself, wholly preoccupied with his private interest and acting in accordance with his private caprice ... for him] the only bond between men is natural necessity, need, and private interest." (quoted by Michael Walzer, 1990).

The work that Rebecca Nye and I did two or three years ago on children's spirituality suggests that in its essence it is diametrically opposed to such individualism. Our work uncovered 'relational consciousness' as the biological precursor of both spirituality and ethics (see end-note).

Christians have allies
There is a real sense in which religion, when it is operating well, is subversive of the status quo, but to feed into the social and political functioning of the moral commonwealth, this privatised world needs to recover a public face. As our research has shown again and again, a major result of secularization is that spirituality has become a taboo subject for many people (including quite a number of churchgoers). This privatisation of relational consciousness continues to have severe effects on social cohesion. If this is true, it means that Christian mission shares some of the perspectives of non-religious people of good will who are concerned with constructing a coherent society by consent rather than brutality. There are many people who from this secular perspective would feel that the essence of their ethical struggle lies in the protection and promotion of relational consciousness, or from my Christian perspective, spirituality. In other words Christians have a very large body of allies in the secular world, at least in the dimension of concern for relational consciousness.

Listening

Spirituality has the greatest difficulty in feeding into social and political legislation because it no longer has a widely plausible, common public language. How do we rediscover such a language? Well the first step is to engage in simple conversation, but conversation of a type that leads beyond those aspects of self that are concerned with public image, fitting in with what is assumed to be the dominant world view. Our experience of doing qualitative research in this area suggests to me that our methodology is well suited to this kind of religious reconstruction. Our role as listeners, with no purpose other than trying to understand what people are saying to us when they talk about their spirituality, seems to give powerful permission for them to speak about the deeper issues in their lives. Whilst we neither criticise nor evangelise, we do not artificially hide our personal beliefs if we are asked about them, and it is surprising how often that happens, and how it seems to release them to speak still more openly about themselves. From a faith perspective, I believe that what we are doing is hearing how God the Holy Spirit is already communicating with these people. I would also say that talking with them has been an important part of my own religious education over the past two years. In a way what is happening is a kind of mutual reflection on *praxis*, which when it is at a sufficiently profound level, leads inevitably to the consideration of spiritual issues and the discovery of a mode of dialogue across the cultural boundary (Yoshikawa, 1987) that exists between Christians and others in contemporary British society. This I suggest is the work of mission.

References

Beit-Hallahmi, B. & Argyle, M. (1997). *The Psychology of Religious Behaviour, Belief and Experience*. London: Routledge.

Brierley, P. (ed.) (2000). *Religious Trends No. 2: 1999/2000*. London: Christian Research.

Hampton, J. (1986). *Hobbes and the Social Contract*. Cambridge University Press.

Hardy, A. (1966). *The Divine Flame: An Essay towards a Natural History of Religion*. London: Collins.

Hay, D. (1994). "The biology of God": What is the current status of Hardy's hypothesis?', *International Journal for the Psychology of Religion*, 4(1), 1-23

Hay, D. & Heald, G. (1987). 'Religion is good for you', *New Society*, 17 April.

Hay, D. & Nye, R. (1998). *The Spirit of the Child*. London: HarperCollins.

Lukes, S. (1973). *Individualism*. Oxford: Basil Blackwell.

MacPherson, C.B. (1962). *The Political Theory of Possessive Individualism: From Hobbes to Locke*. Clarendon Press: Oxford.

Milbank, J. (1993). *Theology and Social Theory*. Oxford: Blackwells.

Walzer, M. (1990). 'The communitarian critique of liberalism', *Political Theory*, 18 (1), 6-23

Yoshikawa, M. (1987). 'The double-swing model of intercultural communication between the East and the West', in, D. Lawrence Kincaid (ed.), *Communication Theory: Eastern and Western Perspectives*. New York: Academic Press Inc.

End-note

In our book *The Spirit of the Child* Rebecca describes this as having two aspects:

- An unusual level of consciousness or perceptiveness, relative to other passages of conversation spoken by that child.
- Conversation expressed in a context of how the child *related* to things, other people, him/herself and God.

This was so contrary to my presuppositions about the solitary nature of spirituality that for a time I was rather disorientated, which I suppose is one of the salutary results of empirical research. But of course once I thought about it, it made eminent sense. Relational consciousness is a pretty good name for the natural awareness that Alister Hardy had in mind. It is because we have such an awareness that we can be religious in the first place. It allows the possibility of relationship to God, or, if we are non-theists, the possibility of an holistic relation to the Other, however we conceive of it. I now see the solitude that is so characteristic of much (but not by any means all) prayer and meditation as merely a setting that is particularly conducive to maintaining the here-and-now immediacy that constitutes spiritual awareness. Thus, Jesus makes it quite explicit that the reason one should retire to one's private room for prayer is to get away from the kind of temptations to hypocrisy that happen when we set ourselves up to pray in public, or give to charity with a trumpet blast, and all the other accoutrements of ego-tripping that are mentioned in the Gospel. Privacy here helps us to remain honestly in the immediacy of the prayer relationship. Once one accepts that relational consciousness is the precursor of spirituality, it also becomes clear that it must be the underpinning of ethics. I know from literally hundreds of conversations with adults about their spirituality, that the typical result of being directly aware of one's immersion in the physical and social matrix is the experience of a shortening of the psychological distance between oneself and one's surroundings. When a person realises this, it matters much more to them when some aspect of reality is damaged, whether it is another person or a part of the environment, for they are much more likely to experience it as a shared damage; the feeling is "I too am damaged by what has happened to the other."

MISSION AND SPIRITUALITY
FOR LIFE

Saunders Davies

God's mission creates, sustains and promotes life, life in all its fullness. Spirituality opens our eyes to that river of life surging within us, among us and throughout creation. We are drawn into its dark, mysterious, threatening flow. As we abandon ourselves to its energies we find life made whole.

That was highlighted by Professor Jürgen Moltmann at your last conference:

> ... in the experience of this life we experience *God's* indestructible affirmation of life and his marvellous joy over life.

That was the clue to God's mission in Jesus. *'Jesus didn't bring a new religion into the world. What he brought was new life.'*

Similarly, he notes:

> The eternal life which God's Spirit creates is *not another life* following on this one. It is the power through which this *life here becomes different*. This mortal and temporal life gains a share in the life of God, and in doing so, itself becomes eternal... So Christian mission isn't concerned about Christianity; its concern is the life of men and women. And the church's mission isn't concerned about the church; its concern is the Kingdom of God. And evangelization isn't concerned about spreading the doctrine of faith; its concern is the life of the world.

We need to hold on to that insight throughout this week's conference. Anything less than attention to *life* can't do justice to mission or spirituality, nor to their dynamic interplay within the divine endeavour.

Before he goes on to provide eight guidelines to pinpoint 'what promotes life', Moltmann dares to ask, 'But what is life?' He suggests that there is more to life than living longer, living more intensively, living more powerfully, living faster.

In contrast to that, don't we seek for a *quality* of living in a 'fulfilled life'? But what is our life to be full-filled with? … It is the *indwelling* of the divine life in our human life, and the *participation* of our human life in the life that is divine. The creative energies of the Spirit flow within us and make us alive in an unguessed-of way.[1]

As he grapples with the mystery of the divine mission touching and invigorating our lives, Moltmann finds himself using picture language. When it comes to theological exploration this seems to be unavoidable. For example, in his attempt to persuade his readers 'to believe in the triune God, and to recognise the profound implications of this belief for the Christian life', Professor David S. Cunningham writes about Source, Wellspring and Living Water (*These Three Are One*). The river of life as an image for the life-giving divine energies occurs throughout the scriptures from Genesis to Revelation.

This use of imagery gives me confidence to share something of the Welsh experience of God's mission by Christ's Spirit throughout the ages as expressed by our poets. 'Poetry is life distilled' (Gwendolyn Brooks).

As a nation we have been gifted with spiritual writers and theologians. However, our long *poetic* tradition has been especially blessed. This struck Dr Oliver Davies as he studied early medieval literature in Wales. He came to the conclusion that:

> If the early Welsh poetic tradition authentically embodies Welsh spirituality, then it is this too which has mediated that spirituality to later ages. Despite the manifold changes in society, religion and culture during the course of Welsh history, the poetic tradition has served powerfully as a social medium for the conservation of perspectives that are intrinsic to, and indeed constitutive of, the Welsh spiritual tradition.[2]

This poetic tradition is still vibrant in Wales and a contemporary poet such as Alan Llwyd seeks to find 'a fitting image for the woe of our times'. After long reflection, he says,

> I perceived one day the water in the depths
> flowing freely, and over it a layer of ice,
> and behold a genuine image for our times:

---

1   *Mission: An Invitation to God's Future*, pp. 29-32
2   Celtic Christianity in Early Medieval Wales, p.144

that river flowing onwards
under the chill of the ice, under the rape of the clammy glass
which freezes the vivacity of each brave heart's stream:
the water with its low passage under the cold blue glass,
life flowing onwards under the ice.[3]

By means of that ordinary image of water flowing under the ice, Alan Llwyd conveys two features of the Welsh experience: the constant threat to life and a resilient spirituality of hope.

Living under threat

Our identity as a nation has been questioned. Our very life has been threatened time and time again. In his poem entitled *Welsh History*, R.S. Thomas sums up our experience in a single line: 'We fought, and were always in retreat'.

That echoes the cry of Aneirin in the sixth century, Llywarch Hen in the ninth century and the slaughter of the last Prince of Wales in 1282. His death dashed the Welsh hope of national independence and called forth this apocalyptic outburst in Gruffudd ab yr Ynad Coch's *Lament for Llywelyn ap Gruffudd*:

With Llywelyn's death, gone is my mind.
Heart frozen in the breast with terror,
Desire decays like dried-up branches.
See you not the rush of wind and rain?
See you not the oaks lash each other?
See you not the ocean scourging the shore?
See you not the truth is portending?
See you not the sun hurtling the sky?
See you not that the stars have fallen?
Have you no belief in God, foolish men?
See you not that the world is ending?[4]

Faced with economic, cultural, social and linguistic threats since then, life has frequently seemed to be all over for the Welsh nation. Although we have survived to this day, that long experience of living under threat has left an indelible mark on our national psyche and spirituality. We know what James Cone means when he says that nations can be divided into two categories: the dominant and the dominated. Welsh people can identify with other groups and nations all over the world which

---

3   *Cerddi Alan Llwyd 1968-1990*, pp. 355 f; trans. Cynthia Davies
4   Gwyn Jones, *The Oxford Book of Welsh Verse in English*, p. 32; trans. Joseph P. Clancy

have been dominated by others, such as blacks and coloured peoples, aborigines and native Americans.

Looking back over a particular century, Dr Kenneth Morgan concluded, 'history was something that had happened to the Welsh.' Nevertheless, he insists that Wales 'also serves as a story of desperate survival against all the odds, of frequent failures and half-fulfilled aspirations, kept alive without self-destructive bitterness and ultimately with much success.'

Would we be justified in translating the historian's 'kept alive' as spirituality? Despite all the threats and frustrations, Dr Kenneth O. Morgan dares to entitle his study, *Rebirth of a Nation: Wales 1880-1980*. He suggests that our experience has relevance for a world living under constant threat: economic and ecological threats, political and nuclear threats.

> The Welsh experience, too, with its past setbacks and subsequent recovery of confidence in a very different social climate after 1945, may have more relevance for the history of Britain in the late twentieth century – clearly the history of a second-class power, at best – than may the imperial path of ascendancy once trodden by the governing English.[5]

Can God's mission be glimpsed in the weakness of the dominated, kept alive by the spirituality of faith, hope and love? At least one could claim that the historian is interested in the whole of a nation's life not merely some religious segment.

Living the Trinity

Who or what has given us life? *Y werin*, the common people, often refer to *Y Bod Mawr*, the Great Being. Instead of feeling alone, totally abandoned, there is a sense of presence, a spirituality of being accompanied. This does not always imply spiritual or theological sophistication. Yet from the very beginning there has been an awareness of the trinitarian God. According to *The Oxford Companion to the Literature of Wales*, 'the Juvencus *englynion* may be said to be the earliest surviving poetry in Welsh' and notes that nine of these *englynion* are 'religious poems celebrating the power of God and urging men to revere the Holy Trinity'[6]. This is Oliver Davies' translation of the fifth[7]:

---

5   K O. Morgan *Rebirth of a Nation: Wales 1880-1980*. pp. 420 f.
6   *Oxford Companion to the Literature of Wales*, p. 331
7   *Op. cit.* p. 51 (tr. O Davies)

He who made the wonder of the world
will save us, has saved us.
It is not too great toil to praise the Trinity.

The tenth century *Armes Prydain* maintains,

How blest will the Welsh be when it can be said,
The Trinity has saved us from the tribulations of the past.

In her collection of early medieval Welsh poetry, *Blodeugerdd Barddas o Ganu Crefyddol Cynnar*, Dr Marged Haycock includes several poems inspired by the Holy Trinity. This is an example from the thirteenth century manuscript, *The Black Book of Carmarthen*:

I praise the threefold *(lit. Three)*
Trinity as God,
Who is one and three,
A single power in unity,
His attributes a single mystery,
One God to praise.[8]

This poem goes on to praise the creative Trinity for forty-four lines. Haycock also quotes poems dedicated to the Holy Trinity from the Taliesin manuscript (14th century). Our greatest Welsh poet, Dafydd ap Gwilym (14th century), began one of his poems by addressing the Three in One and the famous poets of the fifteenth century sang verses to the Holy Trinity. That unbroken tradition has continued to this day.

What is the significance of this firm belief in God as Trinity for spirituality and mission? In *The Promise of Trinitarian Theology* (1991), Colin E. Gunton contends that 'God is being in communion'. That is, being itself, the heart of reality, is communion, fellowship, *koinónia*, shared existence. Gunton quotes Bishop John Zizioulas: 'The substance of God, "God", has no ontological content, no true being, apart from communion.'

Paul S. Fiddes sees it as an invitation to enter into the divine dance:

In *this* dance the partners not only encircle each other and weave in and out between each other as in human dancing; in the divine dance, so intimate is the communion that they move in and through each other so that the pattern is all-inclusive. In fact, I suggest that the image of the dance

---

8   *Op. cit.* p. 57 (tr. O Davies)

makes most sense when we understand the divine persons as movements of relationship rather than as individual subjects who *have* relationships.[9]

A twentieth century Welsh poet, Waldo Williams, sees this divine relating linking every human being.

> Each man alive is knit
> Within God's secret net;
> The full web's unity
> Of I, Thou, He.[10]

Waldo actually uses the word 'Cymod', being together, reconciliation, to convey the effect of being caught up in this divine network. Not only did the early church sense God's purpose to bring everything into a unity in Christ by the power of the Holy Spirit (Eph. 1: 9-14), but glimpsed it beginning to happen as Jew and Gentile sat down to meals together and worshipped together. Age-old enemies were reconciled by the power of the Three in One. The twentieth century poet, Gwenallt Jones, had a similar awareness and experience as he pondered the reality of two world wars:

> Beneath the beasts and the demons in the nature of man
> God speaks: the Trinity is in the depths.
>
> *Tan y bwystfilod a'r demoniaid yn natur dyn*
> *Y mae Duw yn llefaru: y Drindod sydd yn y gwaelodion.*[11]

God's mission can overcome all barriers as we are nurtured by a trinitarian spirituality.

We begin to live the Trinity in community as we become more and more receptive to the 'trinitarian virtues', allowing them to form us and letting God take us up into the divine life. 'Thus,' says David Cunningham, 'on three levels—within the life of God, between God and human beings, and among human beings—participation is an essential feature of Christian life and thought.'[12]

Spirituality provides more than awareness or insight; it draws us into the mission of the Three in One within the human community. Dean Alan Jones puts this vividly:

9   Paul S. Fiddes *Participating in God*, p. 72
10 W. Williams, *The Peacemakers*, pp. 88-9 (Tr. Tony Conran)
11 G. Jones, *Gwreiddaw*, p.82
12 D S.Cunningham, *These three are one*, p186

The doctrine of the Trinity (or better, the very power of the Trinity) begins to come alive for us when we can say with all honesty, 'I cannot be me without you, and we cannot be us without them. *Together* we have a future.'[13]

Living Together

Living in community is at the heart of Welsh spirituality. What life have we if it is not life together? When people meet in Wales they will soon be asking, "Do you know so and so?" To know someone in common provides a link, it fosters community. Waldo Williams asks,

> To know another, what's that? Having
> the same root under the branches.[14]

What is that 'one root'? 'Being' itself, says Waldo.

> There is no withering in the root of Being
> There our pith is retained,
> There is the courage that is gentleness,
> The life of every frail life.[15]

That life in community, participation in Being as communion is invincible.

> The exploiters of iron and oil
> May lick the cities with fire,
> But in vain their lies and exhortation
> To keep us apart for long.[16]

What is the secret of this human fellowship? What is the immortal passion ('*anfarwol nwyd*') that bridges the gap and links us together in community ('*cyfeillach*')? For Waldo it is an inner awareness of the Word, the means of trinitarian communication and the pure light.

> There is a Word, that each heart knows.
> There will be fellowship after this.[17]

No obstacle can prevent that ultimately.

> Their laws and their steel will not avail,
> They will not forever split the old family,
> For the pure light shoots
> Direct from eye to eye.[18]

---

13 A Jones, *Soul Making*, p.195
14 W. Williams, *op. cit.* p.131 (Tr. Tony Conran)
15 James Nicholas, *Waldo Williams*, p.59
16 *Ibid.* p.61
17 *Ibid.* p.61
18 *Ibid.* p.60

This is not just a romantic idea. Pennar Davies saw that happening as he took his grandson for a walk along the Kingsway in Swansea. He noticed the boy make eye contact with a coloured Indian or Pakistani lad. In the light of that pregnant second Pennar sensed the gravitational pull towards communion throughout humanity, throughout history, throughout the whole cosmos – the divine gravity ('glory') that holds everyone and everything together in *koinónia*.

Gravity

Generous space and cunning time and cheerful energy
and light – yes, the light that manages
to travel consistently about six million million
miles a year – conspired
to shape
today, in Kingsway in Swansea,
a meeting which pleased our hearts.

Today in the busy, noisy street,
Owain, nine years old, gave a mischievous nod
full of unconditional friendship
to a brown skinned, swift eyed, comely faced lad,
slender and supple of body,
a lad from India or Pakistan.
After a moment's startled hesitation his smile appeared,
a generous and complete response to the spirited greeting.
For one pregnant second
the colours and the continents were united.
The primitive gravity
that would draw awareness to awareness,
vivacity to vivacity, body to body, was disclosed.
From the eyes of the one to the eyes of the other
flowed the sacred delight.
Between them leapt the joyful electricity
which proclaims
that our humanity is both one and many,
that each living soul is unique and common.

Is it not in this greeting,
in the gravitational pull of the spirit,
that our hope lies?
Was it not to reveal this gravity
that the little boy was set in the midst?
Was it not for this that we were told
to receive the kingdom like a little child?

Is it not the most loathsome foolishness
that fears and jealousies
and the oppression of our maturity
imprison us,
keeping us from acknowledging each other
in such a droll and kindly way?

Foreseeing this greeting
the morning stars sang.
To join in this greeting
Comely Euclid,
Saint Galileo,
Holy Newton and Blessed Einstein toiled.[19]

God's mission is expressed in this cosmic and local gravitational pull towards holy communion. The good news, the gospel is that this can be lived in community. That is life indeed.

The history of Wales bears witness to that. From the sixth century onwards people have lived in close-knit communities. The Celtic lands were not evangelized by famous individuals striding forth on their own, but by saints living in community, planting other communities of faith, giving more and more people an experience of living the Trinity. Place names beginning with 'Llan-' bear witness to those communities dotted all over Wales to this day.

The mission continued in the medieval period through the great and small monasteries, where communities gradually transformed the life of the areas around them. In the eighteenth century the Methodist Revival took root in Wales by means of those living cells/societies, 'seiadau'. We are witnessing a renewal of the community movement throughout the world today. It needs to grow in Wales if God's mission is to flourish in our day and age.

However, this must not be limited to religious communities. Dr Esther de Waal will remind us of that as she speaks about Celtic and Benedictine spiritualities in relation to Southern Africa.

That awareness of total life community is still alive in Wales, despite everything that threatens it, even in the rural areas. R. Gerallt Jones' poem speaks of the death and resurrection of society on the Llyn peninsula as he sees the old pattern of small fields destroyed, reflecting the destruction of a rural society with its

---

19 Pennar Davies, *Llef*, pp. 13 f; trans. Cynthia Davies

patterns and norms. Yet, in spite of the threat of 'social death', the poet is convinced that the hedges will be restored and a new pattern of society will emerge.

Funeral in Llyn

From the crest of the Cairn
one saw a pattern.

Small fields, hedges of gorse,
a tidy geographic quilt
and a sheep-walk of fern and whinberries
enduring together, though reluctantly,
the scheme.

And so with our society.
Each relationship was patterned,
the fruit of years joined end to end
of careful pruning and digging and enclosing,
of knowing the width of each gap,
of knowing, as there was need, when to lock the gate.

Then death came,
the old volcano in man's geography.
We can only watch its lava flowing,
its shapeless primitiveness penetrating,
cultivated hedges scattered
and everything clear-edged, cornered
today as it was in the beginning,
before the coming of order.

We stand afterwards naked
staring wildly at each other;
no gates to be shut,
one's land in another's fields,
so uncompromising the indiscriminate
sea that flowed within.

Tomorrow, the hedges will be rebuilt,
the breaks closed,
and two days hence will come a new safe pattern;
we will walk decorously through the proper gap.
But today a volcano erupted
and we look
deep into each other's eyes
naked.[20]

---

20 R G. Jones in *Twentieth Century Welsh Poems.* pp. 210 f (Trans. Joseph P. Clancy)

Tomorrow 'and two days hence' – on the third day – there will be the resurrection of a genuine community.

What is the clue? Looking deep into each other's eyes. Dr Michael Crowley will show how Latin America can remind us that mission is fostered by new ways of being church as people meet in communities, not just in congregations. Similarly Pete Ward will show that a 'Liquid church' emerges around the realisation that people are seeking an encounter with the living God – together. It is an experience of connecting and community in a host of different situations. It is the great Orthodox vision:

> Each social unit – the family, the school, the workplace, the parish, the Church universal – is to be made an ikon of the Triunity.[21]

It is fascinating to find a similar vision and experience conveyed by Bobi Jones as he describes 'Having Our Tea'.

Having Our Tea

There is something religious in the way we sit
At the tea table, a tidy family of three.
You, my love, slicing bread and butter, and she,
The red-cheeked tot a smear of blackberry jam, and me.
Set apart for the marvellous doting
Of a world's interchange with each other ... that's tea.
Not proper for us to think of the thing as a sacrament,
And yet all the elements are found to change in our hands.
Because we sit and share them with each other
There's a miracle. There's a binding of unmerited graces
By the cheese, and through the apples and milk is established
A new creation of life, a true presence.
And talking to each other, uttering words over food
Is somehow different from customary chatting.
I know perfectly well that generations have had to,
Of necessity, perform this petty action.
And surely their pattern has long since burrowed
As part of our consciousness. Then too, back beyond the epochs
Is depending, turning back to the fountainhead,
And listening on the connecting wires to a Voice
That is at the same time food—He expresses
Himself here from the beginning. All would acknowledge
The food in itself as a source of pleasure:

---

21 Kallistos Ware, *The Orthodox Way*, p. 49

He strengthens the spirit too in its wake.
Still tea is not worship ... But an overflowing
Of things so the spirit may happily hop
In our hearts. So that swallowing heaven's carol
Into our constitutions, we are a choir, our throats
Blending calories and words together in the presence
Of the unseen Leader who laid the table.[22]

That experience goes far beyond the communion of mother, father and daughter. There is a deep sense of communion with the world of matter, an awareness of

Blending calories and words together in the presence
Of the unseen Leader who laid the table.

A Living Creation

The Trinity's activity is not limited to humanity. The spirituality of God's mission senses the source of creation's life.

He who breathes through all creation,
he is Love, eternal Love. *(Bishop Timothy Rees)*

This means that the whole of life, personal and material, is sustained and transformed by God's trinitarian being. Leonardo Boff puts this nicely:

The Trinity in creation seeks to insert creation in the Trinity. The providence of the Father, the liberation brought by the Son and the indwelling of the Holy Spirit are ordered to the transfiguration of the universe.[23]

That is the scope of God's mission; it embraces all things and imbues all things. In Gwenallt's words,

When the Spirit makes thin the canvas
we see that the universe is a creation.

A genuine spirituality opens the eyes of the blind to see that the universe is a creation, a place where we can encounter the Creator's mission, sharing his life and glory in and through all things, and respond in wonder, gratitude and delight with Euros Bowen:

Gloria
The whole world is full of glory:

Here is the glory of created things,
the earth and the sky,

---

22   Bobi Jones in *Twentieth Century Welsh Poems.* pp. 198 f (Trans. Joseph P. Clancy)
23   L. Boff, *Trinity and Society*, p.230

the sun and the moon,
the stars and the vast expanses:
Here is fellowship
with all that was created,
the air and the wind,
cloud and rain,
sunshine and snow:

All life like the bubbling of a flowing river
and the dark currents of the depths of the sea
is full of glory.

The white waves of the breath of peace
on the mountains,
and the light striding
in the distances of the sea:

The explosion of the dawn wood-pigeons
and the fire of the sunset doves,
sheep and cattle at their grazing,
the joy of countless creeping things
as they blossom,
spider and ant
of nimble disposition
proclaim the riches of goodness.
*

To curse life is to err.[24]

To curse life is to err, because life is the outpouring of God's eternal mission. Spirituality enables us to see that and come alive in its vibrant, life-giving flow.

It seems to me that Welsh spirituality is vividly aware of the ever present, on-going mission of the Three in One. To participate in that divine mission is to experience life in all its fullness. It is a life constantly threatened by the forces of death and destruction and yet is kept alive by the divine energies of endurance, transfiguration and resurrection. Each individual's life is enriched and made abundant as it is lived together with others in human community and finds its full potential in the holy communion of the Three in One. That potential can be glimpsed in a mirror, dimly, within the community of the Church. In every generation

---

24 Cynthia Davies, *Euros Bowen Priest-Poet*, pp. 143 f

and within each culture, that community needs to be reshaped and reformed around specific people as they live out their spirituality, their active faith in response to the life of love flowing through them in the presence of the Holy Trinity. That can well be described as a 'Liquid Church' that meets the thirst of men and women for the life-giving water today and also affirms that the river of life flows through the depths of this earth and the cosmos.

> The roomy river's chambers
> have made my life whole.

That is an example of mission and spirituality bringing fullness of life in Gwyneth Lewis' own experience. She is a Welsh poet, born in Cardiff, writing in both English and Welsh. Her poem, 'Wholeness', distils the experience of life that is threatened, yet kept alive, by means of an image that echoes Alan Llwyd's perception of 'life flowing onwards under the ice'.

Seeing Face to Face

Cherish the dark's obscurity.
Look for the diamonds in debris.
God's gift to man is His mystery.

I was killed by the formalities
of ice, which overturned my world
and changed my old life totally.

We had been skating and, as we left
the shore, I was warned:
"If you fall underneath the ice,
aim for the blackness."
It happened. But instead I tried
for the light and died.

The roomy river's chambers
have made my life whole.
Since I fell through I understand
that everything I saw as shreds,
as pieces – grieving, illness, pain –
is precious, like the jagged glassy hole
that broke me and which pulled me through
into these soft-lit rooms of grace
whose killing gave me ample means
for living, murdering all that I had been.

Had I been ready to see in part
I would still be living.

In the black was the shore,
familiar weather, the sweet honeycomb
of dirty cities and all the hope
of our faulty loving, our human home.
Listen to one who now lies awake
for ever and who longs for the art
of blindness, the kindness of seeing in part:

Cherish the dark's obscurity.
Look for the diamonds in debris.
Thank God for all His mystery
and LIVE! [25]

---

25 Gwyneth Lewis in *Modern Poetry in Translation, No. 7* (Welsh issue) ed Dafydd
Johnston, pp. 87f

MISSION AND THE SPIRIT

Searching for a theology of the Holy Spirit leading us to
respond creatively and as a community in contemporary
Britain and Ireland

Robert Kaggwa

Dear Sisters and brothers, with the energy of the Holy Spirit
let us tear apart all walls of division and the culture of death
that separates us. And let us participate in the Holy Spirit's
economy of life, fighting for our life on this earth in
solidarity with all living beings and building communities
for justice, peace and the integrity of creation. Wild wind
of the Holy Spirit, blow to us. Let us welcome her, letting
ourselves go in her wild rhythm of life. Come, Holy Spirit,
renew the whole creation. Amen![1]

Introduction

This prayer which was said by the Korean theologian, Chung
Hyun Kyung in her address to the Assembly of the World Council
of Churches in Canberra (Australia) in 1991, sets the agenda for
the theme that I would like to explore in this paper: Mission and
the Spirit. What kind of mission theology of the Holy Spirit can
lead us to respond creatively and as a community in contemporary
Britain and Ireland? I am an outsider and I do not claim to have
good knowledge of the British and Irish culture. I can only search
and explore with you, sharing my limited experience of the Church
and society here and hoping that together we can draw some
conclusions for a contextual theology of the Holy Spirit that will
help us to live creatively together as a community. In this paper, I
would like to argue that we are living in a time of uncertainty. We
do not have clear answers to our questions and we do not know
what the shape of mission will be in the years to come. The first
part will describe the mission of the Spirit as a process of
exploration. Second, I will describe the present dilemma of
uncertainty that is characteristic of our age. In the third part I will
argue that it is precisely because of this uncertainty that a

---

1   quoted by S. McFague, 'Holy Spirit' in   L. Russell and S. Clarkson (eds.),
    Dictionary of Feminist Theologies, Lousisville: Westminster John Knox, 1996, 147

missionary theology of the Holy Spirit is urgent. This invites us to participate in the creativity and the community of the Spirit in mission. I would like to suggest that the Spirit's mission is to remind us of and include us in this but in order to do that we need to reclaim the mysterious in the Spirit, the wild rhythm of life, knitting together what is broken, separated, excluded and forgotten.

Mission: A Process of Exploration

One of the most beautiful definitions of mission was given to us by the American theologian, Carl Braaten, who described mission as *"the process of exploring the universal significance of the Gospel in history."*[2] Exploring is adventuresome. Explorers go searching for knowledge without knowing beforehand the result of their explorations. Exploration is a learning process. For example, explorers who went to Africa were a varied group. Some where ethnographers, others were natural scientists, physicians and missionaries. Whether they knew it or not, there was something that united all these people. They all embarked on a journey that led them to learn about the continent of Africa and its peoples.

Mission understood as a process of exploring the universal significance of the Good News in history involves an attitude of looking forward, discovering and learning. I wonder whether this can be said of God. Contemporary missiology insists on the missionary nature of God, on *missio Dei*. In this understanding the Triune God moves towards us in history, exploring the depths of the universe, healing and transforming all creation.[3] This rediscovery of *missio Dei* and insistence on the missionary nature of God is something we can all applaud, yet in these post-modern times there is also a great distrust in theories from above and hence also mission theologies "from above". We are moving toward recognising the missionary God, not as one who comes from above, the 'beyond in our midst' but rather as the one who is present in the ordinary times and places in this universe. God is present and active in ways *unknown* to us, in unexpected places and ways. This is an ongoing process of exploration. As Ivone Gebara writes, "to speak of knowing as a process means that the

2   C. Braaten, *The Flaming Centre. A Theology of the Christian Mission*, Fortress: Philadelphia, 1977, 2.
3   I. McCabe, "Mission for the Third Millennium", Talk given to the General Chapter of the Missionaries of Africa, Rome, May 1998, published in *Petit Echo*, n. 893/7 (1998), 327-8.

process by which new elements are being added to overall human knowledge does not necessarily follow a predictable causal path."[4]

We, therefore, need to discover movements of the Spirit in contemporary Britain and Ireland or what British theologian, Mary Grey calls '*trajectories of the Spirit*'[5] in our midst. We need a new level of imagination to read the signs of our times.

It seems to me that if we speak of mission as exploration and transformation, we are speaking of the Holy Spirit as the principal agent of this searching and renewing of the depths of the universe. Elizabeth Johnson expresses this vividly when she writes: "Whether the Spirit is pictured as the warmth and light given by the sun, the life-giving water from the spring, or the flower filled with seeds from the root, what we are actually signifying is God drawing near and passing by in a vivifying, sustaining, renewing and liberating power in the midst of historical struggle. So profoundly is this true that whenever people speak in a generic way of God, of their experience of God or of God's doing something in the world, more often than not they are referring to the Spirit, if a triune prism be introduced."[6] From the very beginning of creation, the Spirit is present like "a mighty wind that hovers over the waters" (Gen. 1:2). The Spirit is present in the long journey of Israel and of the nations, as giver of life or vivifier (Gen. 2:7), and speaking through the prophets (Ez. 2:2). The Spirit is present in the conception of Jesus (Lk. 1:35) and is poured upon Jesus from his baptism and his ministry right through his passion, death and resurrection. The same Spirit is then promised and given to Jesus' disciples to teach them and lead them to the truth (Jn. 14: 26;15:26). "Thus the Spirit *precedes* the coming of Jesus, is active *throughout* his life, death and resurrection, and is *also sent* as the Paraclete by Jesus to the believers, who by this sending and receiving are constituted [as] the Church"[7]

---

4   I. Gebara, *Longing for Running Water. Ecofeminism and Liberation*, Minneapolis: Fortress Press, 1999.
5   *The Outrageous Pursuit of Hope. Prophetic Dreams for the Twenty-first Century*, London: DLT, 2000, 62-66.
6   E. Johnson, *She Who Is. The Mystery of God in Feminist Theological Discourse*, New York: Crossroad, 1992, 127
7   "The *Filioque* Clause in Ecumenical Perspective" Part I, Memorandum, L.Vischer (ed.). *Spirit of God, Spirit of Christ. Ecumenical Reflections on the Filioque Clause*, London: SPCK, 1981, 9 (italics in original).

But the Holy Spirit has often been described as " the Cinderella of theology", "the Unknown", "the faceless", "the half-known", "the shadowy", "the Mysterious One" of the three in the Godhead and it has almost become monotonous to repeat this. Writing in 1991, Jürgen Moltmann remarked that complaint about the 'forgetfulness of the Spirit' had been the starting point of many studies about the Holy Spirit and "it gave way to a positive obsession with the Spirit."[8] Can we say that the situation has now changed? What are the results? Is a new paradigm of the Holy Spirit evident and in place today? In this paper I would like to argue that this is not clear today. The Holy Spirit still remains 'unknown' but this dimension of the unknowability of the Spirit need not to be taken negatively. It could be taken as a pointer to an important dimension of mission, namely the presence, mysterious and elusive character of the mission of the Spirit, One whom we can never close in our traditions and belief systems. The Spirit of God is elusive and Christian reflection on the Spirit has been far less developed than on God Abba and on Jesus Christ. The Christian understanding of the Holy Spirit is grounded chiefly in the intersection of the Christian tradition about the Spirit and contemporary Christian experience of God's presence. But the Spirit blows where it wills (John 3:8). "Divine Spirit is … the creative and freeing power of God let loose in the world. More than most terms for God's dynamism it evokes a universal perspective and signifies divine activity in its widest reaches."[9] The Spirit is one, who is always exploring the depths of the universe and allowing us to explore the universal significance of the Good News in history and space; finding the Spirit in places and times unknown to us; inviting us and unifying us to everything and everyone; creating diversity and unity. The elusiveness of the Spirit can be a positive dimension in mission.

The Present Dilemma:
the uncertain and the unknown in our midst

When I speak of the 'unknown' and the 'uncertain' I am not referring directly to the Spirit but to the present climate in society. Postmodernism[10] and globalisation are some of the descriptions

---

8   J. Moltmann, *The Spirit of Life, A universal Affirmation*, London: SCM, 1992 (English translation), 1.

9   E. Johnson, *She Who Is,* 83.

10   Michael Paul Gallagher makes a distinction between 'postmodernism' and 'postmodernity'. He writes: "The two realities are not completely separable. Both

people give of today's culture and society. We must admit that these terms have an elusive character as well. First of all, there is no agreement on what the term "*post-modern*" means. There are several valuations of post-modernity. Some consider it as a phenomenon that is radically new, others as the continuation of modernity and therefore not really different from it. Thus Anthony Giddens thinks that talk about post-modernity is rather premature "because the consequences of modernity are becoming more radicalised and universalised than before."[11] But others see post-modernity in nostalgic and pre-modern or counter-modern terms,[12] that is, a resource for ideas and values in a conservative reaction against modernity. As the title of the book by Paul Lakeland shows, we can say our Christian faith today is being lived in a *fragmented age*.[13] Some have called this the time when the West is experiencing the same ambivalences or contradictions felt by the rest of the world. It is the time of the *shaking of foundations*. There is nothing that has not been put into question. Even the very notion of truth has been challenged. But what are the implications of post-modernity for mission? How can the gospel be communicated within a culture whose very foundations are now shaken and fragmented?[14]

The second term '*globalisation*', however seems to be preferred by certain scholars. Richard H. Bliese writes that "[J]ust as postmodernism was *the* concept of the 1980s, globalisation may *be* the concept of the 1990s, a concept which tries to express and analyse human development and change at the inauguration of the third millennium."[15] And he adds: "Curiously, 'globalisation' is being treated as less controversial in sociological circles than

---

share a certain questioning of the achievements of modernity but whereas postmodern*ism* seems to remain largely in a mode of refutation, cultural postmodern*ity*, as will be seen, goes beyond negative critique and, in some instances, represents a search for liveable languages beyond the narrowness of modernity". See M. P. Gallagher, *Clashing Symbols. An Introduction to Faith and Culture,* London: DLT, 1997, 87.

11 A. Giddens, *The Consequences of Modernity,* Cambridge: Polity Press, 1990, 3.

12 One can see this in J. Milbank, *Theology and Social Theory: Beyond Secular Reason,* Oxford and Cambridge: Basil Blackwell, 1990.

13 Paul Lakeland, *Postmodernity. Christian Identity in a Fragmented Age,* Minneapolis: Fortress, 1997

14 A recent book deals with this: A. Kirk and K. J. Vanhoozer (eds.), *To Stake a Claim. Mission and the Western Crisis of Knowledge,* New York: Orbis, 1999

15 R.H. Bliese, "Globalization" in K. Mueller et al., *Dictionary of Mission,* New York: Orbis, 1997, 172.

'postmodernism'.[16] However, Timothy Radcliffe is sceptical of globalisation as being the new context of mission and observes that perhaps "what is really distinctive about our world is a particular fruit of globalisation, which is that we do not know where the world is going. We do not have a shared sense of our history".[17] This is what Anthony Giddens calls "the runaway world".[18] Mary Grey borrows the metaphors of *fragmentation* and the *shaking of foundations* from Paul Tillich to describe the break-up of culture and society that we experience today.[19] "Culture is cracking – but who will fill the cracks?"[20]

It seems to me that whichever term one prefers to describe the context of mission today, one must also admit that the old certainties are gone. In her address to SEDOS in Rome, Mary McAleese, President of Ireland expressed this as she narrated memories of her childhood in Belfast: "There was little space in those days for modern day concerns about cultural diversity or religious imposition. Even if there had been, no doubt we would have stared blankly in amazement. For the world I grew up in was one of very stark divisions and utter certainties. It was a world where on the same narrow street, Catholics and Protestants lived side by side, yet a world apart. For my family God was male, Irish and Catholic. For my Protestant friends, God was still male – no gender bending allowed – but with equal certainty, they knew him to be Protestant and British."[21]

Among other things we can mention these characteristics. The Churches in Britain and Ireland are losing popular support. Many children from Christian homes have turned their backs on the Church. The credibility of the Church is being challenged in many ways, not least by the many scandals of its pastors reported so

---

16 Ibid. 173. See also R. Schreiter, *The New Catholicity. Theology between the Global and the Local*, New York: Orbis, 1997, 1-14.

17 "Mission to a Runaway World: Future Citizens of the Kingdom, in *Sedos Documents* (http://www.sedos.org/english/Radcliffe.html), 1.

18 A. Giddens, *Runaway World. How Globalisation is Reshaping our Lives,* London, 1999

19 See M. Grey, "The Shaking of Foundations – Again! Culture and the Liberation of Theology", in *Louvain Studies*, 20 (1995), 347-361. See also her other books: *Beyond the Dark Night. A Way Forward for the Church*, London: Cassell, 1997, 9-17, *The Wisdom of Fools? Seeking Revelation for Today*. London: SPCK and *The Outrageous Pursuit of Hope. Prophetic Dreams for the Twenty-first Century,* London: DLT, 2000, 58-78.

20 M. Grey, *The Wisdom of Fools?*, 1.

21 M. McAleese, "Mission – A Hand of Friendship across the Divide", Address to SEDOS in Rome, 12 Feb 1999, 1, http://www.sedos.org/english/McAleese.html.

much in the media. The historically established Churches are growing smaller and smaller. The general applicability of Greek and Roman patterns of thought have been seriously put in question. The 'great' figures in theology whose influence was crucial in the first two thirds of last century are now dead. Their influence is still recognisable but new themes and new problems for which they were not prepared have come up: rearmament, the cold war and its end, the energy crisis and the ecological problem, the spread of AIDS and other incurable diseases, mad cow disease, foot and mouth disease, world famine, discrimination against large minorities, ethnic conflicts and cleansing, liberation movements, women's movements, overpopulation, global warming, pollution, unstable markets, genetic engineering, the tension between the North and the South, the new ecumenical situation, the new movements in the historical world religions, the revaluation of indigenous spiritualities, the pluralism of philosophies and ideologies.

Finding solutions to these problems is harder than anything comparable in the past. Books on theology which had a high reputation fifty years ago will now strike us as being generally simplistic. For all their scholarship and all their efforts, maybe today theologians and missionaries need to humbly accept that they are not well equipped for working on solutions to all these problems. As Christians we need to admit that we do not know the consequences and answers to these questions. We do not have special knowledge. There is a profound anxiety that arises out of all this. Our contribution can only be part of the whole of humanity's search for meaning.

Yet in all this we can see movements or trajectories of the Spirit, possibilities for re-imagining a new future. The Spirit works in all times and places and in this post-modern situation, we will discover both blessings and demonic elements. It is a world of conflicting spirits. The discernment of the movements of the Spirit in the midst of all these spirits is mission itself, a process of exploring the significance of the Good News in history.

Today we can say that gone is the confidence in progress. The 20th Century may go down in history as the most destructive century of all time. A new sense of evil and collective human sin was demonstrated in the two world wars, the Holocaust, Hiroshima as well as in Chernobyl, and in numerous ethnic, denominational and interreligious cleansings all over the globe. Gone also is the confidence in reason and in a monolithic culture. Our world has been transformed from a set of self-contained tribes and nations into a global reality. During the Enlightenment, the unity of humanity was an idea in the minds of a few visionary intellectuals. Today it is a concrete reality. This is in itself a pointer to a much more profound truth, namely that humanity is converging towards a single community (with the same ecological destiny). The survival of each depends on the co-operation of all. Modern means of communication have made this possible and today we may speak of a *"global village"*, a single *"geopolis"*. This world with its pluralism gives us a new perspective for building a meaningful human community. However, it can also not be denied that despite this unique chance of coming closer that is set before us, we still tend to live by outdated divisive patterns which concentrate on sectarian interests. Human beings have never been so close to each other as they are today, and yet never have they also been so divided. Elisabeth Schüssler Fiorenza laments how modern means of communication "are not an increase in global awareness, international literacy, human solidarity, or an active contribution to the solving of such problems. Rather, media discourses generate great anxiety and the sense of absolute powerlessness in the face of such complex problems. They foster a quiet resignation and create political paralysis that concerns itself with little beyond individual survival."[22] Some today speak even of the 'globalisation of poverty'[23] or the 'Third-Worldisation' of Britain with the irruption of so many people from poor countries into the affluent Britain – and because of the deficiencies in the health and education systems. While some prize dominance, others search for a new transcultural humanity in which ethnic particularity is prized while the human race is valued as one. A world that has become a global village may face the danger of the suppression of differences. However, God has created a world full of vitality and variety. It is not uniform. How can we acknowledge others in their otherness? How can we be enriched by religious and cultural differences? Dialogue among cultures and religious traditions become even more important today.

---

22   E. Schüssler Fiorenza, *Jesus, Miriam's Child, Sophia's Prophet*, New York: Continuum, 1994, pp. 6-7.
23   See M. Chossudovsky, *The Globalization of Poverty, Impacts of IMF and World Bank Reforms*, London: TWN, Penang and Zed Books, 1997.

What is the concrete meaning of divine providence in all this? In the context of Christology, Roger Haight has pointed out new and positive possibilities that could be gained from the post-modern cultural climate.[24] On the positive side, a radical *historical* consciousness provides the possibility and creation of new meaning. This age calls for a critical *social* consciousness. Social structures "are ultimately functions of human interest and freedom, and they can be changed. The dramatic negative experiences of social oppression and annihilation of last century, precisely in their negativity, mediate encounters with transcendental values."[25] But this time also involves a *pluralist* consciousness. At no other time have people had such a sense of the difference of others, of the pluralism of societies, cultures, and religions and of the relativity that this entails. One can no longer claim Western culture as the centre, the higher point of view, or Christianity as the superior religion. The world is pluralistic and polycentric in its horizons of interpretation. This seems to be an attack on universal values and shared truth. A reflection of this is found in young people who are unable to define any absolute or universal values; all is reduced to opinion; every opinion must in principle be tolerated. It is impossible in post-modern culture to think of one group as a "chosen people" or that one religion can claim to inhabit the centre into which all others are to be drawn. These myths or "metanarratives" are simply gone. On the negative side, this situation has left a vacuum, which is deeply threatening, for many have lost a source of identity. But post-modernity provides an opportunity for a dramatic new theological meaning. The discovery of pluralism is precisely a discovery of the "other", other people who are different and valuable, but who are excluded or suppressed by "universal" assumptions. The Holy Spirit becomes one who authorises the other *as other,* and hence functions as a principle of unity that respects differences.

This age involves a *cosmic* consciousness as well. The new concern for our planet has helped people to understand that human beings are not the centre of the universe. Today the utopian dream that there could be no limits to human progress and, therefore, that market-orientated democracy rightly applied would guarantee every human being the maximum fulfilment in a consumer society,

---

24 R. Haight, *Jesus, Symbol of God*, New York: Orbis, 1999, 331-4. I am indebted to his analysis.
25 Ibid., 332

has come to a sudden end. Our planet will not be able to sustain such a dream. The survival of human being depends on the survival of the earth. If there is anything that we come to realise today, it is our limits. This world is limited and we need to work towards a human society that accepts limits and seeks a decent life for all within them. "In this sense, showing that Christian theology opposes both injustices and ruthless exploitation of the earth is not enough."[26] As followers of Christ we are sent to lead in envisioning a more habitable planet. One does not have to be a prophet to foresee that the issue of *ecojustice* is becoming one of the most pressing issues to be dealt with at present.

Concerning the impact of 'globalisation' in Europe, Robert Schreiter argues that three areas will be important for theologising contextually and, therefore, for the context of mission in Europe[27]. These are secularisation, de-christianisation and multiculturalism. Older sociological theories about secularisation may no longer be valid. Religion has not disappeared, contrary to what was predicted. Though institutional religion may seem to be fading away, religion is emerging in different ways, particularly in forms of fundamentalism and diffuse spiritualities, in the face of challenged identities. Some forms of Pentecostalism provide those at the periphery "an antimodern haven in a world that forces change on them without any of the benefits that change might bring."[28]

The de-christianisation of Britain, and maybe, of Ireland is another area that we need to look at. Large groups of Muslims, Hindus, Buddhists and people of other faiths live side by side in this country. A new Britain and a new Ireland will be multireligious. Adherents of these religious groups sometimes practise their religions much more than Christians do. Moreover, multiculturality has become a striking phenomenon, particularly in Britain. All this has changed the social climate of both Ireland and Britain.

This changing climate needs to be addressed. There is certainly talk of a post-modern paradigm in mission today and scholars and

---

26 J.B. Cobb, Jr., *Sustainability: Economics, Ecology and Justice*, New York: Orbis, 1992, 5. See also J. Fuellenbach, *The Kingdom of God. The Message of Jesus Today*, New York: Orbis, 1995, 163-7.

27 R. Schreiter, *The New Catholicity*, 86-97.

28 Ibid, 88

missionaries are becoming aware of the inadequacies of earlier paradigms. In her article, "Postmodern Mission: A Paradigm shift in David Bosch's mission theology",[29] Kirsteen Kim has shown how Bosch's highly acclaimed *Transforming Mission. Paradigm Shifts in Theology of Mission*[30] falls short of presenting a truly post-modern paradigm in mission. One of the criticisms that Kim makes is the absence of post-modern issues, such as ecology, feminism and indigenous spiritualities. But the most important criticism has to do with Bosch's pneumatology, which according to Kim, is church-centred and a Jesuological after-thought ignoring the Spirit as an equal divine person whose mission is present even before the coming of Jesus. Kim concludes that: "The post-modern paradigm will take into account not only the Spirit of mission but also the mission of the Spirit which takes place in the context of other spirits. In any truly missionary encounter, these spirits need to be recognised and their natures discerned by the Spirit of Christ."[31]

With all this in mind, we must say that the context of Christian mission is one of uncertainty and we do not know which direction it will take. This introduces me to the dimension of the Unknown Spirit in our midst and its profound implications for mission.

The Unknown in our midst:
retrieving the mystery of the Holy Spirit
"From early on, God's Spirit has been experienced as a power that exercises deliverance by means of appearances and processes that are difficult to grasp – appearances and processes that can be termed 'emergent'".[32] The uncertain situation and intellectual climate of today has affinities with the way we should speak of the Spirit and the mission of the Spirit. In Western theology Spirit was

---

29 In T. Yates (ed.), *Mission – An Invitation to God's Future*, Sheffield: Cliff College Publishing, 2000, 99-109 and also in *International Review of Mission*, LXXXIX, n. 353 (April 2000), 172-179.

30 New York: Orbis, 1991. Kim does not mention a later book that Bosch wrote shortly before his death: *Believing in the Future. Toward a Missiology of Western Culture*, Valley Forge: Trinity Press, 1995. But Kim's criticism is justified. Even in this later work, Bosch only speaks of ecology and contextual theologies in a short paragraph in the conclusion. Other post-modern themes mentioned by Kim such as feminism and indigenous spiritualities are completely overlooked.

31 K. Kim, "Postmodern Mission", 109

32 M. Welker, *God the Spirit*, Fotress: Minneapolis, 1994, 28

very often linked to ecclesiastical authority and was deprived of its mysteriousness. William Burrows writes:

> Although theology in the West has generally confined the Holy Spirit to the status of mysterious energy making for the efficacy of ecclesial activities, 'Spirit' functions biblically as a name that moves beyond and disrupts attempts to define Jesus or mission in straightforward language. 'Spirit' injects an uncontrollable, effervescent element into the structure of Christian existence – a dimension scarcely explored by theology. Recovering the ability to factor the mysterious event (not primarily conceptual character) of the process of generation of new life into our understanding of Christian mission and vocation, I believe, is central to Christianity recovering its health and being able to deal more vitally with other traditions. [33]

Earlier I mentioned that in theology the Spirit has often been described as 'the Unknown' or 'the faceless'', "the half-known", "the shadowy'', "the Mysterious One" of the three in the Godhead. The Spirit is discreet. "[T]he Spirit largely ignored in theologies of mission, introduces a *non-categorical* mysterious dimension in religious life."[34] Here I would like to plead for reclaiming this dimension of mystery in a missionary theology of the Spirit.

In popular language a mystery is something beyond our understanding, something inexplicable. Very often mystery also means something that we do not yet know, e.g. a mystery story that will be solved at the end of a book, a film or a puzzle in nature that scientists are working to answer. In the Christian and Jewish tradition, however, there is a strong abiding sense that God will always exceed our comprehension. Mystery is reality that is so rich that our understanding can never exhaust it. Mystery can be defined as a known unknown. Mystery is "a mixture of certitudes and uncertainties; of probabilities, hypotheses, realities that surpass us, and fundamental questions to which we have no answers. ... It is one of those words that is indefinable, but that can in the final analysis be part of any definition."[35]

---

33 W. R. Burrows, "A Seventh Paradigm? Catholics and Radical Inculturation", in W. Saayman and K. Kritzinger (eds.), *Mission in Bold Humility: David Bosch's Work Considered*. New York: Orbis 1996, 128.

34 Ibid, 128 (italics – original)

35 I. Gebara, *Longing for Running Water*, 133.

This explanation of the word mystery is indeed paradoxical! But mystery itself is about paradox in life. In his book, *The Courage to Teach*, Parker Palmer describes how we have become masters of 'thinking the world apart'.[36] We live in a polarising culture. We are trained neither to voice both sides of an issue nor to listen with both ears. Most of us are trained in becoming experts of polarisation. "Tell me something and I will find any way, fair or foul, to argue the contrary!"

We look at the world through analytical lenses. We see everything as this or that; either... or; on or off, positive or negative; in or out; black or white. We fragment reality in an endless series of "either ... or". In short, we think the world apart. Of course this has given human beings a great power over nature, a lot of success, many gifts of modern science and technology. But we can say that we have also lost the sense of mystery. This dualism of "either ... or" thinking has also given us a fragmented sense of reality that destroys the wholeness and wonder of life. It misleads and betrays us when applied to the perennial problems of being human in this world. Therefore, we need to move away from an "either ... or" attitude to a "both ... and" attitude. In certain circumstances, truth is a paradoxical joining of apparent opposites, and if we want to know that truth we must learn to embrace those opposites as one. Obviously in the empirical world there are choices to be made: an apple tree cannot be both an oak tree and an apple tree. But there is another realm of knowing and here binary logic ("either ... or") misleads us. This is the realm of profound truth – where, if we want to know what is essential, we must stop thinking the world into pieces and start thinking it together again.

Profound truth rather than empirical fact is the stuff of which paradoxes are made and this is so common in our daily life, even if we are not aware of it often. We are ourselves paradoxes that breathe! We are mystery! Indeed breathing itself is a form of paradox – requiring inhaling and exhaling to be whole. The poles of paradox are like the poles of a battery: hold them together and they generate electricity, pull them apart and the current stops flowing. Consider other paradoxes, for example, our need for both solitude and community. Human beings were made for

---

36   P. Palmer, *The Courage to Teach*, San Francisco: Jossey Bass, 1998, 61-66. In this section I am largely indebted to Palmer's analysis of 'paradox'.

relationships. Without a rich and nourishing network of connections, we wither and die. It is a clinical fact that people who lack relationships get sick more often and recover more slowly than people surrounded by family and friends. But at the same time we are also made for solitude! Our lives may be rich in relationships, but the human self remains a mystery of enfolded inwardness that no other person can possibly enter or know. If we fail to embrace our ultimate aloneness and seek meaning only in communion with others, we wither and die. The farther we travel towards the great mystery, the more at home we must be with our essential aloneness in order to stay healthy and whole.

We need to embrace all these apparent opposites. This means entering into mystery. The result is a world more complex and confusing than the one made simple by either-or thought – but as simplicity is merely the dullness of death, entering into Mystery is characterised by a creative synthesis of "both – and".

To speak about God who is infinite is another way of entering into Mystery. For Christians, the invisible, infinite God is made visible in Jesus of Nazareth. And yet God who is revealed in this particular, historical, limited individual remains nonetheless concealed, hidden, veiled. It also means that God is 'personal'. As humans we speak of a person revealing herself or himself to us. By that we do not mean knowing facts about that person's life but seeing with the "eyes of the heart" who that person is, grasping through love her or his ineffable and inexhaustible mystery. The more intimate our knowledge of another, the more we are drawn to that person's unique mystery and the deeper that mystery becomes.

The Spirit is the point of contact between God and ourselves in history.[37] The Spirit reminds us that God remains mystery and will always remain mystery.[38] How then should we come to the knowledge of the 'Unknown'? The Spirit is not directly knowable but the experience of the Spirit can be known. It is 'tangible' and 'visible'. 'Long before the Spirit was an article of doctrine it/he

---

37 K. McDonnell, "A Trinitarian Theology of the Holy Spirit", 208.
38 This understanding of mystery has nothing to do with Michael Welker's critique of the modern consciousness and the distance of God. Welker links mystery with terms like 'otherwordly', 'supernatural', 'numinous' and transcendent'[*God the Spirit*, 2-7]. J. Moltmann proposes the expression '*immanent transcendence*' to describe this 'mysterious' experience of God's presence not only in humans, in the community but also in nature. See J. Moltmann, *The Spirit of Life*, 34.

was a fact in the experience of the primitive Church'. It is this fact which explains an attitude to the Spirit in the New Testament: viz., that the presence or absence of the Spirit in a person's (or community's) life was directly knowable – not the Spirit as such, but his presence or absence could be ascertained not just directly as a deduction from some rite or formula but immediately. John V. Taylor writes: "From within the depths of its being [the Spirit] urges every creature again and again to take one more tiny step in the direction of higher consciousness and personhood; again and again [the Spirit] creates for every creature the occasion for spontaneity and the necessity, and at every turn [the Spirit] opposes self-interest with a contrary principle of sacrifice and the existence for the other."[39] Of course the experience of the Spirit was "multifaceted"[40]. The book of Acts, sometimes called the gospel of the Holy Spirit, attests to this. So do various manifestations already in the Hebrew Bible and other passages from the Christian scriptures.

But from the Hebrew Bible through the New Testament, the apostolic and patristic period, as well as through the later history of theology, the Spirit remains elusive. The Scriptures do not give us a fully reflective doctrine of the Spirit. At the level of biblical testimony, there are many unanswered questions about the Spirit. For example, is the Spirit, power, presence of God or person? "Does the Spirit lose identity in the Johannine conception of the risen Christ, so that the Spirit is the 'personal presence of Jesus in the Christian while Jesus is with the Father'?"[41] Does Paul identify the Spirit with the risen Christ or with the pre-existent Christ? How is it that Paul knows nothing about the Pentecost experience? Interesting to note is what Jacques Matthey points out in disagreement with David Bosch. Concerning the question whether the Gentile mission would have been possible if the Jews had not rejected the gospel, Bosch writes that "It is therefore incorrect, or at the very least insufficient, to say that the Gentile mission only became possible after the Jews had rejected the

---

39 J.V. Taylor, *The Go-Between God. The Holy Spirit and the Christian Mission*, London: SCM, 1972, 36.

40 J.D. G. Dunn, "Rediscovering the Spirit (1)" in J.D.G. Dunn, *The Christ and the Spirit*, Edinburgh: T& T Clark, 1998, 47

41 R. Brown, *The Gospel according to John* Garden City: Doubleday, 1970, 669, 1139. K. McDonell, "A Trinitarian Theology of the Holy Spirit", in *Theological Studies*, 46 (1985), 203.

gospel."[42] Matthey thinks otherwise. "It needed repeated hints and some forceful convincing by the Spirit to force the church of the origin to admit the fact that mission was not directed only to people of Jewish origin. Acts is an interesting illustration of John 16:13, showing that the Spirit's interventions cannot be reduced to the *anamnesis* or remembrance of already known and understood messages. The Spirit, conducting us in full truth, can push us further to unknown theological territories, present in the message, but not yet developed."[43] Similar questions can be asked about the lack of clarity we find in the patristic writings. Even authors such as the Cappadocians, who are responsible for the formulation of the doctrine of the Holy Spirit at Constantinople betray a clear hesitation about the person of the Spirit.[44] When Killian McDonnell says that "anyone writing on pneumatology is hardly burdened by the past and finds little guidance there",[45] this should not be understood as if nothing clear can be found in the Bible or in the history of theology about the Holy Spirit. We should rather understand it as referring to the mystery of the Spirit, one whom we can never contain or on whom we can never put a full stop.

Of course much is said about the Spirit both in the New Testament and in the Hebrew Scriptures. In the New Testament, there is no Spirit independent of Christ. Life in Christ and life in the Spirit are mutually interdependent (Rom 8:9). And in Johannine thought, all manifestations of the Spirit, though they come from the Father, also come through Christ. Luke 1:5 links the conception of Jesus to the power of the Spirit, and in Acts 2:1-14-36, Peter's Pentecost sermon speaks of the crucified and risen Jesus. Hilary of Poitiers is cautious about talking about the Spirit alone in a non-Trinitarian way. He warns that "concerning the Holy Spirit we should neither be silent nor should we speak" and goes on to add: "He whom in our profession we must join with the Father and the Son cannot be separated in such a profession from

---

42 D. Bosch, *Transforming Mission*, 95.
43 J. Matthey, "The Spirit's Mission Manifesto. Jesus' Hermeneutics − and Luke's Editorial", in *International Review of Mission*, Vol. LXXXIX, n.352, 1 (January 2000), footnote 15 (p.10). Matthey writes that "Here exceptionally, I disagree with Bosch. It seems evident to me that in Acts, the first apostles did not grasp the breadth of Jesus' own ministry, of the Spirit's sending. For them, it remained limited to the renewal of Israel, which then would attract other people (hoping for the nation's future pilgrimage toward Zion)."
44 K. McDonnell, "A Trinitarian Theology of the Holy Spirit", 198.
45 Ibid, 191.

the Father and the Son."[46]   However, we must heed William Burrows' warning against an "over-objectification of the Christ-event".[47]

The primacy of the mission of the Spirit

All this points to the fact that the mission of the Spirit is as important as the mission of Christ and according to biblical testimony the mission of the Spirit *precedes* the mission of Christ, accompanies the mission of Christ by anointing Christ and continues afterwards in creating faith communities after Christ's departure. But the *primacy* of the mission of the Spirit must be stressed.[48] Frederick Crowe writes:

> We have simply to reverse the order in which commonly we think of the Son and the Spirit in the world. Commonly we think of God first sending the Son, and of the Spirit being sent in that context, to bring completion to the work of the Son. The thesis says that, on the contrary, God first sent the Spirit, and then sent the Son in the context of the Spirit's mission, to bring completion – perhaps not precisely the work of the Spirit, but the work which God conceived as one work to be executed in two steps of the twofold mission of first the Spirit and then the Son[49]

I speak of the mission of the Spirit *preceding* the mission of the Son in purely functional terms (in the economy of salvation or at the level of the economic Trinity) - therefore, not in ontological terms. Both missions are co-equal. They go forth hand in hand[50] but in terms of salvation history, it is the Spirit who comes first. And this does not mean that the Son has to be subordinated to the Spirit. Coming before does not in any way mean that the Spirit is more important but it has profound implications for mission. First,

---

46 *On the Trinity* 2, 29 (CCL 62, 64; tr. FC 57, 58). See K. McDonnell, " A Trinitarian Theology of the Holy Spirit", 206.

47 W. R. Burrows, "A Seventh Paradigm? Catholics and Radical Inculturation", in W. Saayman and K. Kritzinger (eds.), *Mission in Bold Humility: David Bosch's Work Considered.* New York: Orbis 1996, 124-128. An 'objectification of the Christ-event' would mean controlling the gospel message as if it could be clearly and exhaustively expressed in objective, rational categories.

48 J.D.G. Dunn, "Rediscovering the Spirit (1)" in J.D.G. Dunn, *The Christ and the Spirit,* Edinburgh: T& T Clark, 1998, 44.

49 F. Crowe cited in S. Bevans, "God Inside Out: Notes Toward a Missionary Theology of the Spirit", in *Sedos Documents*: http//www.sedos.org/english/Bevans.html, 1.

50 Irenaeus refers to the two missions as "the two hands of the Father". Cf. K. McDonnell, "A Trinitarian Theology of the Holy Spirit", 206.

God acts even before the coming of the Son. Western theology had neglected the role of the Spirit and concentrated on Christology thus subordinating the third Person. Second, we cannot even recognise the Son if it were not in the power of the Spirit. Paul writes (1 Cor 12:3) that no-one can say that Jesus is Lord except in the power of the Spirit. Thus being in Christ and living in the Spirit are two sides of the same coin. The Spirit is the sole possibility of any knowledge of the Father and the Son. The Spirit is the point of contact where the Father and the Son touch history. Maybe we can say that the Spirit is the '*how*' and Christ is the '*what*'.[51] In other words, we cannot get to that centre without the power of the Spirit. This view opens the way to the understanding of God's action outside the Church and also to realise that God can always surprise us in many and different ways. Other faiths, other cultures, other peoples are also bearers of the Spirit (something that the absolutism of imperial Christianity had denied). Of course this has always to be discerned and in that way we can never say that all religions and all religious experiences are equal. That would amount to relativism or vague pluralism, which helps no one.

If we put the primacy of the Holy Spirit at the centre of mission, this will have enormous and profound consequences. I will now sketch a few of these implications. I have suggested earlier that the Spirit is the contact point between the Triune God and history. All experiences can mediate the divine Spirit. This requires that we re-examine our way of knowing. In the remaining part I would like to concentrate on this and how we can re-imagine and respond creatively to the mission of the Spirit in our times.

1. *Knowing in community*

All knowing begins in experience. If, as I have suggested, the Spirit is the contact point between God and history, our experiences mediate the presence or the absence of the Spirit. James Dunn has shown that for the early Christians "the experience of the Spirit was a social experience, an incorporating

---

51 Ibid., 227. "Both Christ and the Spirit are at the centre but in different ways: Christ as the 'what' and the Spirit as the 'how'. As this 'how', the Spirit is a way of knowing Jesus and the Father; as a 'how', the Spirit is a way the Father through Christ has contact with history and the Church. The contact function is a mode of the 'how'."

experience, the basis of community, of a Christian group."[52]
Following his mentor, C.F.D. Moule, Dunn insists that Paul's use
of the expression *hé koinónia tou pneumatos* in 2 Cor.13:13 has to
be understood as *"participation in the Spirit"* and not "fellowship
of the Spirit" as we usually say. It refers to the shared or common
experience of the Spirit that the believers have. This is the basis of
community. If we apply this to the mission of the Spirit, we realise
that the Spirit brings about both unity and diversity in those who
share in the Spirit's experience. Not only glory but also sufferings!
In this sense, the Spirit is the energy of connectedness that unites
all.

Community is essential to all reality. It is the matrix of all
being and "we know reality only by being in community with it
ourselves."[53] Modern scientists have rediscovered this way of
relational knowing. Knower cannot be separated from the known
and nuclear physicists cannot study subatomic particles without
altering them in the act of knowing. "On the contrary, objects can
be known and understood very much better if they are seen in their
relationships and co-ordinations with their particular environments
and surroundings (which include the human observer) ...".[54] It is
thus impossible to maintain an objectivist gap between reality 'out
there' and the detached observer 'in here'. How can a historian or
a literary critic study a text of the past without leaving the mark of
his or her personal experience? This relational knowing is a
strength as it connects us. Today we can celebrate being part of a
cosmic community precisely because of this rediscovery of
relational knowing. The question is, do we draw appropriate
conclusions from this experience? Openness to the Spirit is what
saves us from both absolutism and relativism. In relational
knowing we are empowered by the Spirit to discover the 'other',
who has often been suppressed. We learn to embrace diversity. In
absolutism we claim to know the intentions of the Spirit, so there is
no need to dialogue with the 'other'. The missionary possesses the
truth and has only to transmit those truths. With relativism, we
claim that knowledge depends on where one is. Once again there

---

52 J.D.G. Dunn, "The Spirit and the Body of Christ", in J.D.G. Dunn, *The Christ and the Spirit*, 343.

53 P. Parmer, *The Courage to Teach*, 95

54 J. Moltmann, *God in Creation. An Ecological doctrine of Creation*, London: SCM, 1985, 2-3.

is no need to continue dialogue because each one has his or her own truth and the difference is not important.[55]

Mary Grey has developed her theology insisting on this idea of connectedness. "The creative power of the Spirit at the dawn of creation, breathing life into all creatures, is a fundamental trajectory of the Spirit faith traditions. Here is the energy of connection (which has been fundamental to my [Grey's] own theology)."[56] The unpredictable and hidden Spirit is this energy that binds and connects, leading into the unknown, overturning our categories and boundaries. Thus God's Spirit and the human spirit are connected and have a mutual dependency and all are connected to "the life-breath of all living things"[57]. This is an idea that is not so uncommon in indigenous spiritualities,[58] which have often been written off as animism and paganism. American theologian, Sallie McFague, uses the metaphor of 'Body of God' to speak of the universe. "It is a body enlivened and empowered by the divine spirit."[59]. This is also central to Moltmann's ecological doctrine of creation.[60]

In a theology of the Holy Spirit this ecological dimension needs to take centre stage once again. In an age of ecological destruction a Spirit theology that insists on the interconnectedness and integrity of creation[61] is a matter of urgency.

---

55 Is this not the dilemma of absolutism and relativism which cohabit in today's world? The recent Vatican document, *Dominus Iesus*, (5 September 2000) is legitimately worried about modern forms of relativism in what concerns salvation in Jesus Christ but unfortunately its response only accentuates the absolutist dimension. No wonder that this document is lacking in pneumatology!

56 M. Grey, *Outrageous Pursuit of Hope*, 66.

57 Ibid. 68.

58 In his article ["The Place of Traditional Religion in Contemporary South Africa", in J.K. Olupona (ed.), *Traditional Religions in Contemporary Society*, Minnesota: Paragon House, 1991, 35-49] Gerhadus Cornelis Oosthuizen sees African traditional religions as having affinities with post-modern era world views. The close link that traditional Africans make with the natural environment in their spirituality is one of the aspects that Oosthuizen brings out. See p. 45.

59 M. Grey, *Outrageous Pursuit of Hope*, 69. See S. McFague, *The Body of God*, London: SCM, 1993.

60 See J. Moltmann, *God in Creation*, 2-7. See also J. Moltmann, *The Spirit of Life*, 97 and "Mission of the Spirit: Gospel of Life", in T. Yates (ed.), *Mission an Invitation to God's Future*, 29-32.

61 Some prefer to speak of 'the care for creation'. But I find this expression wanting, in as much as it does not necessarily bring out the dimension of interconnectedness and may even hide the fact that humans are part of nature.

2. Creativity: re-imagining and recognising the trajectories of the Spirit

A theology of the Spirit will require a lot of imagination. It will require us to abandon old certainties. As John Taylor writes, "To think deeply about the Holy Spirit is a bewildering, tearing exercise, for whatever [the Spirit] touches [the Spirit] turns it inside out"[62] and K. McDonnell has already been quoted: "Anyone writing on pneumatology is hardly burdened by the past and finds little guidance there".[63] Prophetic imagination is a gift that we will always need. The Spirit, who speaks through the prophets, gives the freedom to dream and create metaphors of connection. Mary Grey speaks of 'epiphanies of connection'.[64] In her recent book she provides us with a beautiful metaphor of "the cosmic egg."[65] In similar words Elizabeth Johnson describes the Spirit as one who "hovers like a great mother bird over her egg, to hatch the living order of the world out of primordial chaos."[66] If the Spirit is associated with bringing to birth ('Fill the earth, and bring it to birth' as the old hymn put it), then the imagery of the cosmic egg is timely. The Spirit is watchful for the moment where the cracks in the discourses of violence appear, where humanity at last admits vulnerability in having no answers, and "commits itself at last to a different kind of listening."[67]

It may be that in our culture, so full of cracks and uncertainties we need a different kind of listening: listening to the experiences of the marginalised, listening to the 'eccentric' (were the prophets not often declared eccentric?), listening to secular movements of liberation, listening to the aspirations of so many young people who have been disillusioned by the institutional Church, listening to their apathy, listening to the resistance coming from the underside of history, listening to the women and to the contribution of feminist spirituality, listening to the immigrants and asylum seekers who come with their indigenous spiritualities. Of course discernment will be necessary. There is a lot of creativity in contextual theologies and we need to listen to this creativity. But let us not be cautious of this in such a way that we stifle the Spirit

---

62   J.V. Taylor, *The Go-Between God*, 179.
63   K. McDonnel, "A Trinitarian Theology of the Holy Spirit", 191.
64   M. Grey, *The Wisdom of Fools*, 60-66
65   M. Grey, *Outrageous Pursuit of Peace*, 72.
66   E. Johnson, *She Who Is*, 134.
67   M. Grey, *Outrageous Pursuit of Peace*, 72.

of God. The prophecy of Joel (2: 28-32), repeated in its entirety in Peter's sermon at Pentecost refers to a multiplicity of experiences and testimonies of the Spirit (Acts 2: 17-18). It is an all-inclusive vision.

> I will pour out my Spirit on all flesh;
> your sons and daughters shall prophesy,
> your old people shall dream dreams,
> and your young people shall see visions.
> Even on the male and female slaves,
> in those days, I will pour out my Spirit.

Conclusion

There are different movements of the Spirit in history to remind us of and include us in the mission of the Spirit. Who knows what the Spirit has in store for us fifty years from now? The fifties, the sixties and the seventies saw the flourishing of the Pentecostal and Charismatic Renewal movement as a legitimate trajectory of the Spirit exploring the Good News in history. Many fruits of this wave of renewal are still with us and they have transformed the face of the Church and society. Today there are other trajectories that need to be discerned. New themes in our so-called 'globalised' and 'post-modern' world invite us to the creativity of the mission of the Spirit. New theologies that address the contradictions inherent in our global systems (liberation theologies; feminist theologies, ecotheologies, ecofeminism and theologies of human rights) are precisely theologies of the Holy Spirit[68] inasmuch as they really explore the universal significance of the gospel of the inclusive God in history. The Spirit intercedes for us with sighs which cannot be uttered (Rom 8:26). Today liberation and feminist theologies that have spread virtually to all corners of the globe are leading us to this renewed understanding of the Spirit as the energy of connectedness, one that is "experienced as the breath of life, the vitality of the rhythms of creation, a force that leads to justice-making and as a memory connecting us with the suffering of our ancestors (memoria passionis)."[69] It is the relational power that binds community. It searches new manifestations of the gathered people of God (in all its diversity) and in new and unexpected places. Paul does not describe the fruits of the Spirit in cognitive terms linked to belief

---

68 See M. Welker, *God the Spirit*, 16-21.
69 M. Grey, *The Wisdom of Fools*, 128.

systems and traditions but in ethical terms (Gal 5:22-23).[70] Mission is not so much about leading people to adhere to articles of faith.[71] It is rather about continuing the career and praxis of Jesus who was anointed with the Spirit (Luke 4: 14-30) to proclaim the Good News of liberation to all those who are excluded, 'faceless' and forgotten. The Spirit is the Inclusive God; the God of the Periphery and of the Underside of history; the God of risks, the God of surprises, empowering us to explore new avenues in our midst. The mission of the Spirit then forbids us to think of one religious tradition or culture as the centre into which all others can be drawn. It is the exploration and discovery of the 'other', who is different and valuable but excluded or suppressed by universal assumptions. It is a Spirit of dialogue, unity and reconciliation with the whole of creation. The Spirit has many names!

> Bring many names, beautiful and good
> Celebrate in parable and story
> Holiness in glory
> Living, loving God
> Hail and Hosanna!
> Bring many names!
>
> Strong mother God, working night and day,
> Planning all the wonders of creation,
> Setting each equation,
> Genius at play:
> Hail and Hosanna!
> Strong mother God!
>
> Warm Father God, hugging every child,
> Feeling all the strains of human living,
> Caring and forgiving
> Till we're reconciled:
> Hail and Hosanna!
> Warm Father God!

---

70 B. Hoedemaker, "Toward An Epistemologically Responsible Missiology", in A. Kirk and K. Vanhoozer(eds.), *To Stake a Claim. Mission and the Western Crisis of Knowledge*, Maryknoll New York: Orbis, 1999, 223.

71 The recent Vatican document *'Dominus Iesus'* seems to ignore this important dimension of mission. It seems as if it is designed to judge, to condemn and to exclude rather than to value, understand and include as the Spirit of God would do. The sincere search for religious peace, based on the radical experience of the ineffable Mystery of God and Jesus' message of the radical inclusiveness of this God are absent in this document. The point of ecumenical dialogue is also to establish peace and justice and the integrity of creation. However, these important aspects have no place in the language of *Dominus Iesus*. The Christian faith represented in this document does not reflect the loving and all-inclusive Triune God.

Old, aching God, grey with endless care,
Calmly piercing evil's new disguises,
    Glad of good surprises,
    Wiser than despair:
Hail and Hosanna!
Old, aching God!

Young, growing God, eager on the move,
Seeing all, and fretting at our blindness,
    Crying out for justice,
    Giving all you have:
Hail and Hosanna!
Young, growing God!

Great, living God, never fully known,
Joyful darkness far beyond our seeing,
    Closer yet than breathing,
    Everlasting home:
Hail and Hosanna!
Great, living God!

Brian Wren[72]

---

72   B. Wren, *What Language Shall I Borrow?* London: SCM, 1989, 137-8.

ACTIVISM AS MISSION SPIRITUALITY: THE EXAMPLE OF WILLIAM CAREY

Brian Stanley

1. A Contradiction in Terms?

I have chosen a deliberately provocative title - is it really possible to be an activist and possess an authentic missionary spirituality? For obvious reasons connected with the style of mission in the colonial era, activism has little place in contemporary ecumenical missiology. It is almost a dirty word among Christians today, even amongst significant sections of evangelical Protestantism, the branch of the church which has traditionally been most closely associated with an emphasis on frenetic missionary activity. The leading historian of British evangelicalism, Professor David Bebbington of the University of Stirling, counts activism – a determination to be busy in the cause of the gospel - as one of the four defining characteristics of the whole evangelical movement, along with conversionism, crucicentrism, and biblicism.[1]

Activism speaks to us of hustle and bustle, of a remorseless compulsion to be up and doing - a lifestyle which is all Martha and no Mary. It also tends to conjure up in our minds pictures of the invasion of Christian mission by the norms and methods of modern business culture: of goals, measurable objectives, packages and programs [!] for the evangelization of the world in the next ten years, the quantification of 'success' or 'failure' in terms of crude statistical criteria. Surely activism in the life of the church leaves no time for genuine reflection, asking the hard questions about the goals and methods of mission, unhurried prayer, stillness in worship. Surely activism such as this is very stony soil for development of a true spirituality of mission?

---

1   D. W. Bebbington, *Evangelicalism in Modern Britain: A History from the 1730s to the 1980s* (London: Allen & Unwin, 1989), pp. 2-3.

Certainly activism can be an attempt to cover up the poverty of the inner spiritual life with the externals of a preoccupied busyness about Christian things. This is a disease to which all Christian professionals, and also many lay people, are particularly prone, and many of our churches suffer from it. Yet there must be a sense in which activism is integral to the dynamic of a gospel which is rooted in the sending and redeeming *activity* of God. Gospel people must have something of the activist about them: we must be, like Jesus himself, 'about our Father's business'. Neither can it be said that this is an *exclusively* Protestant emphasis. At the heart of the spirituality of medieval monasticism, after all, was the central place afforded to *work* in the Benedictine rule. To my mind activism in its best and most authentically Christian sense is exemplified by the career of that remarkable missionary pioneer, William Carey (1761-1834). Carey's understanding of Christian mission may not be our understanding, though I wish to suggest that it is actually not so far removed from contemporary missiological enthusiasms as we might imagine. But whatever our theology of mission, Carey has, I think, something to teach us about the place of a properly qualified activism in the missionary life of the church.

2. Obligation - Bane or Blessing?

William Carey was born in the small Northamptonshire village of Paulerspury in 1761. His father, Edmund Carey, was the parish clerk and village schoolmaster. Much of the church of Carey's youth was indifferent to claims of mission, both within Britain, and even more, overseas. The Church of England, within which Carey grew up, had succumbed in considerable measure to the twin temptations of 'reasonable religion' and social respectability - any hint of religious *enthusiasm* was suspected as a sign of incipient Methodism or incipient madness, and it was hard to distinguish the two. Yet much of nonconformity was no better. Many dissenters had succumbed to their own brands of rationalism - either to Unitarianism - or to a hyper-Calvinism which left all to God and cut the nerve of human moral responsibility. Many in the Particular Baptists – the denomination to which Carey had attached himself by 1783 - had fallen for this latter option. Hyper-Calvinism was the prevailing theological influence among the Baptist churches of Northamptonshire and Leicestershire - the circles in which the young Carey moved.

According to this hyper-Calvinist tradition, the divine commission in Matthew 28 to go and make disciples of all nations could not conceivably apply to us. After all, the commission had been given to the apostles at the birth of the church, and they had been given the extraordinary Pentecostal gift of tongues to enable them to discharge it. This understanding of the Great Commission was in fact shared by most of mainstream Protestant thinking from the late sixteenth century onwards: in the apostolic age God had equipped his church for the extraordinary demands of taking the gospel to the pagan world by bestowing on the church the extraordinary spiritual gifts of the ability to speak in foreign tongues and of supernatural healing. It was reasonable to suppose that if God wished the contemporary church to repeat such apostolic endeavour by attempting to preach the gospel to the barbarous heathen beyond the boundaries of Christendom, he would signal his intention by a new outpouring of these extraordinary apostolic gifts.

In September 1785 the 24-year-old William Carey was newly settled in his first pastorate in the sleepy Northamptonshire village of Moulton. In that month he attended his first meeting of the local ministers' fraternal. Instead of keeping modestly quiet, as a young newcomer might normally be expected to do, Carey had the temerity to propose as a fit topic for formal theological discussion the question: 'Whether the command given to the apostles to "teach all nations", was not obligatory on all succeeding ministers to the end of the world, seeing that the accompanying promise [I am with you always] was of equal extent?'

The response of the chairman was peremptory in the extreme:

> Certainly nothing could be done before another Pentecost, when an effusion of miraculous gifts, including the gift of tongues, would give effect to the Commission of Christ as at first ... he was a most miserable enthusiast for asking such a question.[2]

This was a put down analogous to being called a fundamentalist today! There is doubt over the date of this incident, the identity of the chairman (allegedly J. C. Ryland of Northampton), and over the precise words he used: the most commonly cited version - 'Sit

---

2   J. W. Morris, *Memoirs of the Life and Writings of the Revd Andrew Fuller* (London: 1816), pp. 96-7.

down, young man, when God pleases to convert the heathen, he'll do it without your help or mine' - first appears in a biography published in the USA in 1853, and its authenticity must be suspect.[3]

We should notice Carey's focus on obligation. Against Christians of his own day who had denied any responsibility to bring the gospel to those beyond the frontiers of western Christendom, he drew attention to the continuing and universal obligation imposed on all Christians by the command of Christ and the purpose of God. This theme of obligation was, of course, central in the pamphlet which Carey began writing in Moulton and completed after his move to Leicester in May 1789 to become pastor of the Baptist Church at Harvey Lane: *An Enquiry into the Obligations of Christians to Use Means for the Conversion of the Heathens.* The pamphlet was published in Leicester on 12 May 1792 at the price of 1s 6d.

For Carey obligation demanded action. The *Enquiry* was a call to all Christians, and especially his own Baptist denomination, to get off their backsides and actually *do* something to bring the knowledge of Christ to the world beyond the boundaries of so-called 'Christian' Europe: it was not enough for Christians simply to pray for the spread of God's kingdom - they must add to their prayers a readiness to use *means*, 'every lawful method to spread the knowledge of His name'.[4]   Others shared his evangelical Calvinist theology, but it is Carey above all who keeps insisting in 1791-2 on the necessity for *action*, as, for example, at the meeting of the Northamptonshire Baptist Association (covering the Baptist churches of the whole East Midlands area) on 30-31 May 1792. On Wednesday 30 May, Carey preached his so-called 'deathless' sermon on Isaiah 54: 2-3, urging his fellow Baptists to heed the prophet's call to 'lengthen their cords and strengthen their stakes' in anticipation of what God was about to do in greatly expanding the scope of his people. More of this sermon later. We know that the sermon made a great impact on its hearers. Yet the following morning, in the business meeting of the Association, nobody was

---

3   J. Belcher, *William Carey: a Biography* (Philadelphia: 1853). For a discussion of this episode see my *The History of the Baptist Missionary Society 1792-1992* (Edinburgh: T. & T. Clark, 1992), pp. 6-7.

4   William Carey, *An Enquiry into the Obligations of Christians to Use Means for the Conversion of the Heathens* (Leicester: 1792), facsimile edition (London: Carey Kingsgate Press, 1961), p. 3.

willing to make a proposition to take any action in response. Carey then seized the hand of his friend, Andrew Fuller, minister of the Kettering church, and inquired whether they were again going away without '*doing* anything'.[5] As a result, a resolution was passed that a plan should be drawn up for forming a Baptist society for propagating the gospel to the heathen. Without Carey's repeated insistence on the imperative for action, the Baptist Missionary Society – the first of the modern evangelical mission agencies - would not have been formed in the back parlour of Mrs Beeby Wallis's home in Kettering on 2 October 1792.

Now to emphasize moral obligation in response to the command of Christ as a central ingredient in theology of mission is not very popular today, even in evangelical circles. A theology of mission that is all obligation and nothing else will produce nothing but barren legalism and frustration. But equally, if we remove all trace of compelling obligation from our understanding of mission, we are left with a complacent and indulgent spirituality, in which mission is reduced to an invitation to others to share the religious *experience* which we ourselves have enjoyed - i.e. a human-centred rather than God-centred mission theology. These questions are especially pertinent today, when the church is less confident than it was of the soteriological necessity and urgency of mission. In Britain at least, if you want to hear today an appeal for urgent and imperative action in response to the desperate needs of the world, you would, sad to relate, be best advised *not* go to a church to listen to a sermon: you are much more likely to hear such a summons to urgent sacrificial action on behalf of humanity by turning on your television on Red Nose Day.

2. Divine Sovereignty and Human Responsibility: or, God's Mission and Ours

In Carey's thought and writing, emphasis on human obligation is always held in close relationship to an equivalent emphasis on mission as the plan, purpose, and activity of God himself. The basis of obligation in mission is not solely or even primarily the command of Christ - for such an approach too often leads to a guilt-induced and legalistic approach to mission. The commission of Christ to his church itself reflects and depends on the loving purpose of God: the missionary movement of God himself towards

---

5   J. C. Marshman, *The Life and Times of Carey, Marshman, and Ward*, 2 vols (London: 1859), I, p. 15.

all humanity. My central contention in this paper is that true spirituality in mission depends on the maintenance of a proper balance between God's sovereign and all-embracing redemptive purpose and our human responsibility. I wish to consider five aspects of this union between confidence in God's purpose and commitment to action in accord with that purpose – a union which to my mind the church today has largely lost.

(i) God's salvific purpose and activity are the basis of confident missionary action

What Carey attempted in going to Bengal as one of the first two missionaries of the BMS in 1793 was widely regarded as little short of lunacy. For a largely self-educated dissenting pastor-cum-shoemaker to travel half-way round the world, try to force his way illegally without a licence into British India, and then seek to convert those who were regarded as poor, benighted Hindus to Christianity seemed preposterous in the extreme, and attracted ridicule. Carey's response to such criticisms was simply to appeal, not merely to the clarity of God's command, but even more to the certainty of his redemptive purpose and activity.

Carey's confidence in the fulfilment of God's missionary purpose is most famously exemplified in his sermon on Isaiah 54:2-3 to the Northamptonshire Baptist Association ministers' meeting in Nottingham on 30 May 1792. In the plight of exiled Judah, apparently forgotten by God her husband, Carey saw a picture of the barren and desolate church of his day, and in the promise of a new and wider destiny for Judah lay the promise of countless new children in the Christian family to be drawn from all the earth. However, God's promise was also his command. God was about to do great things by extending the kingdom of Jesus throughout the globe, and for that very reason Christians were bound to attempt great things by spreading the gospel overseas. Hence Carey's most celebrated and much misquoted slogan. Go to Calcutta today, to the site of the first church which Carey planted in Calcutta – the Lal Bazaar church, and you will find that appropriately enough there is now a Bible College adjacent to the church building. Over the main entrance to the College, you will see this slogan displayed:

> 'Attempt great things for God
> Expect great things from God.'

The reversal of the quotation is in fact symbolic of what happened to the Protestant mission movement in its dominant Anglo-American form in the course of the nineteenth century. Gustav Warneck's famous criticism of Anglo-American activism, expressed at the New York Ecumenical Missionary Conference in 1900, ably delineates the form of debased activism which progressively infected Protestant missions in the century after 1792: a form of unreflective activism rooted in the self-absorption of increasingly sophisticated and hence domineering western mission organisations had progressively distorted the balance in Carey's Calvinistic theology between divine and human initiative. The 'attempting of great things for God' had come to dominate the expectation of great things from God:

> The mission command bids us 'go' into all the world, not 'fly'. *Festina lente* applies also to missionary undertakings. The kingdom of heaven is like a field in which the crop is healthily growing at a normal rate, not like a hot-house. Impatient pressing forward has led to the waste of much precious toil, and more than one old mission field has been unwarrantably neglected in the haste to begin work in a new field.

> The non-Christian world is not to be carried by assault. Mission history should also teach us not to specify a time when the evangelisation of the world is to be completed. It is not for us to determine the times and seasons, but to do in this our own time what we can, and do it wisely and discreetly.[6]

It is probable that what Carey actually said was simply 'Expect great things ... attempt great things' – the words 'from God' and 'to God' appear to be a later textual interposition, but one that fully reflects Carey's meaning.[7] That does not much matter, but the order does. The expectation of great things from God is theologically and chronologically prior to the attempting of great things for him. As that other missionary son of Calvin, David Bosch, emphasised, the *missio Dei* is theologically and

---

6 Ecumenical Missionary Conference New York, 1900, *Report of the Ecumenical Conference on Foreign Missions, Held in Carnegie Hall and Neighboring Churches, April 21 to May 1*, 2 vols (London: Religious Tract Society, and New York: American Tract Society, n.d.), I, p. 290.

7 Stanley, *History of the BMS*, p. 14.

chronologically prior to all human activity in mission.[8] That is why the role of the Spirit must be central in both missionary theology and missionary spirituality. This was certainly the case for Carey: the final section of the *Enquiry* begins with an exposition of the fact that all human means used in mission will be ineffectual without the *'fervent and united prayer'* of the people of God: 'If a temple is raised for God in the heathen world, it will not be *by might, nor by power*, nor by the authority of the magistrate, or the eloquence of the orator; *but my Spirit, saith the Lord of Hosts.*'[9] In that statement Carey repudiates reliance on the two false sources of confidence that were to prove the undoing of missions over the next century: the leaky umbrella of imperial power (the authority of the magistrate); and the Enlightenment expectation that Christian rational apologetic (the eloquence of the orator) would convince people of the superiority of Christianity.

For all Carey's attack on the passivity of hyper-Calvinism, he remained, like his theological mentor Andrew Fuller, thoroughly Calvinistic in his theological framework (by today's standards, a high Calvinist). In common with almost all pioneers of the Protestant missionary awakening, Carey placed his confidence in what he held to be the promises of Scripture that through the preaching of the gospel in the power of the Spirit the 'heathen' would be brought to make their glad submission to the lordship of Christ (Psalm 2). Now I have questions about this postmillennial eschatology - does it not lose sight of the contrast between this age, in which the submission of the world to the lordship of Christ will always be incomplete, and the new creation of the age to come, in which every knee will bow and every tongue confess that Christ is Lord? Does it not lose sight of the second coming of Christ as the focus of the Christian hope? But at least it expresses one half of the witness of scripture, namely that God's saving purpose cannot ultimately be defeated, and that the good news of the kingdom is the power of God unto salvation to all that believe. The vision of the ultimate triumph of God's saving and new-creating purpose is the basis of confident missionary action. This leads directly to the second point.

---

8   David Bosch, *Transforming Mission: Paradigm Shifts in Theology of Mission* (Maryknoll, N.Y.: Orbis, 1991), pp. 10, 370, 390.
9   Carey, *Enquiry*, p. 77.

(ii) The promised reign of God is the basis of persistent endurance in mission

Carey greatly under-estimated the magnitude of the task which awaited him in Bengal. He was staggered on arrival in India by the nature of Hindu religion and society, especially by the caste system, which seemed to him to imprison the population in bonds which made conversion to Christ appear virtually impossible: then as now, for a caste Hindu to become a Christian meant ostracism from the community. It is no wonder that it took seven years before the conversion of the first Hindu, Krishna Pal, and even thereafter conversions were relatively few. In such circumstances it was easy to lose heart: 'When I first left England', Carey wrote in 1794, 'my hope of the conversion of the heathen was very strong; but among so many obstacles it would utterly die away, unless upheld by God, having nothing to cherish it'. He found his resources for endurance and encouragement in the promises of God in Scripture: 'Yet this is our encouragement, the power of God is sufficient to accomplish everything which he has promised, and his promises are exceedingly great and precious respecting the conversion of the heathens.' [10]

In June 1796, Carey wrote to Fuller, the BMS secretary in Kettering, about the work he and his first colleague, John Thomas, were doing:

> Mr T[homas] and I are Men and Fallible, but we can only desert the Work of Preaching the Word of Life to the Hindoos, with our Lives, and are thro' Grace determined to hold on tho' our discouragements were a Thousand times greater than they are - we have the same ground of Hope with our Brethren in England. Viz. the Promise, Power, and Faithfulness of God; for unless his Mercy break the Heart of Stone either in England, India or Africa, nothing will be done effectually; and he can as easily convert a superstitious Bram[in] [*sic*] as an Englishman.[11]

Now even if we accept the fundamental legitimacy of Carey's quest for the conversion of Hindus, there are theological questions to be asked here. In point of fact, of course, for the last 200 years it *has* generally proved more difficult to convert a Brahmin than your average Englishman, and this raises questions of theodicy for

---

10 *Periodical Accounts relative to the Baptist Missionary Society*, I, p. 175.
11 Carey to Fuller, 17 June 1796, IN/13, BMS archives, Regent's Park College, Oxford.

any conversionist theology of mission which sees conversion to Christ as a result of the work of the Spirit and not simply human persuasion (in my view an indispensable emphasis given the controversial nature of religious conversion in India and other contexts today). It is no accident that it was among missionaries with experience of India that the first serious theological doubts were raised about the entire project of seeking to convert those of other faiths to Christianity. Our generation cannot avoid confronting this pre-eminent missiological issue. I would simply make two comments here. The first is to stress that in Carey's theology the imperative to call 'the heathen' to faith in Christ is not grounded primarily in any claim that they are eternally lost without faith in Christ: Carey refers very rarely to hell, though he regularly uses language such as 'pagan darkness'. The basis for calling Hindus to conversion to Christ is rather the revelation of God's purpose to establish his kingdom among all humanity. A second comment is that even if our theology of mission has no place for calling those of other faiths to conversion, the essential theological point remains that our motivation for endurance in the missionary task – *however* we define it – must derive from the word and purpose of God, not on the uncertainties of the human response which our work for God evokes. If our activism focuses on the level of response, without reference to what we can discern of the purposes of God, it soon degenerates into frenetic and manipulative activity.

(iii) God's providence transforms disasters into mercies

Central to Carey's work in Bengal was his supervision of the printing and translation of the Bible into various Indian vernacular languages: a reflection of the premium which the Serampore Baptist missionaries, rather in contrast to Alexander Duff of the Church of Scotland mission in Calcutta, placed on Christian education in the vernacular. On 11 March 1812 fire swept through his printing workshop at Serampore, destroying several of Carey's precious manuscripts and a large collection of printing fonts and paper, to the value of 70,000 rupees. In human terms it was a shattering disaster. Carey estimated it would take twelve months' hard labour to replace what had been lost. Yet in reporting the fire to Fuller, he describes the fire as a 'providence' and rapidly passes from detailing the losses to a list of eight 'merciful circumstances' attending the fire, for which he wished to give thanks. The last of these was the fact that 'we have all of us been supported under the affliction, and preserved from discouragement. To me the consideration of the divine sovereignty and wisdom has been very supporting; and indeed, I have usually been supported under afflictions by feeling that I and mine are in the hands of an infinitely wise God – I endeavoured to improve this our affliction last Lord's Day, from Psalm XVI.10 'Be still and know that I am God'.'[12]

Thus to Carey the disaster of the fire was simply another reminder of the infinitely wise and inscrutable providence of God, and hence also of the ultimate certainty that his missionary purposes would triumph. As it happened, it was precisely the news of the fire which did much to make Carey a well-known figure in Britain, and substantially increased levels of public interest and support. Again, we may have questions to address to this quaintly Puritan theology of providence, but we need also to ask what our own Christian generation has lost by its general repudiation of an active belief in providence – of a God who really is involved in the warp and woof of everyday human history. There is something rather impressive about the capacity of faith of this kind to transform disasters into mercies. True Christian activism is sustained by an inner serenity, which can take quite appalling reverses in its stride, and yet press on with the divinely-appointed task. For Carey, that was possible because he had been captivated by the demands of the gospel of grace – here is the concept of obligation again!

(iv) Missionary vocation imposes absolute demands and hence creates radical freedom

In Section IV of the *Enquiry* Carey deals with a number of practical objections to the missionary task, including the objection that missionaries in tropical lands would not be able to procure the necessities of life; i.e. that food and comforts would not be available to enable English ministers to live at the level to which they had become accustomed. His reply is to acknowledge that European food might not be obtainable, but to insist that making the adjustment to a native diet would be no more than a further application of the basic commitment which anyone makes on entering God's service. Carey continues with a powerful passage which reinforces again the obligations intrinsic to the gospel of Christ:

---

12 Carey to Fuller, 25 Mar. 1812, IN/13, BMS archives, Regent's Park College, Oxford.

A Christian minister is a person who in a peculiar sense is *not his own*; he is the *servant* of God, and therefore ought to be wholly devoted to him. By entering on that sacred office he solemnly undertakes to be always engaged, as much as possible, in the Lord's work, and not to chuse his own pleasure, or employment, or pursue the ministry as a something that is to subserve his own ends, or interests, or as a kind of bye-work. He engages to go where God pleases, and to do, or endure what he sees fit to command, or call him to, in the exercise of his function. He virtually bids farewell to friends, pleasures, and comforts, and stands in readiness to endure the greatest sufferings in the work of his Lord, and Master. It is inconsistent for ministers to please themselves with thoughts of a numerous auditory, cordial friends, a civilized country, legal protection, affluence, splendor, or even a competency. The slights, and hatred of men, and even pretended friends, gloomy prisons, and tortures, the society of barbarians of uncouth speech, miserable accommodations in wretched wildernesses, hunger, and thirst, nakedness, weariness, and painfulness, hard work, and but little worldly encouragement, should rather be the objects of their expectation.[13]

The Christian minister, proclaims Carey, is committed to being an activist - 'he solemnly undertakes to be always engaged, as much as possible, in the Lord's work'. There is in Carey none of that conceptual division between 'ministry' and 'mission' which still bedevils so much of the church in the western hemisphere. To be committed to Christian ministry or service is also, Carey insists, to be committed to mission, for the minister 'engages to go where God pleases, and to do, or endure what he sees fit to command'. In his splendid book, *A Vision Betrayed*, Andrew Ross has shown how the fourth vow of the professed members of the Jesuit order, binding them to go wherever the Pope might send them in sole submission to his authority, proved a powerful and radical liberating dynamic in mission history, forming the basis of the Jesuit missiological tradition of dissociation from western political authority and cultural norms.[14] In the same way, Carey argues that commitment to mission necessarily involves a radical preparedness to distance oneself from the comforts and security of one's own

---

13 Carey, *Enquiry*, p. 72.
14 Andrew Ross, *A Vision Betrayed: the Jesuits in Japan and China 1542-1742* (Edinburgh: Edinburgh UP, 1994), pp. 202-3.

society and culture. Is it reading too much into Carey's words here to suggest that this emphasis on absolute personal vulnerability was the basis of the considerable measure of cultural identification and flexibility which most historians now discern in the early Serampore missionaries, in contrast to so many of their successors in nineteenth-century missions?

(v) God's grace puts all human achievements in mission into perspective

By any standard, Carey's achievements were extraordinary. In biblical translation, he was primarily responsible for the translation of the entire Bible into six Asian languages, and of parts of it into a further twenty-nine (though we should stress that this translating achievement was a collaborative enterprise involving a team of Indian pandits or assistants, both Hindus and Christians). Serampore College was founded in 1818 as an institution to train Christian Indians to be missionaries to their own people and offer Hindus and Muslims a higher education on Christian principles. It still stands today as the oldest theological college in India and one of the premier institutions of higher education in West Bengal. To these achievements should be added his major contributions to Bengali literature and culture, social reform (such as the abolition of *sati* in Bengal), and Indian horticulture and agriculture. Carey exemplifies the fact that a theology of mission that is strongly committed to the goal of extending the church is not *necessarily* a narrow or what would now (quite wrongly) be called a 'pietist' theology of mission. Carey was deeply committed to agricultural improvement in India, recognising that on such improvement was 'suspended the comfort and happiness of the larger part of … numerous millions'.[15]

All of this was accomplished against the background of acute domestic tragedy. His first wife, Dorothy, did not share her husband's sense of call to India, and soon after arrival in Bengal, developed an acute mental illness which required her to be locked in her room with little interruption. She died in 1807. Yet Carey always retained an exceptionally low evaluation of his own spiritual productivity. In 1817, reflecting on recent deaths of colleagues, he wrote: 'The night of death will soon come when none of us can work. I look with deep regret on my past life and

---

15 E. Daniel Potts, *British Baptist Missionaries in India 1793-1837: the History of Serampore and its Missions* (Cambridge: Cambridge UP, 1967), p. 71.

am ashamed to see what a loiterer I have been. I scarcely appear to live to any useful purpose.'[16] Similarly, on his 70th birthday in 1831, Carey wrote to his son, Jabez, reviewing the story of his life, and concluded that he found 'much, very much, for which I ought to be humbled in the dust': his 'negligence in the Lord's work' had been 'great'.[17]

Carey is buried in a now sadly neglected cemetery in Serampore. His own grave is simple in the extreme. The more grandiose monument adjacent to his own grave marks the tomb of his second Danish wife, Charlotte. But on the side of that monument is an inscription which Carey instructed should be placed on his wife's tomb in his own memory. It contains a couplet of Isaac Watts (which itself draws on Old Testament language from Psalm 22 and Job):
> 'A wretched, poor and helpless worm
> On thy kind arms I fall.'

To our minds, all this may seem faintly comic, over the top, if not positively unhealthy. We are accustomed rather to the need to give self-despising Christians a proper sense of their own self-worth. Encouraging anyone to think of themselves as a wretched, poor and helpless worm is not high on the list of our pastoral priorities. Yet Carey was no evangelical Uriah Heep, 'ever so 'umble' in a false and affected way. He was far from a doormat, a Christian wimp who delighted in being walked over by others. Reading his letters written in the 1820s, when he and his colleagues fought the BMS tooth and nail for what they felt to be their rights in the lamentable 'Serampore Controversy', which led to the separation of the Serampore mission from the BMS in 1827, soon dispels that impression. He insisted that the relationship between missionaries and the home committee which sent them should be one of Christian brotherhood, not a servant-master relationship.[18]

Carey appears to belittle himself only because he is so captivated by the immensity of God's grace in using him to play some part in his eternal purposes. The activist in Christian work can all too easily become someone feeding their own insecure ego, convinced that the future of the church rests on their shoulders and

---

16 Carey to Jabez Carey, 3 Feb. 1817, Angus Library, Regent's Park College, Oxford.
17 Carey to Jabez Carey, 17 Aug. 1831, Angus Library, Regent's Park College, Oxford.
18 See Stanley, *History of the BMS*, pp. 57-67.

theirs alone. However, the true Christian activist retains a clear focus on the grace of God which throws all human achievements into miniature. Carey's epitaph expresses both his own deep sense of unworthiness of how God had used him, and his own equally firm conviction of his security in God – at the end of his life in 1834 he knew, that at the last, his work done, he could throw himself with absolute confidence onto the love of God in Christ - 'on thy kind arms I fall'.

In my book, therefore, activism of the kind which Carey exemplifies is not a dirty word, but rather a proper and deeply spiritual response to the grace of God. Much will, of course, depend on what we believe about the mission of God to the world in which He involves us. Carey believed that the whole of humanity needed urgently and imperatively to hear and receive the good news of the coming of the kingdom in Jesus Christ – that there is to be found in knowing and following Christ a fullness of life and human community that can be found nowhere else and which death cannot extinguish. It is now the churches of the south and the east – the inheritors of the mission legacy of the west which Carey did so much to establish – which hold on to that conviction with greatest confidence and vigour. Churches in the former mission fields, including parts of India, are now the primary senders in global mission. In the western world, by contrast, the church in our day has not found it easy to hold on to that belief, as the pressures on Christians to conform to a pluralist understanding of religious truth are enormous. But perhaps they are not essentially different from the pressures which Carey faced in attempting to persuade the church of the eighteenth century that mission was not some eccentric or preposterous activity but rather a central and inescapable imperative of the gospel of grace.

PART II

CREATIVE WAYS
OF BEING CHURCH

LIQUID CHURCH

Pete Ward

New approaches to Church have been at the heart of contemporary mission in the UK. This has led to considerable creativity and thus we now have youth churches, seeker services, cell churches, alternative worships, youth congregations and so on. These developments have sprung from the conviction that Church itself is a problem, and therefore if the faith is to be contextualised in contemporary culture, then how we do Church must be re-framed in some way. This is a view with which I am in substantial agreement, and yet despite all the new developments, I am more and more convinced that the re-imagining of Church may have some way further to travel. Two key observations have led to this conviction.

The first observation is the evident failure of so called Alternative Worship to attract people in any great numbers. Most groups seem to gather a small handful of enthusiasts. Given the various discourses of the 'post', alternative worship with its emphasis on ritual, symbol, contemporary culture, play, the image, and ambiguity should really be a more impressive solution. Why have these groups largely failed to connect with significant numbers in a 'post-modern' context? The second observation is that events such as Soul Survivor appear to be going from strength to strength attracting young people in their thousands. There is an evident paradox here in that the style of worship associated with Soul Survivor, and other post-Wimber groups, has developed a tendency to become somewhat inflexible and routine. If we agree with the discourses of the 'post' (which I admit I largely do) then how are we to account for the popularity of contemporary charismatic worship?

It is tempting to adopt the view from one of these two opposing camps. The charismatic in me may be drawn to some notion of spiritual superiority. The Holy Spirit anoints and draws the people, and so the numbers are read as a blessing. Yet it seems strange that God should be limited to worship contextualised in a 1980's stadium rock culture. Moreover charismatic ecstasy and the mystical spirituality of image and ritual evident in Alternative Worship are much too closely related to privilege one above the other. To swap sides for a moment as an Alt worshipper of long standing my tendency may be to adopt a framework based on notions of the mainstream and hip culture derived from popular music. Soul Survivor is therefore the equivalent of Tracy's and Sharon's dancing round their handbags to mass marketed chart music. In contrast Alternative worship is to be regarded as, hip, cool, and exclusive, or to use a theological term it is 'prophetic'. Despite an element of truth, this view seems reductive and less than satisfactory. It seems less than credible to write off the enthusiasm of so many young people (who are presumably as 'post' as we get) as deluded or duped. In contrast it seems hard to escape the market logic that must view the Alternative groups as themselves perhaps a little 'sad'.

Looking from one group towards the other is less than helpful, not least because I feel that both have insights to share and both have aspects of the way forward for worship in contemporary culture. Rather than align with one camp (and I confess I find this a little hard because I feel that I have a place in both) I plan to discuss a way forward which I have called 'Liquid Church' – this phrase is based upon Bauman's phrase 'Liquid Modernity'[1] and throughout this paper I will draw upon this work.

Solid and Liquid

Bauman distinguishes between solid or 'heavy' modernity and what he calls liquid modernity. Modernity he argues, was based

---

1   Z Bauman, *Liquid Modernity*, (2000)

on a call to melt the 'solids' and so it emerges from the untying of the economy from traditional (and religious) linkages. The connection to family, the sacred and obligation are replaced by an institutionalised rational system.[2] Modernity, thus substitutes one solid for another, this being a solid built from the sum of individual choosing. Solid modernity is based on the victory of the settled over the nomad, it is a culture linked to production rather than consumption, it is the Fordist principle of expansion, size, plant, boundaries, norms, rules, and class orientated affinities and identities.[3] The liquefaction of modernity is now turned upon itself so that capital is released from location, individuals are no longer afforded the possibility of communal identities, consumption is privileged over production, and the individual has to shape identity apart from community.[4] Bauman's analysis reads as a grim lament for the fate of humanity and seems to have been penned with not a little regret for the passing of previous certainties. Whilst not sharing Bauman's pessimism, his analysis of changes in modernity, as a fluidity (rather than as a 'post'), lend themselves to be used in a discussion of contemporary ecclesiology. The approach adopted is to use 'Liquid Modernity' as a jumping off point rather than accepting entirely its analytical perspectives.

As it is possible to talk of solid modernity, it also seems appropriate to speak of solid Church. A Church based on the maintaining of boundaries, norms and rules, where panopticon like, members and leaders are locked together in relationships of surveillance and control. Expansion is based on increasing the size of the plant and the territorial influence of the congregation. Membership is linked to regular attendance at a central Sunday act of worship. Leaders measure their effect by the size of attendance and followers locate their identity in a collective sense of belonging. Communal life is regulated by house groups and house group leaders and a structure of committees and representation is step laddered from local, to regional, to national, and to international levels: the bureaucratisation of divine economy.

The problem with alternative worship, as I read it, is that it has inherited aspects of this heavy or solid Church. It has done this by developing as 'services' or 'congregations'. Each has a name

---

2   Ibid., pp. 3-4
3   Ibid., p25, p35, p57, and p63
4   Ibid., p5, p7, p13, p29, p31

epicentre, JOY, Grace etc. and each has a meeting linked to a time of service: JOY meets at 7pm. The dynamic is clear, to be a part of this community you must attend. Coffee in the church hall after the service may have been replaced by a trip down the pub but the same 'heavy' social dynamic is to some extent in play. This is solid congregational life, heavy Church, and no amount of irony or visual technology will disguise this fact. Despite our 'post' sensibilities and aesthetics, we have been keen to be seen as real Church. The irony has been that our models of church have been forged in Fordist heavy modernity. In effect our fluid worship has been neatly contained in a very solid container and like any liquid it has adopted the shape of that within which it is placed.

Liquid Church is at this moment an act of imagination but it would attempt to flow beyond the solid social organisation of the 'congregation'. Two quite different worship experiences have led me to feel that such imagining may be possible. The first was the Labyrinth in St Paul's Cathedral which was organised by Alternative Worship Groups based in London. The Labyrinth was set out on a carpet and at various points on the walkway there were stations with activities for reflection, meditation, and prayer. These included a bucket with water in and stones which when dropped into the bucket were to represent past regrets and wrong doing, or a computer screen with electronic images of candles these could be 'lit' by pressing the key board and a prayer said for a friend in need. Each 'worshipper' was given a personal CD player on which there was accompanying music and a spoken meditative guide to the activities within the labyrinth. The second was a brief visit to an Orthodox Church in Greece. The Church was a centre of pilgrimage and many of those making their way to mid-day prayer did so on their hands and knees. Once inside the Church a variety of activities were on offer. Worshippers could kiss the sacred icon, light candles, eat the blessed bread which was available, fill small bottles with Holy Oil, and wander around the church – this offered the possibility of more icon kissing. The service was conducted while all of this was taking place. A few stood and listened to the prayers but the pew ridden ranks of Western congregations seemed entirely absent. As the singing and chanting was continuing the priest was reading petitions quietly in front of the altar. At one side of the church people were writing prayers on small pieces of paper. It was these prayers which eventually found their way to the priest.

The Orthodox style of worship, and to some extent the Labyrinth, represent pre-modern spiritualities and traditions. As such they perhaps represent a glimpse beyond the heavy congregation orientated life of many of our Churches. In both of these examples the relationship to tradition, identity, spiritual discipline, and practise has been re-orientated in ways which are significantly different to our solid social structures and as such they indicate a way forward to a more liquid Church.

Identity Afloat

In solid modernity individual identity was securely located in class and gender norms. So tightly prescribed were these roles that escape was little easier than it had been in the pre-modern world of estates and divine order. In the rapidly changing fluid environment of the present these identity options are no longer in play, either as refuge, or as constraint.[5] Thus contradictions and troubles no longer translate into collective struggles.[6] The consequent individualisation of risk and identity formation means that we are responsible for our own success or failure. The result is individuals seeking a precarious way forward in an environment of increasing choice with little guidance or direction.

'What emerges from the fading social norms is naked, frightened aggressive ego in search of love and help. In the search for itself and an affectionate sociality, it easily gets lost in the jungle of the self...Someone who is poking around in the fog of his or her own self is no longer capable of noticing that this isolation, this solitary confinement of the ego is a "mass sentence."'[7]

Respite is sought in what Bauman variously calls 'peg', cloakroom, or carnival communities. Peg communities offer the chance for individuals to gather for a moment around a 'nail' on which they can peg their individual fears.[8] Cloakroom communities allow individuals to dress for an event, leave their coats at the door, and to enjoy a temporary spectacle. A carnival is similarly a gathering of individuals around an event which offers a brief distraction from the demands and fears of a fluid unsettled search for identity and meaning.[9] These communities of respite and refuge perhaps indicate an interpretative strategy for understanding the

---

5   Ibid., p. 33   6.   Ibid., p. 34ff
7   Ibid., p.37 (Beck)   8.   Idem
9   Ibid., p. 200

attraction of Charismatic worship with its network of celebrations, tours, festivals, newly released albums, and brightly packaged initiatives. Here individuals find some measure of distraction, spectacle, and the offer of security. Events such as Soul Survivor are consumer orientated carnivals of spirituality sustained by frequent tours and promoted products. Far from being surpassed by the 'post' as some have argued[10] the social structures of charismatic worship well adapted to a liquid environment. At the same time a peg community offers only temporary respite and it may not be the long term solution which it is hoped by writers such as Cray.[11] My own observation is that the worship and spirituality offered by Soul Survivor is ideally suited to younger teenagers. The security and spiritual package on offer connects very well with the insecurities and struggles of this age group. As these young people get older the predictable routines of the worship and the teaching become less relevant. Refuge and respite may very soon turn to containment and restraint. Thus the solutions offered by contemporary charismatic worship may eventually be a little too restrictive to carry an individual through an extended voyage through the sea of modernity. As a point of departure, and maybe return, it certainly has its place but there is need to search for a more fluid solution.

Shopping for a Liquid Church

Shopping characterises all of contemporary life. Individuals, says Bauman, are constantly comparing prices, casting their eyes along the shelves, feeling the goods, and assessing the balance on our credit cards.

'Whatever we do and whatever name we attach to our activity it is a kind of shopping, or an activity shaped in the likeness of shopping. The code in which our "life policy" is scripted is derived from the pragmatics of shopping.'[12]

Heavy Church is not geared up for the shopper, it is a 'one size fits all' environment. Heavy Church is a culture based on production rather than consumption, its social reflexes are geared to norms and rules based on the possibilities and disciplines required of good and productive worshippers. In these climes

---

10 D. Tomlinson, *The Post Evangelical* (1995)
11 G. Cray et al., *The Post Evangelical Debate* (1997) p. 18
12 Z. Bauman, op. Cit., p 73

leaders are authorities who know better and offer an as yet unseen way forward. Liquid Modernity has left this kind of Church and these kind of leaders somewhat adrift with a refuge community their only option to exercise their learned responses.

Liquid Church would reshape itself around worshippers as consumers. Spiritual life would recognise that shopping is the natural way of interaction with all aspects of life including the spiritual. A fluid Church would abandon congregational structures in favour of a varied and changing diet of worship, prayer, study and activity. The assumption that what we offer in our morning service may be boring or unpalatable but ultimately is 'good for you', will be challenged. In its place will be a responsive, flexible pattern of Church life which seeks to deliver not only what individuals want, but also which draws on the depth and variety of the Christian tradition. Such a consumer orientated Church would be likely avoid the dumbing down of the, 'middle path', 'we must not offend', 'we need to carry the congregation with us', mentality of heavy Church. Instead a variety of spiritual expressions drawing on the riches of a number of Christian traditions would be available. A mixed diet of the profound and the accessible would enable the liquid Church to reflect the breadth and depth of the Gospel. A choice of prayer styles, activities, mission challenges, opportunities for study, and music expression, would be basic to Church life. These choices of course need to be on offer at different times and in a variety of locations. Membership would be replaced by participation and involvement. Individual choice would guide and influence the creativity of Church leaders. Liquid Church would be continually on the move responding to the Spirit and the Gospel of Jesus, the imagination and the creativity of leaders and the choices and experiences of worshippers.

From Need to Desire

Heavy Church is set up to convince people of their need (of God) and then deliver salvation in response to this need. Need in this sense has been prescribed, anticipated, it is related to a paternalistic authority that 'knows best'. Need is limited, boundaried, part of a common human condition, it can be met and satisfied. Spiritual need is taught and policed in heavy Church. A fluid culture is not based on the reasonable limits and prescribed notions of need. Liquid Church replaces need with desire. Desire is not imposed; it emerges from the worshipper. To desire God is to seek him rather than to learn or be taught that we need him. Desire may be stimulated by what is on offer, but it remains the responsibility of the individual and in this sense it is non-referential.[13]

A Liquid Church would be built around the realisation that people are seeking after encounter with God. Spiritual hunger, desire, and pleasure are just below the surface. A trip around the High Street Shops is all that is required to demonstrate that this is true. Spiritual desire, albeit inchoate, is evident in the sale of candles, art, music, holidays, garden products, etc. Encounter with mystery, with the divine, is clearly sought after by many more people than those who are drawn into the heavy routine of the congregation. The Church may well own the rights to the genuine article but it has not learned to locate itself in the new market place of the fluid. Solid Church is seen by many outside the faith as a club demanding exclusive commitment and as such it is not perceived as part of the wider market. This is what is meant when people use the phrase "I am spiritual but I'm not religious". The exclusive club of traditional heavy 'religion' has been rejected, but the search for God continues. Indeed there is some evidence that spiritual quest is alive and well in the floating world of modernity.[14]

Liquid Church would take this spiritual searching as its starting point and identify it as a desire for God. Desire is a motivating force that drives many people to seek after God. Liquid Church will gain confidence from this fact. Solid Church has a tendency to down play the spiritual in a concern to keep everyone happy. The extremes of commitment and discipleship are often discouraged because they threaten the comfortable, stable, and static majority. Heavy Church wants to keep the maximum numbers together in same 'meeting'. It therefore tends to confuse attendance with commitment and faith with compliance. Liquid Church will need to be more acute, more exacting, more demanding and in turn offer profound and costly encounter with God. In the fluid market place the distinctive rather than the routine, and the vibrant rather than the normal will be sought after and desired. Need may be satisfied and met. Desire will be continually in play. Worshippers in the Liquid Church will desire to meet with God and to continue to meet God. Liquid Church will therefore avoid the regular and the mundane in favour of the profound and the colourful.

---

13 Ibid., p. 74
14 D. Lyon, *Postmodernity* (2000) W.C. Roof, *Spiritual Marketplace* (1999)

From Authority to Example

Need in heavy Church is related to authority, a leadership which prescribes spiritual malady and their solutions. In contrast, desire is located in the perceptions of the worshipper. In liquid modernity authority is replaced by example. Bauman, in relation to this shift, discusses Jane Fonda's Workout Book and Video. Individuals seeking guidance in the deregulated world of the consumer turn to celebrities such as Jane Fonda for a way forward. What is on offer is a clear and an uncompromising message. The author has taken control of her body and her life. She has made a difference to her own life and she sets out what is involved for anyone wanting to know.

'Jane Fonda is quite outspoken about the substance of her offer and straightforward about what sort of example her readers and watchers ought to follow; "I like to think a lot of my body is my own doing and my own blood and guts. It's my responsibility".'[15]

In the Liquid Church leadership will move from reliance on appointment and authority to example. When worshippers are free to shop they will gravitate towards those they perceive as being enlightened and in the know. In the Liquid Church holiness, discipline, and passion will mean that the leaders will be people who are sought out as teachers. Those who are perceived to have met with God and been in his presence and been changed by his Spirit will be the guides. Heavy Church ordains those who are safe and steady and willing to hold the fort. The priorities of the worship consumer are different. He or she seeks those who are saintly, inspired, and full of the Spirit of God.

Those who desire God will be willing to follow these kinds of leaders along the demanding paths of spiritual discipline. Liquid Church will replace 'norms' and routines with clearly expressed ways of living in the presence of God. The spiritual path may be presented as an exacting and testing 'way' for followers of Jesus. Leaders relocate themselves as fellow travellers telling tales of wondrous sights and risky pathways. The way of the Cross of Jesus will be seen to involve committed engagement and some suffering. To live in the grace and energising of the Spirit will arise from the exercise of submission and repentance. These Gospel perspectives will be shared by those who are seen as examples rather than taught by those who assume authority based on outside appointment.

---

15 Bauman, op. cit., p. 66 (Radnor)

Liquid Church will remain committed to Gospel perspectives but it will try to re-express these in the new fluid environment.

The lowest common denominator of congregational life will be replaced by the pursuit of the Holy. This corresponds to Bauman's discussion of the difference between health and fitness. Health is located in solid modernity and is based on conforming to basic norms, rules and standardised expectations. Fitness in contrast is an openness to the unexpected, a readiness for what life may throw at you.[16] Liquid Church will have more akin to fitness than health. The growth in the retreat movement and in spiritual direction indicate that people are already searching for spirituality which goes beyond the safe norms of the congregation. The comfortable lifestyle of heavy Church is being supplemented by more demanding spiritual routines and exercises. The religious in convents and monasteries are currently being sought out as holy examples and guides. These developments indicate that the Liquid Church may be seeping under the doors of our solid institutions.

Refuge to Network

The factory system of Heavy Church requires that we all get along and accept each other as part of the Christian community. Heavy Church demands a measure of social interaction and routinises these processes. As Heavy Church mutates into a place of refuge, Bauman's peg community, true social diversity is slowly eliminated. Congregations are made up of similar people with similar incomes and similar fears.

Liquid Church would grasp a vision of connection and community that moves outside the solid refuge of the congregation. Connection would be located in common cause, similar desires and pleasures. Liquid Church would follow the fault lines of social connection based on networks. The informal would be privileged over the formal. Meeting together on the basis of doing things with each other, or attending social activities together. Bauman's portrait of the consumer is as isolated and frightened individual forever unsure of their place in the world.[17] Liquid Church would be based on the belief that this need not be the case, but in striking this course it will not return to the refuge mentality of solid Church, instead it will work towards patterns of connection which move out into the social landscape.

---

16   Ibid., p. 77
17   Ibid., p. 163

RECAPTURING THE ORIGINAL MODELS
Creative Ways of Being Church in East Africa

Laurenti Magesa

Introduction

I am a Tanzanian and a Catholic. I mention these two facts first because they will influence my remarks this evening,

Reflecting on "creative ways of being church" - which is the theme of this conference - I will concentrate my remarks on the East African experience, with which I am quite familiar, and I'll do so mainly from the situation of the Catholic Church, in which I grew up and have been ministering as a priest for the last twenty-six years.

In all the three East African countries of Kenya, Uganda and Tanzania, the Catholic Church is well over one hundred years old now. The Catholic missionaries who arrived there first to formally preach the gospel at the end of the nineteenth century were from the British Isles and France. They came from Britain because she was the colonial master of the whole region at the time. Kenya was directly under Great Britain as a colony; Uganda was a protectorate and Tanganyika a territory, both entrusted to British administration by the League of Nations. Catholic missionaries from France come into the picture as prominently as their British counterparts because they were members of the missionary congregations and societies that sent pioneer evangelizers to the region. Some of these societies were founded specifically for the evangelization of Africa. The Missionaries of Africa (popularly known as the White Fathers) are an example that quickly comes to mind. There were others as well, such as the Holy Ghost Fathers who were among the first Catholic missionaries to arrive.

German Protestant missionaries had arrived earlier in the region when Germany ruled a big part of East Africa before the First World War, but had stayed too briefly to make a lasting impact. Now, however, because the region was under British admin-istration, British Protestant missionaries also came at the same time as the Catholics. The history of these two groups in East Africa, and most notably in Uganda, shows that there was no friendship lost at all between them.

Necessity for an historical review

I am aware that all of this history is well known, so I am sure some will argue that it does not need retelling, particularly at a conference of missiologists like the present one. Yet, in my opinion the very theme of our conference demands that some of these facts need to be mentioned, indeed *must* be mentioned. This is important not only to place the theme into proper perspective, but - and this seems to me even more important - in order to appreciate the very nature of the struggle for new ways of being church, for a creative spirituality, that has been and is taking place in the East African region.

For "struggle" it indeed is. When we talk about being creative in this context, we do not at all mean fashioning something *ex nihilo,* after the manner of God. On the contrary: we must have in mind a certain history of church in East Africa, that is to say, a way of being church the first evangelizers brought with them, and the effect this has had on the African people in this region up to the present time. It is in response to the shortcomings of this particular history, this context, if you like, that East African Catholics attempt to read the message of the gospel anew and fashion a new model of church that is relevant for them.

As I see it, the initial history of mission in East Africa - or indeed Africa in general - must be repeated in any discussion about past, present and future ecclesiology there. It must not be allowed to fade away from memory, for to do so risks a fourfold danger. First, we risk having a static church, confirming the missionary model as the only valid one, and consequently overlooking its shortcomings. In that case, it makes no sense to speak of new ways of being church. Secondly, we risk frustrating the work of the Holy Spirit whose purpose it is to ever expand our understanding into the Truth of Jesus Christ. Thirdly, we risk disturbing the visible unity of the church by alienating from it, through too hasty and incorrect judgements, people who may otherwise be genuinely inspired by the Holy Spirit to seek the Truth. This has happened in Africa in the case of some of the founders of the African Initiated Churches. Finally, we risk relegating the church in East Africa to a state of eternal juniority, where it will always wear a foreign face such that it will not become a truly local church but will always depend on others for its theology, personnel and finances.

To some extent, an historical review and vision will help to free the church in East Africa from the captivity of such perspectives and positions as these. It will help it to appreciate genuine initiatives into new ways of being church as a gift of the Holy Spirit, given to Christians in various places in order to express their faith in Christ in ways that are meaningful to them. It will teach the church to accept and celebrate legitimate diversity in unity as a blessing, and not to view it as a threat to its identity and existence.

Since the church in East Africa cannot explain her present situation, nor chart out her own desired future without understanding its past, we must therefore briefly consider what model has governed it up to the present time.

A dominant missionary model

In attempting to paint a picture of missionary ecclesiology in East Africa, I do realize that in this short space and time I risk constructing a caricature of a complex situation and an extremely involved process. The picture is not as simple as can be drawn in a few broad and quick strokes. For, to be sure, there were those voices from individual missionaries that from the very beginning were prophetic. They protested that the dominant model of church operating in the region was somewhat flawed and not quite in keeping with the message of the gospel the church was supposed to preach. Yet, by and large, one has to say that the ecclesiology whose characteristics I am about to describe prevailed and moulded the church in East Africa, and largely still does. If some East African Catholics are now looking for a new way of being church that is more relevant to their situation and needs, it is *vis-à-vis* this missionary model and its consequences.

In its encounter with the culture and religion of the indigenous people of the East African region, five major attitudes characterized missionary ecclesiology. These may be summarized as derision, exclusion, imposition, passivity and individualism. Of course, they were not entirely, or even largely, the creation of missionaries *per se*, but of the European socio-cultural and "scientific" environment reigning at the time. Being children of this intellectual environment of social Darwinism and European colonialism, the early missionaries to East Africa constructed their ecclesiology based on the perception of the African peoples that was then prevailing everywhere.

The European perception of Africans at the time placed them at a lower level of human being, or being human, than practically all other peoples of the world. This is why it was thought that they could be colonized or exploited for commercial and other purposes. Africans were "instrumentalised" in these ways because, as it was generally accepted in Europe at the time, they had neither culture nor religion. So Europeans generally believed that it was legitimate, compassionate and "Christian" both to civilize them and to give them religion, specifically Christianity. The three "Cs" guided Europe's relationship and dealings with Africa: Christianity, Civilization and Commerce. The colonial government and the Christian churches saw it as their "burden" to undertake these things, and indeed they worked hand in hand to achieve this purpose.

As a consequence, Catholic (and Christian) missionary ecclesiology in general despised any and all expressions of African religiosity. It sought to discourage them by various means: it laughed at them and legislated church (and sometimes persuaded the government to legislate civil) law against them, African rituals, for instance, and even ways of socializing and relaxing (in this case, in the form of indigenous dances), and methods of physical healing (indigenous medicine and medical practices) were proscribed. They were also considered primitive in the negative sense of the word. No Catholic dared to attend to or to do these things in public view without running the risk of being considered a backslider, an apostate, and therefore almost certainly being excommunicated from the church.

Legislation was a particularly effective way, psychologically and morally, to deter Catholic believers from involving themselves in their indigenous customs because, in the African people's worldview, adherence to the law, to custom, to tradition, makes the person to belong, and in the African worldview, "belonging" is a central principle of being human. In the case of the church, then, for the African, you are either a member or not a member of the church basically if you keep or break its laws. Nevertheless, even after baptism, many Catholics chose not to accept totally the laws of the church, but to hold on to some of their own indigenous customs and belief systems. They found it impossible to abandon the latter completely as the church then absolutely required.

Moreover, in its pastoral practice, the missionary church was seen to be rather exclusive. It was good at proselytizing, but it welcomed to its rituals only its own, baptized Catholics. Missionaries saw nothing wrong with the practice, of course, but in the eyes of most Africans, even to many African Catholics themselves, this practice was somewhat perplexing. The practice of exclusion applied most stringently to the reception of the Eucharist, but it was for African Catholics hard to understand this. Why should they exclude relatives and friends from a sacred meal, which was meant to signify unity and friendship, they silently wondered? Despite the teaching on the Eucharist learned from the catechism, the practice continued to be a scandal in the eyes of most of the people. In Africa generally, you never refuse to share a meal with anyone, neighbours or strangers, except a sworn enemy.

Furthermore, these restrictions were imposed by a governing structure that in its day-to-day operation consisted of few built-in avenues for conversation, so as to allow the base in some way to influence the top. The system was simply hierarchical, differing significantly from the traditional type of government Africans in this region were used to, which, although not democratic, allowed some form of exchange of ideas. In most ethnic groups before colonialism, government consisted in rule by elders, a system of gerontocracy, and in its processes, it at least allowed some degree of input from and by the base. Yet in the church many of the leaders were not in actual age even 'elders'; they had to be given the title by ascription. But how were East African Catholics expected to understand this kind of leadership? As a proverb in the region has it, "The shoulder is not higher than the head": the young have no business telling the elders what to do.

But the system persisted in the church. It encouraged the attitude of passivity among East African Catholics, a situation which was further enforced by the teaching that the faithful were strictly "a learning church". Not only was all church doctrine given to them but also its application in their particular circumstances was predetermined. The question "Why are you as a Catholic acting in such and such a manner" usually elicited the answer, "Because Father said so". This not only indicated spiritual infantilism, but also the fact that there was little personal appropriation of the faith.

In those cases where Catholics were actively involved in the Church, it was primarily out of the desire for individual salvation, not social concern. In the Catholic teaching at the time, the individual's personal relationship with God overshadowed that concerned with the social dimension of salvation. The conviction that "To be human is to be in relationship", which African religiosity emphasized so much, was not underlined enough in Catholic ecclesiology.

So the phenomenon that prevailed was that often people gathered in churches without really gathering together, and congregated without experiencing fellowship. In many ways, this was not the *ekklesia* as it was meant to be in apostolic times that we find described in the New Testament. It was not as well the community of believers that satisfied the African heart's desire for human communion, which, according to their religiosity, signified also communion with God and other spiritual powers. The liturgy, for instance, was for African Catholics too intellectual and not physical or emotional enough. It lacked a sense of activity, such as dance and touch.

For a long time in the one hundred odd years of the Catholic Church's existence in East Africa, nothing could be done about this situation. In the context of the doctrinal environment of the universal church, this model seemed etched in stone, impossible to change as much in East Africa as anywhere else in the world. So those African Catholics who were dissatisfied with it and had the courage to do so voted with their feet and left the church, a few to start their church communities more imbued with a New Testament and African spirit. These became the African Initiated (or Independent) Churches (AICs). These churches have prolif-erated throughout the region.

According to one observer, Teresia Hinga, in Kenya, for example, from very early on, AICs ranged "from the cult of 'Mumbo' and 'Dini Ya Misambwa', which movements advocated total rejection of Western culture and religion and a conscious revival of traditional religious practices and spirituality. There were also religious movements which sought to separate Christ-ianity and the western garb in which it was clad. The 'Akurini' ... and the 'Karinga' movements both among the Kikuyus of Kenya, insisted on their rights to be Christians in a manner that allowed them to continue to be Africans. Though these movements embraced Christianity, they were repelled by the idea that to be Christian, one had to abandon being African; that there is a certain incompatibility between being both."[1]

Still, for various reasons we shall not go into here, many people chose to live with the ambiguities and stayed within the Catholic Church.

General reasons for dissatisfaction

The main reasons for African dissatisfaction with the missionary model of church are contained within the missionary ecclesiology itself, as we have outlined it above. The social sciences, however - anthropology in particular - have since the beginning of the last half of the twentieth century (the 1950s) shown us that culture is a central element in the identity of a people. Although it mutates of its own with the passage of time, and especially when it comes into contact with other cultures, it can hardly be totally shorn off from a people, as the Catholic Church intended to do in East Africa. Therefore, however much the Catholic system despised them, major elements of African cultural values remained with the people, even with those who chose to stay in the Church. In my own observation and experience, I continually notice that things like belief in spirits, human causation of disease and witchcraft persist to this day as an element of the Catholic religious consciousness of most Africans. These include the highly educated in the new Western system that reject these things and that the church and the civil systems have been advancing for the last hundred years. I sometimes notice it even among the indigenous clergy and religious, as well as among politicians and professors. (Do not let me be understood by saying this, however, that I am taking a position in favor of these or other indigenous beliefs and practices. For the purpose of this presentation that is not the point. What I am doing is simply making a statement of fact).

Positively, the kind of church the majority of Africans were looking for was one that provided them with dignity as Africans, with companionship according to their own understanding of

---

1   Hinga, Teresia, 1994. "Inculturation and the Otherness of Africans: Some Reflections," Peter Turkson & Frans Wijsen, eds., *Inculturation,* Kampen: KOK, pp. 10-18.

relationships, and with a certain degree of freedom and involvement in the church's affairs and activities. Those who decided not to join the church, or to leave it after baptism, did not find these elements there. As some scholars have put it, they hardly found in the church "a place to feel at home".

Over a hundred years on since first evangelization, African Catholics still find it hard to understand why the church was, and in many cases still is, against aspects of their traditional worship practices and other customs. For instance, one man of a parish in Musoma, Tanzania, was baptized in the Catholic Church in 1958. He cannot participate in the sacraments today because he is married to four wives. But, explaining his situation during a research interview in 1999, he said he could not understand why the fact that he was polygamous would warrant his exclusion from the sacraments of the church, especially the Eucharist. He argued:

> I am a good Catholic and a regular churchgoer. I was baptized and got married to my first wife in church. But later I married three others because it is acceptable in our tradition. I know it goes against church teaching, but I do not see why I should be discriminated from receiving the sacraments just because I have four wives.

During the same interview, another man, who also identified himself as a good Catholic, said he still regarded his cultural values very highly. He said that he often experienced conflict when confronted with Catholic and traditional precepts on matters central to his life, in spite of being a Catholic for a long time. Among the things he mentioned that he likewise did not agree with were the rule against polygamy, the Catholic regulation against offering sacrifices and libations to ancestral spirits in times of crisis, and visiting diviners and medicine men when affliction strikes. Quoting a proverb he concluded, *"Mwacha mila ni mtumwa"* (a person who abandons his/her cultural values to embrace others cannot be free, i.e. he/she becomes a slave to the latter).

Citing another, perhaps less radical, example a woman interviewee seemed indirectly to blame the church for causing what she described as the corrosion of moral values she was experiencing in society. She felt that her own people's cultural values of respect for the elders had been ignored by the church, and so she thought that it should be encouraged alongside all other Christian teachings. "The youth", she argued, "have lost respect for the elders, and therefore for all those values which gave us a sound foundation for our communal life".

These few examples illustrate the tension that many African Catholics still feel as Catholics. It relates to the ambiguity that arises because one does not know for sure whether one is "inside" or "outside" the church. Are they good Catholics, as African Catholics themselves who practice these things would like to think, or are they not? Are they inside as members of the church, or by their actions and behaviour are they outside it?

With the freedom ushered into the church by the Second Vatican Council, subsequent synods of bishops, particularly the synod on evangelization in 1974 - and Pope Paul VI's famous and celebrated Apostolic Exhortation *Evangelii Nuntiandi* - this unease, experienced by many Africans in the church on account of the dominant ecclesiology, could more openly be acknowledged, discussed and initiatives towards new ways of being church tried.

The contribution of politicians and theologians
Vatican II took place at the very time that many African countries were becoming autonomous nations by getting independence from the colonial governments. The three East African countries of Tanganyika, Uganda and Kenya became independent successively in 1961, 1962 and 1963. All the three first presidents of these countries were either practicing Christians or had been trained in Christian schools, and were quite familiar with both the contributions and the shortcomings of Christianity in the region. One of them was a staunch Catholic, who professed his faith very openly and ardently, and counted missionary priests and bishops among his best friends. However, all of them were quite critical about the close association between the church and the colonial governments in their attitude towards African culture and religiosity. African politicians in the region were thus the first to openly articulate the feet that Africa is culturally different from, and cannot be the same as, Europe. This was a platform that gained them a political hearing from people of all faiths. They were articulating a truth that was close to the heart of most Africans also in matters of religious significance.

Within the church, catholic intellectuals, especially the few trained theologians among the priests at the time, also began speaking openly and writing about the shortcomings of the

101

ecclesiology then in force. They demanded the construction of a model of church that was more "relevant" to the African situation. In their theological writings, they used such terms as "African-ization", "localization", "indigenization", and "contextualization" to describe the model of the church they envisioned. They wanted a church "acculturated" and a theology "adapted" to African political cultural and social realities. They were talking about a church that would accept the local languages as valid for use in worship, together with the most meaningful of its symbols, metaphors, values, myths and so on. In other words, they were hoping for a church that would view African culture positively in its encounter with Christianity as also a place where God dwells. As one theologian later put it: "It is not the missionaries who brought God to Africa, rather it is God who brought the missionaries to Africa".

Pope Paul VI provided further forceful encouragement. During his visit to Uganda in 1969, he emphasized that the African continent had to recapture its own historical, cultural and spiritual identity. It had to do so, the pope said, proudly, thanking God for this gift that was its people's culture. Urging all Africans to work for an African form of Christian faith, he declared: "You may, and you must, have an African Christianity".

The African bishops throughout the continent had been following this debate and these developments carefully. Many of them were now indigenous, and these developments touched issues close to their lives. Even the non-indigenous bishops were familiar enough with the situation in the continent to identify with Pope Paul's words. During the synod on evangelization in Rome in 1974, therefore, they all seized the opportunity to tell the world that the adaptation of foreign models to Christianity in Africa was not the way to go. There was need, they said, for a theology and an ecclesiology of Incarnation. Like the second person of the Trinity who became human in everything but sin, the church in Africa had to become African in everything except only that which was clearly wrong.

In the Catholic Church: SCCs a new way of being church
Following upon all of these events, the theologies of Inculturation and Liberation began to develop and take root in East Africa. Their most practical expression in terms of new ways of being church has been the formation of Small Christian

Communities (SCCs), which the bishops throughout Eastern Africa declared since 1973 to be their number one pastoral priority.

The bishops wanted the church in the region to learn from the model of the early church described in the Acts of the Apostles and in some of the epistles of the New Testament. The early church functioned essentially on the level of neighbourhood groupings. The faithful met together and celebrated the supper of the Lord in neighbourhood households. These were people who lived near one another, knew one another well, and helped one another in times of need. The book of Acts describes this model in ideal terms: in Jerusalem, all Christians sold everything they owned and brought the proceeds to the feet of the apostles. From the common pool thus established, food and other requirements were distributed to everybody on the basis of need, so that, according to Acts, none of the members of the community was in want. The early Christians shared everything in common. Close to the apostolic period, there is said to have existed a principle in church government that helped to consolidate this model. It said that a bishopric had to be split if the point came that the bishop did not know by name all the faithful in his area of jurisdiction. This was in order to preserve the intimacy among Christians that the apostolic church appears to have valued so much.

Although SCCs in East Africa were not intended to go that far, they were founded to share with the early church some of its characteristics: namely, being neighbourhood churches in which people know one another well, and can help one another in times of need. Just as in the early church at Jerusalem, with the appointment of the seven deacons to minister to the widows, who did not feel justly treated in the distribution of food, ministries were also to be formed in SCCs according to the needs of the particular community. In other words, needs would dictate the kind of ministries required in the community, rather than pre-established forms of ministry creating needs to be filled, as was the case in missionary ecclesiology. So, early on in their formation, we find in SCCs all over East Africa men and women being appointed to minister to the sick, the poor, the lapsed, and so on. And these were not fixed ministries; they changed as circumstances required.

The SCCs were intended in East Africa then to be the basic church, the center of Christian life and activity. They were intended to be self-governing and essentially self-ministering in those areas that did not need orders. They were also intended to be self-supporting financially, though always mindful of the welfare of other communities wherever they were, in the interests of unity, for the church is one. And perhaps most importantly, they were invited to give in the context of their existing situation the answer to Jesus' question: "But you, who do you say I am?" In other words, SCCs were invested with the task of developing an appropriate theology in all of its branches, and to form pastoral practices suited to their place and time.

In this ecclesiology, the parish was to be a communion of SCCs and the parish priest a symbol of their unity. On the larger level, the diocese, with its bishop, was the symbol of unity of the SCCs and the parishes in the geographical area. In ordinary circumstances, however, neither the parish nor the diocese was to play a central role in the Christian life of the communities, in the sense of determining and controlling their day-to-day activities.

I explain the situation of the SCCs in Eastern Africa in the past tense because, in the majority of cases, ecclesiastical bureaucracy and fear have frustrated their original intention. As I have noted, it was a model very close to that of the scriptures. But we all know what happened to the latter when the church began to expand beyond Jerusalem and its environs and became established in the Roman provinces. The apostolic model slowly caved in under pressure from the monarchical and hierarchical ecclesiology that is evident already in the second century CE, and all but disappeared until Vatican II.

Similarly in East Africa: it did not take long before the ecclesiology of SCCs (although clearly inspired by the scriptures and clearly intended to be the basic church by all the bishops of the region) was perceived to be encroaching on the authority and "power" traditionally enjoyed and wielded by the parish priest and the bishop in the former model. In the new model, the parish priest did not control the money of the SCCs and, as a consequence, neither did the bishop. Where SCCs were well established and strong, the priest did not control even their pastoral decisions. He participated in the discussions as first, indeed, but only as "first among equals" (as *primus inter pares*). The members of the SCCs decided, for example, who among them would receive the sacraments, and either they themselves imposed the sanctions on those of their members who went astray or asked the parish to do so. In other words, by doing this they were seeking to identify their own relationship to Jesus in pastoral action. Formerly, however, the procedure had been different: all the answers had come from "above", namely from the parish priest acting for and in the name of the bishop.

In those few communities here and there in the region that have been left to develop fully because of the commitment to them of some bishops and priests in the region, there is felt a strong sense of dignity and participation in the affairs of the church. This extends further than the SCC level to the level of the parish and diocese. As an example, during my time as parish priest of two different rural parishes of my diocese in 1986 and lately in 1995-2000, these are the king of communities that contributed most to the upkeep and other needs of the rectory and diocese, most often in kind, offering foodstuffs and livestock to feed the priest and support the seminarians and other diocesan causes. They did so happily time after time, and challenged other communities to do the same.

But most significantly, and perhaps most unsettling to the church authorities of the traditional Catholic mindset, these communities are not loath to draw from their own traditional religiosity in answering Jesus' question cited above: Who do *you* say that I am? In a number of ways, they challenge the exclusivity of the dominant Catholic model. In my last parish, they repeatedly elected to leadership positions men and women who were in "irregular" unions - which for that area means polygamy - resisting constant pressure from me not to do so because it was against diocesan policy as well as "the explicit teaching of the church". The answer I always received when I asked why they were doing so was that the people elected participated in and co-operated well with members of their community in every way, that they were good Christians and, that anyway, they were the most suitable people in the community to lead! As far as they were concerned, it seemed that no amount of explanation from me, short of painful arm-twisting, could change their mind.

It was also in these communities in my two parishes where I noticed that the inferiority complex cultivated by the missionary church's prejudice against African religiosity was most effectively overcome. At funerals, for example, traditional rites indicating belief in the union of the people with their ancestors were openly performed. When at a neighbouring parish the parish priest banned them, many of the older Christians just transferred membership to another parish where the practices were tolerated. I observed that attention given to traditional religiosity by Catholics extended to many major areas of life, with people performing some sort of traditional rites at birth, marriage and so on, in combination with, or apart from, the "official" Catholic rites - and not feeling guilty about it.

For inculturation as incarnation, something that is still far from having been achieved in East Africa,[2] this to me indicates a hopeful direction: it recaptures the original models of being African and being Christian.

Breaking ground in this trail of a new way of being church in terms of doctrine, structure and practice are the African Initiated Churches (AICs). They have tried to remain faithful to both scripture and their own God-given African religiosity. It is true they have their shortcomings and even errors, but, as Hinga again writes:

> ... Whatever else can be said about Independent Churches, it is clear that they have emerged through the initiative of a people who are very much aware of their cultural heritage and can be said to have incarnated Christianity in Africa in a very significant and spontaneous way. This they did long before the term inculturation became in vogue, particularly in the post conciliar era. As early as 1963, Gaudentia Aoko, a cofounder of the Legio Maria Church in Kenya insisted that they were Catholics, but they were Catholics in Africa not in Europe, and that, to her and her followers, made a difference.[3]

The ways of charismatic groups

Apart from the AICs other groups that have emerged in East Africa as a Christian response to the contemporary world order. I shall refer to them as "Charismatic groups". Some exist as part of the Christian churches and operate within them, others function as

2   Magesa, Laurenti, 1994, 'The Present and Future of Inculturation in Eastern Africa', Ibid, pp.57-71.
3   Hinga, Teresia, op. cit., pp. 15-16

independent groups. But all of them are imaginative new ways of being church and share similar characteristics.

In the first place, each of these groups originates from and owes allegiance to a leader or leaders who are perceived by their followers to possess exceptional saintly qualities and powers, especially the power of spiritual and physical healing. Secondly, they all at some point in their worship services make use of ecstatic forms of prayer which may or may not include changes in the state of consciousness of the persons praying, leading to the phenomenon of speaking in tongues (or *glossolalia*). This is interpreted as being possessed by the Holy Spirit and leads to healing, known as "faith healing". Finally, all of them in various ways espouse an apocalyptic hope that for the chosen (meaning themselves): there is a future time of great prosperity and happiness which they will achieve by fulfilling the conditions the group through the inspired leader lays out.

Their regulations rarely restrict membership in any one of them to a particular class of people. They are as a rule very inclusive, thus their attraction. They include the very rich, the middle class and the very poor, and are growing spectacularly in number in East Africa. Their popularity seems also to be due to the fact that they address directly problems in the contemporary world situation which many people can relate to. These include economic, social, political or moral issues that are perceived to be unsettling and threatening. Charismatic groups provide immediate and clear answers to them. In this sense, these charismatic groups can be called "communities of affliction", that is, communities that come into existence on account of and in response to a particular disturbing situation and which come to an end when the situation no longer exists.

The main concern of the charismatic groups in the East African region is: Is it possible to lead an ethical life in the circumstances of the contemporary world? With only variations of degree, they answer the question negatively. Some focus their attention on a single issue, such as sexual promiscuity, which they see as the climax of moral decay, and link it with the HIV/AIDS pandemic as a punishment from God. Others, however, are more broad in their interpretation of the world's malaise. They point to contemporary developments in science and technology as contributing factors towards the breakdown in Christian morals.

For the charismatics, "conversion" is the only appropriate response. They understand conversion to mean that people must reject the reign of Satan, which is much of what happens in the contemporary world, and must institute the reign of the saints, as the leaders define it.

A clear, though tragic, recent example of these groups in East Africa is the Movement for the Restoration of the Ten Commandments of God, founded by one Miss Credonia Mwerinde in Uganda. Founded in 1990, the movement's central motive was to inspire all of its followers to turn against this sinful world by adhering to the ten commandments of God. According to Credonia, these were instructions from God revealed to her in apparitions by the Virgin Mary. Drawn by the promise of a future paradise which she announced would come in 2000 with the end of the world,

> Credonia was joined by hundreds of followers. These were people whose country had been ravaged by a brutal military regime, by civil war and by the HIV/AIDS pandemic. They were people who had little or nothing to live for. They were also people who believed in miracles as part of the ordinary experience of life, being unable to distinguish between verifiable fact and religious fantasy. They were ready to give all their money and possessions to Credonia, to live on a starvation diet, to keep total silence and spend long hours in prayer, secure in the knowledge that when the world came to an end in the year 2000, they would accompany their leader to heaven.[4]

Even though mostly poor and uneducated, as A. Shorter and J. Njiru describe Credonia's movement above, its members included a few middle class and even upper class, very educated people. One of the top leaders of the movement with Credonia was a former Catholic priest. It also is well known that the government in general was well disposed towards it. When Credonia realized that the end would not come as she had predicted in 2000, and that her followers were getting restless having taken from them all the means of their existence, she set on fire the house they were gathered for prayer in the village of Kanungu, thus burning them alive on March 17th 2000.

---

4   Shorter, A. and Joseph N. Njiru, *New Religious Movements in Africa*, 2001, p. 12

Credonia's group is perhaps an extreme example, but hundreds of similar groups exist in the region. They are both local and foreign. A well known one in Tanzania is the Marian Faith Healing group (known locally as *Wanamaombi*). It was founded and is led by a (now suspended) Catholic priest by the name of Felician Nkwera. It claims as some of its devoted members people very high up in government and in educational institutions. In its healing prayer sessions, it likewise does not discriminate against people on the basis of creed. Everyone is welcome to attend and to benefit from the prayers and Nkwera's healing power. In Kenya, the most conspicuous of these groups are of foreign origin, and are active in the form of crusades. A regular visitor there (and elsewhere in Africa) is the German-born evangelist Reinhard Bonnke. He draws thousands to his meetings, often including the State presidents of the countries he visits.

The Catholic Church usually views these groups officially with suspicion, closely supervising and controlling those that operate within its structures. Those that operate outside its structures the Church always disowns, as it did Father Felician Nkwera of the *Wanamaombi* in Tanzania and, further afield, Archbishop Emmanuel Milingo, formerly of Lusaka, Zambia. However, this does not diminish their popularity: they respond, perhaps better than the official church to the felt needs of their congregations. They are models that Africans relate to and feel at home in, despite their shortcomings.

The charismatic groups, taken as a whole, are a complex phenomenon. There are those among them which want nothing to do with politics or social advocacy, concentrating only on prayer. But there also are those whose most obvious characteristic is the "revival of religion in the public sphere". The latter reject secularism understood in the sense that people can lead their lives meaningfully without reference to God or religion. They view capitalistic materialism as a threat to religious belief. Their basic point is that secularism is a consequence of the globalization process, and that globalization endangers people's cultural identities and much of what is beautiful in them.

On the other hand, there are those charismatic groups that are diametrically the opposite of this view. They propound the "prosperity gospel", literally saying that poverty indicates God's disfavour. For them, globalization is not something to be questioned, it is a blessing to be unconditionally welcomed. These groups are usually silent even in the face of massive corruption in the region. Their leaders, for example, often fraternize publicly with known embezzlers of public funds in the State machinery. In such cases, these groups lose completely their prophetic value.

Nevertheless, charismatic groups are often tightly knit communities, responding to Africa's desire for close human relationships and fellowship. The larger more loosely knit among them, compensate for this by the intense involvement that their worship services engender. Whatever else they may be, they are therapeutic services. The members depart from them refreshed and healed in mind and soul, carrying a new hope for life in their hearts.

Conclusion

Inculturation as incarnation means that the Gospel must transform culture at the same time as it is being transformed by it. In Pope John Paul II's expression, it means that the "Gospel must become culture". The way to do so, it seems to me, is to construct ways and forms of Christian living that "make space" for people's cultural identities to be expressed. It is to have various models of Christian expression within the one Christian family. SCCs, AICs and various charismatic groups are all trying to do this in East Africa. It does not mean that none may be critiqued, but it does mean that in this age of ecumenism, of churches learning from one another towards ever better understanding of the fullness God's revelation through the spirit of Christ, they must accept and learn from one another. Their ecclesiological orientations must learn to be at home in Africa, drawing inspiration from both the Gospel and African sources.

ECCLESIAL MISSION:
critical lessons from Latin America on ways of being church

"'Listen, what do you do to reach the people?
How do you do it?"
We don't reach the people, we are the people...'[1]

Michael Crowley

I Introduction

This BIAMS conference theme – 'Creative ways of being church'- expresses our common interest in exploring the possibilities of promoting in some sense a renewal in ecclesiological development especially in Western culture. This case study drawn from Latin American popular culture approaches the issue from a distinct contextual perspective - emergent grass-roots ecclesial movements that arise out of real social and cultural conflicts and are responsive to the pressing spiritual necessities of personal and community survival amidst the changes provoked by the impact of modernity and post-modernity. It is this vital search for salvific space that has led many from the poorest and marginalized masses to embrace renewed and inculturated expressions of Catholic and evangelical Christian community in Latin America. Creative they may be, but these movements are more instinctively conceived, not abstractly planned ecclesial responses.

Superficially these Latin American ecclesial developments seem to contrast with those in Europe from the late 19th century onwards but in fact they also reflect in a distinct context the continuing decline in historic structures and forms of Christian community in the post-Colonial conditions pertaining in the continent during the same period. The remarkable feature of the

---

1   Question asked by Emilio Castro, former General Secretary of the WCC of Chilean Pentecostal bishop Francisco Anabalon, Iglesia Pentecostal Apostólica, cited in I. Palma (ed.), *En Tierra Extraña: Itinerario del Pueblo Pentecostal Chileno* (Santiago: Ed. Amerinda, 1988) 153.

Latin American ecclesial experience is that the disintegration of Christendom has not 'de-ecclesiafied' or 'de-sacralised' society but has rather led to a multiplication of new popular ecclesial movements and communities on the margins of the fragmenting older historic notions of church as alternative, sometimes dissident, responses to them. Thus the pervasive underlying socio-ecclesial crisis in Latin America is reflected in the established Roman Catholic ecclesial structures as well as in the Catholic ecclesial base communities. At the same time the minority historic Protestant churches have suffered a crisis over their identity and mission in the face of Pentecostal movements whose own ecclesial crisis reflects their particular struggle over their notion of church and its relationship to society.

Thus, whilst crisis, restructuring and realignment characterises ecclesial movements in Latin America, it is the continuing popular religious response to new forms of church that contrasts with the apparent ecclesiastical demise of influence of historic Christendom structures in Western European society. However, an increasing functionalism pervades many aspects of ministry and church practice in Latin America, heightening the missiological need to foster the emergence of biblically inspired models for Christian community and related notions of the role of church in the world. The question then is not what will happen to Christianity in the continent (assuming present trends continue) but what it will actually do there. The demand is not so much for 'an analysis but a confession and a commitment.'[2] Even the historic Roman Catholic Church in Latin America recognises it has no other option than to be missionary in the continent.[3]

The precarious life situation of the majority of Latin Americans is extremely susceptible to external social, political and economic trends and the maintenance of a two class society (with a tentative and small middle class in between). Moreover, the fragile existence of democracies are maintained with considerable hierarchical control that provokes social discontent and protest. Yet no major structural or revolutionary changes are to be expected in Latin American society.[4] The religious factor continues to

2   J. Miguez Bonino, 'The Condition and Prospects of Christianity in Latin America', in G. Cook (ed.), *New Face of the Church in Latin America* (Maryknoll: Orbis, 1994) 266.
3   Ibid., 262.
4   Ibid., 260.

provide 'a subjective compensation in an increasingly objectified, and mechanised world.' Grass-roots ecclesial movements recruit millions at the social base seeking 'a refuge from social anomie and uprootedness.'[5]

The older religious categories of 'sects' and 'cults' are still applied misleadingly by some conservative sectors of the Roman Catholic church[6] but this is reflective of an entrenched attitude that barely masks an aspiration to return to the security of an older ecclesial hegemony.[7] Moreover 'Catholic' and 'Protestant' are very generic designations and careful distinctions need to be made within the two historically broad movements. Roman Catholicism established its dominant cultural-religious presence in the continent in the sixteenth century, but grass-roots dissent from the 'official' religion, whilst pervasive, is not readily acknowledged by the hierarchy. 'Roman Catholicism is not today - if it ever was - a monolithic, totally homogeneous reality.'[8] Despite growing scholarly interest, no adequate taxonomy of Latin American 'Pentecostalisms' yet exists. The generic term 'Pentecostal' often refers to quite a heterogeneous movement.[9]

The impact of modernity and the processes of secularisation only gathered pace in the Latin American republics from the late 19th century but by the 1940s there was a growing realisation that traditional Catholic religiosity could not hope to cope.[10] Talk of 're-evangelisation' or 'new' evangelisation' gained ground as inescapable evidence accumulated that the Catholic church would need to redouble its efforts to become a missionary church again in Latin America.[11] Traditional popular Catholic religiosity in the

5   Ibid. Míguez Bonino finds parallels with Pauline ecclesial mission. See Acts 17:22.
6   The term 'sect' is often used disparagingly by the Roman Catholic Church to refer to the non-historic Protestant churches i.e. those with low ecclesiology and not just groups with a low non-Chalcedonic Christology. See Conferencia Episcopal de Chile, *Evangélicos y Sectas* (Santiago: CEC, 1992); F. Sampedro (ed.), *Pentecostalismo, Sectas y Pastoral* (Santiago: CEC, 1989).
7   C. Duarte, *Las Mil y Una Caras de la Religión: Sectas y Nuevos Movimientos Relgiosos en América Latina* (Quito: CLAI, 1995) iv; 1-15.
8   Míguez Bonino, 'Prospects', 261.
9   Some contemporary studies create the impression that a single homogenous movement is being spoken of and even interchange 'Pentecostal' with 'Protestant' with little qualification. See D. Stoll, *Is Latin America Turning Protestant?* (Berkeley: University of California Press, 1990).
10   Cf., Jesuit Alberto Hurtado's controversial work for the time, *¿Es Chile un País Católico?* (Santiago: Ediciones Esplendor, 1941).
11   Míguez Bonino, 'Prospects', 262.

rural environment and to a certain extent in the poor urban periphery remained particularly resistant to the church's 'romanizing' and institutional reforms.

The reforms of Vatican II and their Medellín sequel in Latin America seemed to open up new possibilities for Catholicism in the continent as it engaged modernity but, ironically, some four decades on from the council, the Catholic church's strength at the popular level, despite new initiatives and the efforts of the progressive wing, seems even weaker, whilst new ecclesial movements dispute the place Catholicism once held.[12] We might describe the three ecclesial currents in the following way:

1. Catholicism: institutional power losing popular presence

CELAM II in Medellín in 1968, marked the radical application of the reforms of Vatican II to the continent through grass-roots innovations in pastoral practice, the prioritising of the option for the poor, the stimulus of the CEBs and the reordering of theological and missiological precepts in a new liberation theology whose concern was with a doctrine of God not merely related to his being also to knowing which 'side' he was on.[13] Thus liberational initiatives and progressive contextualized ecclesiology were prioritised by a 'modernising' institution.[14] The break with the historic ecclesial *status quo* produced a counter response from conservatives in CELAM and the Vatican curia. By the time of the CELAM IV in Santo Domingo in 1992 the official line of the Catholic hierarchy, as presented in the papal address and final document, was to speak of a 'new evangelisation' that sought to recreate a fundamentally Catholic society inspired in the Social Doctrine of the Church and effectively aspiring to a contemporary a 'neo-Christendom'. This official policy however seemed to have 'no historical possibility of realisation'[15] for a popular piety was unlikely to flourish within such official neo-Christendom ecclesial structures.[16]

---

12 Ibid.
13 D. Bosch, *Transforming Mission* (Maryknoll: Orbis 1991) 439.
14 L. Luzbetak's anthropological-missiological framework for distinguishing ecclesiological models provides a basis for analyzing ecclesial developments in the continent. L.Luzbetak, *The Church and Cultures: New perspectives in Missiological Anthropology* (Maryknoll: Orbis, 1988). See especially 374-397.
15 Míguez Bonino, 'Prospects', 263.
16 Ibid.

The burgeoning threat to Catholic grass-roots ecclesial initiatives continued to be Pentecostal mission and ecclesiality. Despite all the internal Catholic reforms stemming from Vatican II and Medellín, steady decline and loss continued. With the beginning of a global implosion of world socialist structures and states in 1989, the underlying shift to a world-wide predominance of neo-liberalism, combined with the growing conservative trends within the Vatican hierarchy, a re-evaluation of the progressive project was forced, as utopic projects in Latin America increasingly seemed non-viable. Cultural concerns have tended to replace earlier socio-economic projects.[17] An 'axial shift'[18] was taking place as revolutionary notions began to give way to ethical, religious and cultural projects. Thus, as the temptation to revert to a *status quo* mentality re-surfaced after the demise of authoritarian regimes across the continent in the late 1980s, Catholicism still faced an unresolved fundamental crisis: how it would achieve an effective but popular ecclesial presence amongst the masses.

2. Historic Protestantism: limited presence lacking popular empowerment

Protestant and Evangelical movements were governed by a very different ecclesiastical agenda marked by a common historic reformational heritage. Largely ecumenical, liberal and middle class in ethos they were mostly committed to the educated classes and thus have struggled to keep pace with Latin American socio-cultural shifts. Popular religious grass-roots movements, not historic Protestantism, proved to be the real alternative to Roman Catholicism. Historic Protestant churches have been affected by the crisis of the middle classes squeezed on the social spectrum between the popular masses and the dominating upper classes and élites. Some have seen their best prospect at present to be providing 'a valuable theological and spiritual service to the larger Protestant [Pentecostal] movement.'[19]

---

17 Literature on this shift is extensive and concurrent. For a critique of the ideological changes see J. Casteñada, *Utopia Unarmed* (New York: Vintage, 1994); G. De Schrijver, 'Paradigm Shift in Third World Theologies of Liberation' in G. De Schrijver (ed.), *Liberation on Shifting Grounds: A clash of socio-economic and cultural paradigms* (Leuven: Leuven University Press, 1998) 3-83; J.C. Scannone, '"Axial Shift" instead of "Paradigm Shift"', in Schrijver, *Liberation* 85-103.

18 This phrase is first attributed to Pablo Richard a Chilean progressive. Cited by Scannone in '"Axial"', 95-96.

19 Míguez Bonino, 'Prospects', 264.

3. Pentecostalism: popular presence and empowerment at the grass-roots

The indigenous Pentecostal churches have been little concerned with systematic doctrinal development, nor, until the 1980s, with civic projects. They have tended, rather, to adapt the Methodist, Baptist or Reformed theology of their origins to their particular contexts in a process facilitating an autochthonous expression of Christianity that has amply demonstrated its capacity to penetrate and flourish amongst the marginal and working class areas of the continent. Pentecostalism's capacity to achieve indigeneity has been aided by key distinctive characteristics: 'expressive (charismatic) worship', 'fraternal solidarity', and the security offered by a 'closed integrated community'.[20]

Yet the impact of Pentecostal ecclesial communities in Latin America had been consistently underestimated ever since an early 'well-informed correspondent' reckoned one of the first indigenous Pentecostal movement had 'reached its climax...in a short time the field will have been burned over and the movement die out...'[21] The autonomous future potential of Pentecostal communities within an apparently Catholic culture has been consistently misjudged by Protestant and Catholic Churches until the 1960s when the studies of E. Willems and C. Lalive D'Epinay drew serious academic attention to the religious and social significance of Pentecostalism in Brazil and Chile.[22] By the 1990s the theses of D. Martin and D. Stoll amongst others were highlighting the religious and cultural potential of the Pentecostal communities in the continent.[23] The emergence of 'neo-Pentecostal', or even 'post-Pentecostal'[24] ecclesial movements has added to the developing plurality of the 'religious market' and the wider utilisation of media communications has spawned new forms of

20 Ibid., 265.
21 Cited in W.E. Browning, *The West Coast Republics of South America*; J. Ritchie; K.E.Grubb. (eds.), Chap., IV by Webster E. Browning (London: World Dominion Press, 1930) 48.
22 E. Willems, *Followers of the New Faith: Culture Change and the Rise of Protestantism in Brazil and Chile* (Nashville: Vanderbilt University Press, 1967); Christian Lalive D'Epinay, *Refugio de las Masas* (Santiago: Ed. Pacifico, 1968) English edition, *Haven of the Masses* (London: Epworth, 1969).
23 D. Martin, *Tongues of Fire* (Oxford: Blackwell, 1990); Stoll, *Is Latin America turning Protestant?* (Berkeley: University of California Press, 1990)
24 See N. Saracco, 'The Pentecostalization of Latin America and the beginning of the post-Pentecostal era', paper given at the Oxford consultation of 'Currents in World Christianity', July 14-17, 1999 (Cambridge: CWC,1999) 12-14.

ecclesial networks and grass-roots movements. Catholicism has attempted to defend its historic constituency but ultimately the permanency of its officially sponsored ecclesial models will ultimately now depend on their being inculturated Christian communities.[25] The ecclesial re-entrenchment within Roman Catholicism in the face of the progressive demise and continuing Pentecostal expansion raises critical questions about ecclesiology, social justice and the integrity of the gospel.[26]

II Shifts in religious allegiance

The ecclesial and religious changes in the continent have occurred in the context of wider cultural transformations[27] and have provoked speculation that Latin America might eventually 'turn Protestant'[28] and see an 'evangelical majority'.[29] The expansion of 'popular Protestant' churches was an unexpected and 'puzzling' missiological development even for some Protestant observers,[30] challenging as it does the stereotypical Latino-Católico presuppositions.[31] However, 'Pentecostality' as a type of spiritual emphasis within Christianity should not necessarily be seen as a deriving solely from Protestantism [32] and some like J. P. Bastian argue that Pentecostalism should be regarded more as a religious movement derivative of a popular autonomous Catholicism expressing an implicit protest against the

---

25 Luzbetak sets out what the key features of inculturated gospel community would be. Luzbetak, *Church*, 82-3.
26 Míguez Bonino, 'Prospects', 267.
27 The change of religious affiliation and growth of a 'popular' form of Protestantism in traditionally homogenous Roman Catholic societies 'takes place in one of the most critical periods of social transition for Latin America, in which the condition of the poor urban and rural masses continues to deteriorate, reaching levels of bare subsistence.' J. S. Escobar, 'Conflicts of Interpretation of Popular Interpretations', in G. Cook (ed.), *New Face of the Church in Latin America* (Maryknoll: Orbis, 1994) 113. Escobar talks of 'the religious source for new forms of social and political participation of the emerging classes and subcultures that are changing the sociological and political maps of the region.' Ibid., 112.
28 D. Stoll, *Turning* xiii.
29 J. McCoy, 'Robbing Peter to Pay Paul', *Latinamerica Press* (Lima: 29 June, 1989) cited by Escobar, 'Interpretations', 122. See D. Stoll, *Turning,* 337, Appendix 3.
30 Escobar, 'Interpretations', 112.
31 W. Hollenweger, 'Pentecostalism's Global Language' in *Christian History*, Issue 58, Vol. XVII, No. 2 (1998) 24.
32 Cf. B.Campos, *De la Reforma Protestante a la Pentecostalidad de la Iglesia: Debate sobre el Pentecostalismo en América Latina*, (Quito: CLAI, 1997) 90-92.

authoritarianism of the church than as a variant of Protestantism.[33] However, 1) this ignores how sixteenth century Protestantism itself emerged and 2) neglects the wider global cultural and religious shifts highlighted by D. Martin.[34] The consequences of a religious' 'reformation' on the prospects for social transformation in a region of the world where it is claimed some 42% of the world's Roman Catholics live are clearly highly significant. The steady shift in ecclesial allegiance has widespread cultural consequences[35] and is the result of a complex and continuous interaction of multiple factors and forces in which historical initiatives of evangelisation in Latin are clearly involved.[36] What is evident is that the narrative, language and imagery of the Christian gospel continues to find manifold responses in Latin American culture of which it has been an intrinsic, though often masked part. Christianity's partly perceived transcendent reality[37] has increasingly been the source of popular contemporary ecclesial and cultural renewal with Brazil and Chile showing the most notable religious changes in the region[38] and hence are sources for this ecclesial evaluation.

III Historic Roman Catholic evangelisation

The conscientious efforts to evangelise the indigenous populations from the sixteenth century onwards by a minority of the Spanish and Portuguese religious should be differentiated from the more typically coercive conquest, by 'Cross and Sword' that

---

33 J.P. Bastian, 'Protestantism in Latin America', in E. Dussel (ed.), *The Church in Latin America*, 1492-1992 (Maryknoll: Orbis, 1992) 313-49. See discussion in M. Quintero, *Un Debate sobre Pentecostalismo y Misión de la Iglesia en América Latina:Jornadas de Actualización Teológica* (Quito: CLAI, 1997) 11, 22.

34 See Martin, *Tongues*, 4-6.

35 Franz Damen, 'Las sectas ¿avalancha o desafío?' *Cuarto Intermedio*, No. 3, cited in Escobar, 'Interpretations', 113.

36 Specialist sociological and anthropological studies too readily 'explain' religious transformations functionally and reflexively as if they could be conformed and methodologically reduced to the theoretical descriptions and determinative premises of the discipline in question. However, people as social actors at the grass-roots act upon as well as are being acted on by the social and cultural forces. People's human autonomy, motivation and cognizance of actions are too easily ignored in a way that 'discounts their own understandings of what it is they are doing'. See, Martin, *Tongues*, 1.

37 This was the argument classically set out by John MacKay, *El Otro Cristo Español* (México DF: Casa Unida, 1952)., English version *The Other Spanish Christ: A Spiritual Study of Spain and South America* (New York: Macmillan, 1932).

38 Cf., also the rising evangelical movement in Central America. Stoll, *Turning*, Appendices, 1, 2 & 3, 333-38.

established the Iberian Catholic hegemony over the continent. However, notwithstanding the later Protestant and secular 'black propaganda' not all Catholic colonial evangelism merits the wholly negative critique of some modern judgements. Nevertheless the overall pattern for Iberian mission was sternly paternalistic at best and bordering on the genocidal at worst.[39] Colonialisation was regarded as the task of building a 'Christian Empire' and although some acted to alleviate the suffering and situation of the indigenous peoples,[40] on the whole there was fanatical intolerance of all non-Catholic culture. The posture adopted was essentially one of *Reconquista*, rooted in the eight centuries long struggle against the Moors in the Iberian peninsula expressed in Gonzalo Fernandez de Oviedo's remark: 'Who doubts that the smoke of gunpowder against the Indians is incense for the Lord?'[41] From the steel of the political, military and religious alliance was forged the blunt and insensitive instruments of the Cruzada in the Americas which harnessed the intolerant religious zeal of the peninsular but which knew little of the counter-reformational subtleties of European Catholicism. Within 40 years colonists had:

> subjugated and decimated the Indians of high culture and driven the nomads back into the virgin forests; they integrated the remainder in the course of time through mixed marriages and finally brought them under the influence of the missions....There was in fact a transplantation of Iberian Catholicism.[42]

The historical outcome of this was a Latin American Roman Catholicism characterised by a marriage of altar and crown administered by a ruling oligarchy of church and state who owned

---

39 L. N. Rivera, *A Violent Evangelism: The Political and Religious Conquest of the Americas* (Louiseville: Westminster-John Knox Press, 1992) 169-79.

40 A minority of priests demonstrated a genuine concern for Indian peoples but the brute aspects of Colonization mostly went unmitigated. G. Gutiérrez has developed liberation themes from some heroic colonial struggles for Indian rights. G. Gutiérrez, *En busca de los pobres de Jesucristo: el pensamiento de Bartolomé de las Casas* (Salamanca: Sígueme, 1993); For a survey see H.J. Prien, *La Historia del Cristianismo en América Latina* (Salamanca: Ed. Sígueme, 1985) 253-54; P.A. Deiros, *Historia del Cristianismo en América Latina* (Buenos Aires: FTL, 1992) 207-390. For Chile see M. Salinas, 'La Evangelización en Chile,'in E. Dussel et al, (ed.), *Historia General de la Iglesia en América Latina, Vol. IX* (Salamanca: CEHILA-Ed. Sígueme, 1994) 42-63.

41 Quoted by Morales Padrón in 'Manual de Historia Universal', 5:265 cited by P.A., Deiros, *Historia del Cristianismo en América Latina* (Buenos Aires: FTL, 1992) 258. *(My own translation from the quote cited in Deiros.)*

42 W. Bühlman, *The Coming of the Third Church* (Maryknoll: Orbis, 1978) 155.

the large estates on which religion was marked by clericalism and high sacramentalism that was:

> religion as the cult of saints, processions and vows...recourse to any means, including spiritualism, to obtain "graces" and miracles ... here we see taken to an extreme the policy of baptising en masse, in the hope that the second and third generation will give rise to better Christians. On the contrary, when the first conversion miscarried, a second is less likely to come later; once a whole population becomes bound by tradition, hardened within Catholic structures, it is that much more difficult to shake.[43]

Only at Independence did the 'shaking' and 'breaking' of this Catholic culture begin as liberation from Iberian control created new conditions for religious and cultural development in the continent. The gulf between the social and ecclesiastical hierarchy and peoples' actual religious world has lingered on long into the post-Colonial period.

IV Protestantism in Latin America

1. Tentative inroads

Early attempts of Protestants in the sixteenth and seventeenth centuries to gain a toehold in the continent met with little long-term success.[44] Latin America was effectively sealed off from any religious change until the demise of the Spanish and Portuguese Empires and political independence from Iberia from 1810 onwards. This led quickly to a fragmentation into competing nation states and exposure to the commercial preponderance of the Protestant nations to the North. Gradually overlapping but progressively more vigorous foreign Protestant evangelisation and expansion occurred in the continent.[45] Expatriate and immigrant ethnic and language groups of Anglican, Presbyterian, Lutheran

---

43 Ibid., 155-56.
44 Protestant colonies in Venezuela (1529-50) and Brazil, [Rio de Janeiro (1555-67); Recife (1624-1654)] were frustrated whilst later colonies in the Caribbean, central America and the Guyanas were aided by the commercial and maritime power of north European states during the period 1655-1810: thus Protestant churches occupied the fringes of the Spanish and Portuguese Empire and culture.
45 This framework of successive initiatives of Protestant Mission is adopted from M. Berg and P. Pretiz's analysis 'Five Waves of Protestant Evangelization' in Cook, *Face*, 56-62.

and Methodist congregations slowly established on the continent against the Catholic clergy's attempt to maintain their ecclesial hegemony.

2. Beyond the ethnic immigrant enclave.

A more avowedly missionary wave of Protestants came in the wake of 19th century immigration as the opportunities for foreign educationalists were offered by liberal and reformist politicians concerned to break the monopoly of the traditional Catholic catechetical approach to education. Whilst a significant number of *simpatizantes* (admirers and supporters) of Protestant education were in evidence during the second half of the nineteenth century, which raised Protestant expectation, few conversions and denominational transference ensued. The hope of a reformation of Catholicism from within[46] failed to take into account the functional role of the cultural, social and religious bonds of the continent. Later, the influence of theological liberalism from Europe and North America had unforeseen consequences for the expansion of popular Protestant churches.

3. Independent Evangelical missions

The arrival of more avowedly Evangelical faith missions led to a third Protestant ecclesial stream popularly characterised by the appearance of the modest 'storefront' chapels and a more extensive Bible and evangelistic witness. Many of the missionary protagonists had abandoned the mainline Protestant denominations over the theological controversies surrounding the fundamentalist-modernist debate in the United States and Europe to spearhead the autonomous and semi-autonomous faith missions whose ranks were further swollen by missionaries expelled from China in the early 1950s. Thus many North American faith missions exhibited elements of ideological anti-communism as well as anti-Catholic sentiments (both belief systems being regarded by some Protestants as causal in the general underdevelopment of the continent).

4. Protestant *Cruzada* and *Conquista*

A more overtly public fourth wave of Protestant activity followed characterised by evangelistic *Cruzadas*, church planting and the formation of Bible cells by independent evangelical and

---

46 The roots of reform in Spanish Catholicism and the need for it from a Protestant missiological reformed perspective in Latin America were set out by Mackay, *Cristo*, 101-29.

Pentecostal groups. A common feature in this phase of Protestant advance was a traditional Evangelicalism marked by a commitment to the Great Commission whose fulfilment looked to hasten the return of Christ. An underlying premise was the commitment to foster the 'enlightened' aspects of Christian (Western) culture in a predominantly 'unmodernised' Catholic society.[47]

By the 1960s 'Saturation Evangelism', followed later by Church Growth inspired strategies, questioned the efficacy of the older models of outreach.[48] D. McGavran's influence[49] later embellished by P. Wagner,[50] initiated an influential but predominantly North American theology of mission of a highly functionalist ethos dependent on an applied cultural anthropology that tended to ignore 'the conflictive nature of social relationships.'[51] A more comprehensively Biblical missiology reflecting the inherent themes of Creation, Salvation History and the Kingdom of God was promoted by the *Fraternidad Teológica Latinoamericana* (FTL) influenced by a renewed evangelicalism that turned the focus from first World 'missions' to the more global expression of Lausanne (1974) with a concern for more 'holistic mission'[52] against some of the assumptions of the 'church growth' approach[53] and the superficialities of earlier Protestant

---

47 G. Cook, 'Protestant Mission and Evangelization in Latin America: An Interpretation', in Cook, *Face*, 45.
48 A. R. Tippet, *Church Growth and the Word of God* (Grand Rapids: Eerdmanns, 1970).
49 Most notably *Bridges of God* (London:1955) and *Understanding Church Growth* (Grand Rapids: Eerdmans, 1970). See T. Yates, *Christian Mission in the Twentieth Century* (Cambridge:CUP, 1994) 214-19.
50 As a disciple, interpreter and successor to McGavran at the Fuller School for World Mission.
51 Cook, 'Mission', 49.
52 Ibid., 49. The inter-continental tension over the priority and meaning of evangelism is reflected in Cook's objection to Arthur Johnstone's inaccurate interpretation of the causes of the decline of evangelism in western churches as 'highly ethnocentric view of recent mission history' as well as being 'theologically inaccurate'. See A. Johnstone, *The Battle for World Evangelism* (Wheaton: Tyndale, 1978) 12, 73, 175-76.
53 'Beginning from certain methodological givens cross-cultural mission theoreticians make sweeping generalizations concerning church growth and expansion across cultural and geographical barriers.' Cook, 'Mission', 49. Cook has in mind the introduction to D. McGavran's *Understanding Church Growth*, 13-63. Nevertheless Cook acknowledges the positive contribution of agencies like MARC World Vision International, Lausanne and Fuller Theological Seminary in the development of Protestant mission in Latin America.

missiological practice.[54]   A key ecclesial question was whether a church that was *not* indigenous could effectively evangelise.[55]

5. Autochthonous Pentecostal Ecclesiality

An authentic popular evangelisation that marked the most significant phase of ecclesial mission in popular Latin American culture was a heterogeneous movement that gave rise to grass-roots indigenous churches, locally led and propagated. This Pentecostal 'ecclesiality' as an autochthonous church development in Latin America can be traced directly to movements beginning in Valparaíso and Santiago in Chile (1909), São Paulo (1910) and Belén (1911) in north-East Brazil. These indigenous Pentecostal churches began to take root in Latin America as a fringe and dissident phenomenon of the Protestant constituency[56] and reactive to Catholicism as it drew from popular culture, the evangelical Holiness movement of Wesleyan heritage and from restoration movements seeking in modernity a more biblical and primitive Spirit-filled church.[57]

This ecclesiology was generally characterised by its formal rupture with denominational structures, foreign mission boards and ecclesiastical organisations.[58] Receiving no subsidies or mission-ry support from overseas it was forced to generate leadership from within its own ranks and thus the lack of formal education ceased to be a barrier to ecclesial leadership. Militant membership, a reckless

54 R. Padilla is critical of the North American Church Growth strategy and views it as a particular cultural expression of North American Missiology. R. Padilla, *Misión Integral: Ensayos sobre el Reino y la iglesia* (Buenos Aires: Nueva Creación, 1986) 159-63. This was also reflected in *the Congreso Latinoamericano de Evangelización conferences* (CLADE) which have been critical of the dispensational approach of much of North American missiology. However, an absence of critical theological reflection about social responsibility exists in many quarters of the evangelical movement as well as a lack of understanding over what cross-cultural mission involves

55 Orlando E. Costas, *The Church and its Mission: A Shattering Critique from the Third World* (Wheaton: Tyndale, 1974) 145.

56 For an essential survey of Pentecostal beginnings and growth in Latin America see W.J.Hollenweger, *The Pentecostals* (London: SCM, 1972) 63-6, 75-110; David Barrett, *World Christian Encyclopaedia* (Oxford: OUP, 1982). A more recent survey is provided by Donald Dayton, 'El Pentecostalismo esta encontrando su destino en América Latina', *Evangelio y Sociedad*, No.11 (Nov.-Dec., 1991) 15-7.

57 An analysis of the sources for Pentecostalism in Christian traditions is provided by D. W. Dayton's *Theological Roots of Pentecostalism* (Metuchen, NJ: Scarecrow Press, 1987). The Spanish edition has a valuable prologue by N. Saracco; *Raíces Teológicas del Pentecostalismo* (Buenos Airies: Nueva Creación, 1991).

58 This was certainly the case with the Chilean Methodist Pentecostal movement and the Brazilian AD and CC.

faith generosity and the accumulative effect of incessant street witness led to unprecedented grass-roots ecclesial expansion.[59]

The Pentecostal expectation even cherished the notion of supplanting Catholicism by 'popular Protestant' movements but this required going far beyond mere quantitative expansion.[60] The diversity of the different socio-ecclesiological options facing the Pentecostal community echoes the dilemma of sixteenth century believers in Europe: whether to be Catholic, Reformed or radically Reformed.[61]

Thus indigenous Pentecostal communities in Latin America emerged, as in the case of primitive Christianity, as a movement at the level of popular culture[62] and in the case of Chile and Brazil they were obliged to generate their own ecclesial structures rooted in local communities considerably isolated and independent of wider world Pentecostalism.[63] North American and European Pentecostalism of missionary origin, came later to Latin America but they struggled to gain a precarious rootedness in the popular culture of the continent because their 'imported' institutional, cultural identity and ecclesial character hampered contextualization and bequeathed 'foreign' Pentecostal movements a financial and organisational dependency. Moreover, leadership and pastoral ministerial training followed more traditional pedagogical curriculum patterns of seminary and Bible institute which marginalized the working classes from leadership.[64]

---

59 J. Sepúlveda, 'The Pentecostal movement in Latin America', 'Jahrbuch Mission 1992: Fokus Lateinamerika', in Cook, Face, 68-81. See Stoll, Turning, 8,9. There is nothing specifically new to Christianity in the Pentecostal search for an intense experience of God through the Holy Spirit, the quest for Holiness, the strong eschatological hope and evangelistic zeal.

60 Míguez Bonino, 'Prospects', 263.

61 David Martin contends that a tussle over cultural ethos typified in the historic anglo-hispanic competitive struggle dating from the Reformation has been played out in Latin America. Martin, Tongues, 10.

62 Ibid., 286.

63 Sepúlveda, 'Movement', 69 .

64 Only gradually have some 'foreign' groups bridged the cultural divide and made the transition into more popular ecclesiality. In the majority of the Latin American republics Pentecostalism of a missionary origin predominates but not, significantly, in Chile or Brazil. In any case it is more accurate to speak in the plural of 'Pentecostalisms' or 'Popular Protestantisms' and their 'ecclesiologies'.

IV The missiological challenge of the people's church

There is a sense that 'Popular Protestantism' is a surprising manifestation of what G.Gutíerrez has called ' the irruption of the poor'[65] and what W. Bühlman called 'The coming of the third Church'[66] highlighted the emergence of an indigenous church in the southern hemisphere[67] that marked the shift from the historic ecclesiastical mission structures to more emancipatory and autonomous inculturated ecclesial communities.[68] As an ecclesial development grass-roots Pentecostalism raises vital missiological issues over what 'popular', 'religious' and 'community' mean in a Christian movement.[69] They have aroused great concern in Catholic circles, producing either reactive conservatism or a renewal of commitment to Catholic missionary efforts.[70] For Latin American Catholicism, Vatican II and the subsequent Medellín conference seemed to inaugurate a new ecclesial engagement but it has been Pentecostalism's ecclesial development and expansion from below that has been the historical surprise for it brought church where none was expected – amongst the socially deprived marginalized in the hostile environs of the Latin American urban periphery.

Despite the fact that 42% of the world's Catholics made up its membership, only 2% of the world wide missionary personnel came from the continent and a large missionary force was required to maintain the Catholic church in the continent[71] whilst in comparison the popular Pentecostal churches continued to demonstrate an innate ability to expand and draw leadership from the popular grass-roots and motivated working class activists.

---

65 G. Gutierrez, 'The Irruption of the Poor in Latin America', in Torres and Eagleson (eds.), *The Challenge of Basic Christian Communities* (Maryknoll: Orbis, 1984) 107-23; 108. See Escobar, 'Interpretations', 129.

66 W. Buhlman, *The Church of the Future* (Maryknoll: Orbis, 1986) 6.

67 A. Walls, 'Culture and Coherence in Christian History,' in *Evangelical Review of Theology*, Vol. 9, No.35 (July,1985) 221, cited by Escobar, 'Interpretations', 129.

68 The African Independent churches reflect a distinct contextual ecclesial response to the crisis of western missiological models under modernity's impact.

69 Escobar, 'Interpretations', in Cook, Faces, 131-34.

70 See D. Irarrazaval, 'Mission in Latin America: Inculturated Liberation', *Missiology*, Vol. XX, No.2 (April, 1992) 229-35.

71 Missionary Conference documents, 'Cuarto Congreso Misionero Latinoamericano', COMLA IV, 1991 (Lima: Obras Misionales Pontificias, 1992) 267 cited in Escobar, 'Interpretations', 129.

V Brazilian Catholic and Pentecostal grass-roots

1. The progressive church and the *CEB*s

Inherent in this movement was an attempt to pursue 'rationalised religion' in a church embodied by popularly religious lay people in order to bring about ' a radical democratisation within the Catholic church.'[72] However conservative trends have affected the hierarchy, clergy, pastoral agents and religious more than the laity and the *CEB* members. The historic religious watershed in Brazil has already past and the hegemony of the Catholic Church and traditional folk Catholicism has been seriously, if not irrevocably, broken. Pentecostal churches, Afro-spiritism and new religious movements responded to modernity but with a spiritual discourse that has led to religious diversity becoming characteristic of modern Brazil's lower classes.

The progressive pursuit of rationalisation that disregarded traditional rituals and religiosity actually increased the poor's marginalisation in the Brazilian Catholic church even further and made more attractive the religious alternatives which provided a notion of freedom, 'enchantment' as well as a response to modernity. Ironically, the CEBs were an attempt by the Brazilian Catholic church to reach the poor it had not been able to assimilate.

Yet whilst there is a material functionality to religion, its election by the poor is not merely functionalist, not materialist. All religions of the Brazilian poor seem to be, at both the subjective and objective levels, related to their struggle for survival and all religious groups that are popular among the poor are materially 'useful'. Ecclesial life offers alternative community possibilities, deepened motivation and strengthened will to endure and overcome impoverished existence in the life journey through the sprawling urban periphery.

The *CEB* 're-invented' Catholic ecclesial life at the grass-roots for the purpose of liberative action amongst those at the base of the social and religious pyramid but the progressive wing of Brazilian Catholicism did not achieve the wider transformation of church and society it had sought through them. The *CEB* neither replaced the parishes nor became 'popular' Catholic churches and substantial institutional, missiological and cultural reasons have

---

72 C.L. Mariz, *Coping with Poverty: Pentecostals and Christian Communities in Brazil* (Philadelphia: Temple University Press, 1994) 16.

meant the *CEB* critical difficulties have not yet been overcome. Ironically, the wider democratisation of Brazil diminished the *CEBs* intended strategic role and the resistance of a restorationist hierarchy has thwarted the *CEBs* becoming sufficiently inculturated to become ecclesially autochthonous, whilst the burgeoning Pentecostal communities progressively· become the ecclesial option of the 'people'. Moreover, the *CEBs* clerical dependence has not yet been resolved in principle nor overcome in practice. The Catholic grass-roots themselves seemed unable to assume the protagonism and critical consciousness necessary for the *caminhada*[73] elected for them by the Catholic grass-roots leadership.[74]

Brazilian Catholicism's progressive ecclesial project failed to achieve a wider transformation of church and society. Moreover, the conciliar inspired motivation to create a 'new mode' of ecclesial life for the purpose of liberative action amongst those at the base of the social and religious pyramid generated conflict with the important conservative elements in the church hierarchy and serious tensions with the Vatican. Hence, institutional restraints have impeded the *CEBs* in developing and inculturating sufficiently to become ecclesially autochthonous at a popular level. They remained caught between institutionality and genuine popular ecclesiality and therefore have often been unable to satisfy either the hierarchy or the wider popular Catholic classes. The *CEBs* sustainability, which is crucially dependent on their being truly ecclesial and popular, needs the grass-roots themselves to assume their own protagonism. The ecclesial option for the poor has to become, if it is to be ultimately and widely transformative, the ecclesial option of the poor. The hierarchical prerogative to decide for the base how such ecclesiality develops negates the sovereignty of the Spirit in favour of the institutionalised authority of the church: thus the potential for inculturated mission as the

---

73 The 'long march through the wilderness.' D. Lehmann, *Struggle for the Spirit: Religious Transformation and Popular Culture in Brazil and Latin America* (Cambridge: Polity Press, 1996) 222. Gutiérrez openly recognises the long term nature of the journey during which an emerging liberative spirituality and ecclesiology will inevitably be taxing and demanding of its protagonists.G. Gutiérrez, *We Drink from Our Own Wells: The Spiritual Journey of a People* (Maryknoll: Orbis, 1984) 72-89.
74 P. Berryman, *Religion in the Megacity: Catholic and Protestant Portraits from Latin America* (Maryknoll: Orbis, 1996) 69-70.

calling and responsibility of the grass-roots community itself is undermined.[75]

3. Brazilian Pentecostalism: from peripheral ecclesial dissent to popular ecclesial mutation

Meanwhile a thriving popular religious culture in contemporary Brazil which draws its roots from a long history of cross-fertilisation of religious beliefs amongst Brazil's marginalized masses[76] is the context for the emergence of a plethora of Pentecostal ecclesial movements.[77] However, whilst earlier Brazilian Pentecostal 'ecclesiologies' represent grass-roots developments of Christian community they mark, in fact, a rupture with many aspects of popular syncretistic religious culture as well as embodying an emancipation from and a symbolic protest against the established Brazilian ecclesiastical order as well.[78]

Pentecostals recognise that their life-blood depends on breaking the cordons of clerical caste, Protestant or Catholic. Religiously that is their raison d'être and in the symbolic realm it dramatises their emigration from the class

---

75 Burrows had argued this in the 1980s in relation to global Catholicism. W.R. Burrows, *New Ministries: the Global Context*, (Maryknoll: Orbis, 1980) 20-21.
76 A.A. Westra, 'La Conducta del Consumidor en el Mercado Brasileño de Salvación', Boudewijnse, Opio, 116.
77 Westra, 'Consumidor', 115-35. Westra's case study examines the religious 'market' in the city of Bahía in the State of Alagoinhas.
78 Lehmann, *Struggle*, 192-93. Historic Protestant church growth began to slowly decline relative to population after the 1930s as the first wave of Pentecostal churches began to gain a national presence.
Estimate of the proportion of historic Protestants to Pentecostals in Brazil 1930-1990:

1930 (a)	1964 (b)	1990 (c)
90.5% / 9.5%	34.8% /65.2%	20% / 80%

Estimates by E. Braga and K. Grub (a), W.R. Read (b & c) cited in L.S. Campos, 'Protestantismo Histórico y Pentecostalismo en Brazil, Aproximaciones o Conflicto,' in D.F. Gutiérrez, *En la Fuerza del Espíritu* (México DF: Aipral, 1995) 113, n. 41. See Martin for 1930 figure, Martin, Tongues, 65. However, there is no agreed method of assessing ecclesial participation. Prien, for example, allows for 'traditional' Protestants to be in a slight majority over Pentecostals in 1970 by a proportion of 50.6% to 49.4% respectively. W.Read and F.A. Ineson, Brazil 1980 (Monrovia: MARCC, 1973) 23 cited in Prien, Historia, 784, n. 242. Freston affirms that by 1995 at least 'two-thirds' of 'Protestants' in Brazil were Pentecostals constituting some 16 million participants. Freston, P., 'Breve Historia do Pentecostalismo Brasileiro' in A. Antoniazzi, et al. (eds) *Nem Anjos Nem Demônios: Interpretações Sociológicas do Pentecostalismo* (Petrópolis: Vozes, 1994) 133.

128

barriers of Brazilian society. They are establishing their own special realm in the world of Brazil...[79]

Whilst earlier Pentecostal movements were reactive to certain aspects of Protestant ecclesial models and to the hierarchical authority of traditional Catholic ecclesiality, contemporary post-Pentecostal movements are more complexly responsive and eclectically related to Catholic, cultural and popular religious notions, most notably the *IURD* (Iglesia Universal del Reino de Dois).

Pentecostal Brazilian developments are not characterised by a sense of ecclesial disarray but by a search for an ordered empowerment and community in a culture impacted by social fragmentation brought on by modernity. Post-modern socio-economic trends are reflected increasingly in a post-Pentecostal ecclesial movement which still retains a sense of the potential of marginal people empowered from below: '*toda revolução cultural, tuda coisa que der certo, começou de baixo*' (every cultural revolution, everything which is certain, comes from below).[80] This represents more of an expectant collective assault on the material promises offered by post-modern culture that contrasts with the earlier posture of Pentecostal ecclesial movements whose hope fixed more on an external eschatological and transcendent vision evoked by the experience of the Spirit.

Both earlier rupture and later continuity with traditional Brazilian society are reflected in the distinct movements[81] as they resonate social change and the masses' needs.[82] Increasingly, paradoxical and apparent cultural and religious contradictions are managed dynamically by juxtaposing older and newer traditions in an on going process of controlled eclectic syncretistic ecclesial mutation.[83] An emphasis on spiritual and social empowerment of all members, whilst expressive of Pentecostal freedom and personal liberation, nevertheless has its limits; hence the need for a supervising authority. Spiritual and emotional expressiveness in

---

79 Martin, *Tongues*, 66.
80 Pastor Rodríguez of the IURD cited in Lehmann, *Struggle*, 213.
81 Droogers, 'Visiones Paradójicas sobre Religión Paradójica: Modelos explicativos del Crecimiento del Pentecostalismo en Brasil y Chile.', B. Boudewijnse, A. Drooger and F. Kamsteeg (eds.), *Algo más que Opio: Una Lectura Antropológica del Pentecostalismo Latinoamericano y Caribeño* (DEI: San José, 1991) 38.
82 Ibid., 37.
83 Ibid., 21.

ecclesial worship helps counterbalance an authoritarian homiletic by creating a semblance of pneumatic freedom.

The social and theological dualism inherent in the rupture of earlier Pentecostalism with the Brazilian social order in its societal 'walk-out' has gradually been reassessed as its membership mushroomed and the potential of its cohesive community structures were recognised. Post-Pentecostal practice has brought more direct engagement in the socio-political realm. This marks a shift in attitudes from earlier Pentecostal ecclesial apoliticism: thus a sinful world which believers are not to embrace, which stands in contrast to the church, also becomes, conversely, the territory for active mission, service and potentially the source of blessing both spiritual and material. Earlier Pentecostal traditions are gradually learning to selectively 'spoil the Egyptians' for the 'adornment of the temple' whilst post-Pentecostalism's utilisation of the mass media and political involvement to propagate its message emphasising materiality, prosperity and health brought the consumer market into a de-ecclesified temple.

Strong eschatological belief in earlier Pentecostal movements bolstered hopes and strengthened resistance of members all too conscious of the profound cosmic crisis affecting the material domain.[84] Increasingly, however, under post-Pentecostal shifts, a pre-millenial eschatology has become over-realised[85] in the predominance given to divine healing and material provision; while seemingly pointing to an emphasis on the spiritual realm it has heightened the movement's more exclusive concern for physicality and the resolution of material issues.

Brazilian post-Pentecostalism, exemplified by the *IURD*, has broken with many of the historical ecclesial boundaries established by the older denominations and earlier Pentecostalism, thus creating a minimised Protestantism[86] and a new religious mentality[87] that challenges historical ecclesial forms that have

---

84 Ibid., 22.
85 P.D., Sierpierski, 'Pos-Pentecostalismo e Política no Brasil' in *Estudos Teológicos*, No.1 1997, Año 37, 52.
86 This may reflect the IURD's throwing off the Enlightenment premises of much Protestant emphasis on fallenness and personal sin. See Shaull, 'Transformation', 77-83.
87 S. Coleman sees the IURD as a 'Faith' and 'Prosperity' movement that adapts worship to 'new forms of religious consumption' that parallel comparable

increasingly suffered a crisis over their ecclesial relationship with the popular grass-roots culture, despite decades of missionary effort. The challenge for both a renewal of the notion of church and the doctrine of God in Latin America is evident.

VI Catholic and Pentecostal Chile

1. Two ecclesial starting points

The Chilean experience of the Base Communities (*CBs*) from the 1960s onwards has raised questions over the traditional hierarchical notion of a clerically dominated church and increasingly advocated a collegial dialogical model linked to communities and implied a 'smaller, more homogeneous, democratic, de-clericalised, and sexually egalitarian institution.'[88] But this was a church that the Vatican under John Paul II found increasingly unacceptable. Chilean Catholicism since Medellín has reflected two distinct experiences of the Christian God.[89] The Chilean grass-roots church pursued a 'Latin American' ecclesial vision, rooted in the conciliar[90] and CELAM conferences in which the mystery of a God of life and mercy is found in the fraternal ecclesial community and communion with those who are oppressed.[91] The struggle of the base communities under dictatorship of the 1970s and 1980s accentuated the need for a 'prophetic' ecclesia of solidarity and communion that emphasised a related and more consciously biblically rooted vision of God.[92]

Whilst the traditional Chilean church mirrored a pyramid of power dominated by a clerical élite the latter grass-roots ecclesiology has sought to be a community and circle of fraternal solidarity, love and friendship:[93] a communion of the Triune God's people who are all uniquely different but nonetheless equal in

movements emerging in a globalising world culture.   S. Coleman, *The Globalisation of Charismatic Christianity* (Cambridge: CUP, 2000) 38.

88   In the mid-1970s 70% of the hierarchy favoured the continuation of its exclusive prerogative to take decisions for the church whilst 51.5% of the nuns and 64.7% of lay leaders advocated a much more consultative institution. Smith, 'Church', 337.

89   R. Muñoz, *Dios de los Cristianos* (Santiago: Paulinas, 1986) 39-40.

90   The claim is not that Vatican II entirely changed the traditional ecclesial model but that it 'relativised' its hierarchical reality.

91   See Boff, *Ecclesiogenesis*, 132-34.

92   Muñoz, R., *El Camino de la Iglesia en América Latina a través de sus Conferencias de Medellín, Puebla y Santo Domingo* (Santiago: SS.CC., 1997) I.5.

93   See L.Boff, *Ecclesiogenesis: the base communities reinvent the church* (Maryknoll: Orbis, 1986) 23-33.

status and dignity[94] in a missiologically incarnated, pneumatic and liberative church. This ecclesial vision has proved vulnerable to the shifts in the Chilean church and society[95] and, as in the case in Brazil, was curiously undermined by the 're-democratisation' of Chile and affected by the hierarchy's return to institutional concerns of the 1990s in the face of the challenges presented by the discourse of neo-liberalism and the weakening of Catholic hegemony by the popular ecclesial proliferation of the Pentecostals.

In Chilean Catholicism there remains a clear tension reflected in two distinct experiences of the Christian God: over against the neo-colonial hierarchical notion of the Trinity, the grass-roots church reflects a Latin American 'ecclesial conversion' inspired by Vatican II and activated by the Medellín vision of a 'prophetic' church that emphasises a 'practice of solidarity' and a more 'popular and biblical' experience of God. This, however, remains precariously incipient in Chile. The Chilean ecclesial 'crisis' arises from the insistence that the church is to be missionary, incarnational, fraternal, diverse, pneumatic and liberative against the traditional notion of church, bolstered by Vatican policies, that mirrors a pyramid of ecclesiastical power under a clerical élite.

2. Chilean Pentecostal advance

In common with Brazilian Pentecostal ecclesiology, the Chilean Pentecostal churches are marked by authoritarian ecclesial government and an autochthonous character derived from early autonomy from foreign institutional mission control.[96] After the mid-1930s the ecclesial proliferation of the Pentecostal movement became increasingly prone to fragmentation. Seen from a different perspective the fragmentation was an integral part of its proliferation as autocratic local and national leadership provoked new offshoots in a cyclical pattern of expansion and division.[97] Whilst the 1932 schism clearly affected ecclesial growth initially, later sub-divisions seem to have accelerated the expansion of the

---

94 Ibid.
95 R. Muñoz, *Pueblo, Comunidad, Evangelio* (Santiago: Rehue, 1994) 50-1.
96 J.B.A. Kessler, *A Study of the Older Protestant Missions and Churches in Peru and Chile* (Goes: Oosterbaan and le Cointre, 1967) 327.
97 F. Anabalon, as one of the present day leaders of Chilean Pentecostalism, accepts that *Caudillismo* rather than doctrinal matters is often the cause of Pentecostal fragmentation. Palma, *Extraña*, 149-50. Interview by the author with F. Anabalon, 12 December, 1997, Union Bíblica, Santiago.

movement. Official census figures indicate the overall rise in the percentage of evangelicals in the population from around 1% before the Methodist schism in 1910 to over 12% in 1992. By 1940 a clear popular movement had begun to register in the official census figures.[98] In general terms it is possible to affirm that from 1930 to 1960 its growth rate was some 100% per decade.[99] Arguably Pentecostal expansion has increased in times of crisis,[100] although this is relative to how each 'crisis' is perceived in different social sectors.[101] Pentecostal ecclesial communities have been an effective survival strategy against poverty for the marginalized. However it is also clear, up to the present, that the growth in membership of Pentecostal ecclesial communities, at a rate greater than population increase, has not declined in periods of relative social peace and prosperity in Chile.

---

98 Official census figures for 'Protestants', 1907-1992 in Lagos, *Evangélicos*, 27.

1907	1920	1930	1940	1952	1960	1970	1980	1992
1.1%	1.44%	1.45%	2.34%	4.06%	5.58%	6.18%	7.5%*	12.4%***
							(10.0%**)	
31,5000	54,800	63,400	118,400	225,000	425,700	549,900	1,132,900	1,278,644

NB All figures up to 1980 consider 'Protestants-Evangelicals-Pentecostals' together.

* No religious data was taken in the official census in 1980 so the figure for that year is supplied by Centro Bellarmino, Santiago, cited in P. Hoff, 'Chile's Pentecostals face problems due to Isolation', *EMQ*, Vol.27, No. 3 (July, 1991) 245. ** Estimate by 'Movimiento' (Table 6.1) 106; *** The 1992 figure does not include the figure for 'historic Protestants' and only considers those over 14 years of age. No reliable figures for earlier years. The total 'Protestant' numbers just before 1930 were calculated at some 62,000 of which up to a third were thought to be 'Pentecostal'. MacKay, *Cristo*, 245. It is calculated for the 1992 figure that 90% of the total are 'Pentecostals', Hoff, Ibid. We argue that the substantial percentage increases in the post 1940 period are due to Pentecostal ecclesial expansion. For a breakdown of the 1980 statistics. See Barrett, *World*, 226. The above figures will be conservative and register only those who directly affirm they are members of a religious affiliation. 'Participants' who with a lower level of formal commitment and children not baptised will not register in the figures. Catholics, on the other hand, who have been baptised but may still be nominal and non-practising, will register in the census figures.

98 N. Sepúlveda, 'Breve Síntesis Histórica del Movimiento Pentecostal en Chile', C. Alvarez (ed.), *Pentecostalismo y Liberación: Una Experiencia Latinoamericana* (San José: DEI, 1992) 40-4.

99 C. Parker, *Las Iglesias y su Acción Social en Chile* (Santiago: Unicef, 1996) 93; Sepúlveda, 'Nacimiento', 256.

100 H. Lagos, and A. Chacon, *Los Evangélicos en Chile: Una Lectura Sociológica* (Concepción: Presor-Lar, 1987) 26-38.

101 Ibid., 34.

133

At least 400 legally constituted Pentecostal denominations had been registered in Chile by the mid-1990s, with more than 1,000 other unregistered grass-roots groups and movements being in existence.[102] By the same period, some 1,150 'evangelical' places of worship were established in Santiago, the capital, as compared to 470 Roman Catholic parishes.[103] By the early 1990s even the most conservative estimates considered Pentecostal communities to represent the second religious option in Chile after Roman Catholicism. Whereas Catholics totalled 7,409,526 (76.7% of population total) Pentecostals were approximately 90.0% of the evangelical-Protestant population of a total of some 1,278,644 (12.4%) in the country.[104] In fact the figures do not fully represent the religious impact and following of Pentecostalism as only 20% of Catholics attend Church regularly (once a week) and could be regarded as practising Catholics (at 'official' Church services.) 80% attend occasionally or hardly ever whereas amongst evangelicals some 50% attended weekly.[105] In some areas of Santiago and Chile's VIIIth Region, Pentecostals would be more numerous than Catholics in places of worship on Sundays. The Catholic concern over the clear decline in allegiance has not generated, as yet, any effective measures to reverse the present trend. At the same time Pentecostal unity and reconciliation is made more complex by the need for congregations to be legally registered' thus perversely encouraging the secular institution-alisation of divisions that arise from pastoral conflicts and disputes over church assets.

As Chilean law finally shifts to 'officialise' dissident ecclesiology[106] the character of the gospel of 'rupture' and symbolic protest of social 'walk-out' becomes subject to

---

102 Ibid., 20. Many groups are not legally registered and so the figure could be more than 2,000. C. Parker, *Iglesias*, 97.

103 Fontaine, T. and H. Beyer, 'Retrato del Movimiento Evangélico a la Luz de las Encuestas de Opinion Pública, *Estudios Públicos* No. 44, Primavera (Santiago: Centro de Estudios Públicos, 1991) 67.

104 Official 1992 census by Censo de Población, Instituto Nacional de Estadísticas, Santiago. Census did not include people under 14 years of age. Fontaine, 'Evangélico', 61-124. The survey reported higher figures for evangelicals [16%] and lower for Catholics [73%]

105 Parker, *Acción*, 20-5; 32-5.

106 See J. Sepúlveda, 'Pentecostal Theology in the Context of the Struggle for Life', in *Faith born in the Struggle for Life: a rereading of Protestant faith in Latin America today*, Dow Kirkpatrick, (ed.), trans. L.McCoy (Grand Rapids: Eerdmans, 1988) 313.

Constantinian restraint as 'militancy' gives way to nominalism[107] and democracy and 'free-market' philosophy brings greater material and civic rewards. As the distance between the Pentecostal churches and the world is diminished in Chile[108] the 'ecclesiology of exclusion' extolled in the rhythmic plaintive hymn of the Chilean pilgrim Pentecostal soul may echo with less conviction in the decades ahead:

> Soy extranjero aqui, en tierra extraña estoy;
> (I am a stranger here, in a strange land I am)
> Mi hogar está muy lejos, del sol más allá... [109]
> (My home is far away , beyond the sun..)

A crucial key to the emergence of Chilean Pentecostal communities was the religious peripheral and dissident culture in which the movement sprang up: the growing social awareness of the nominally Catholic urban working classes, their underlying religious anticlericalism and the slow easing of religious and cultural constraints as moderate industrialisation impacted Chile. Modernity, whilst weakening institutional Catholic authority and fragmenting traditional social structures, at the same time created greater cultural space for the emergence of popular religious movements and provided a milieu of religious dissidence to assure Pentecostal communities a fertile breeding ground.

The relative failure of the Enlightenment responsive Protestant mission reflective of the 1916 Panama Conference's 'preferential option to the educated classes' in Latin America is qualified by the vindication of a contextualized ecclesiality derived from a dissident missiological 'self-supporting' policy that became foundational in the origins of an autochthonous Chilean Pentecostal movement initiated by the *IMP* (Iglesia Metodista Pentecostal). An ecclesiality of dissent, rupture and separation has become less pronounced as Pentecostal communities have become

---

107 An authoritative survey revealed that although over 62% of professing 'evangelicals' attended their church about twice a month, some 21% attended only sporadically whilst just under 17% attended hardly at all. Fontaine, T. and H. Beyer, 'Retrato del Movimiento Evangélico a la Luz de las Encuestas de Opinion Pública, *Estudios Públicos* No. 44, Primavera (Santiago: Centro de Estudios Públicos, 1991) 93.

108 E.Cleary and J. Sepúlveda, 'Chilean Pentecostalism: Coming of Age', in E.L. Cleary & H.W. Stewart-Gambinho, *Power, Politics and Pentecostals in Latin America,* (Boulder: Westview Press, 1997) 114-15.

109 IMEC, 'Soy extranjero aqui' Hymn No.162, Himnario Metodista Pentecostal (Santiago: Ossa Imp. n.d.) 155.

more institutionally established as a predominant grass-roots church presence in Chile. Increasingly 'post-Pentecostal' movements are appearing in Chile, including the *IURD*. Functionalist ecclesiologies carry the seeds of their own instability and inculturated communities which lose their ontological roots in the doctrine of the triune God and the disciplines of biblical reflection on *praxis* are in danger of assimilating with little resistance or transformation some incongruous popular and post-modern cultural trends.

VII Transformational paradigm in community

Pentecostalism has a theological precedent for conscientisation which is a transformative hermeneutic of *praxis* that works out truth and knowledge, not abstractly, but in the experience and reality of life that is covenantal in its relationality with God and others.

Pentecostal communities share the same social context as the CEBs and thus there exists the potential for an ecclesial dynamic which would integrate greater affective, oral and communal dimensions of human interaction into a transformative paradigm.[110] However, Freire's transformative model which was so influential in the CEBs, relied on an ideologically questionable 'hierarchy of consciousness'[111] and a promotion of liberation amongst the poor that was ironically obliged to denigrate their perception of reality in order to elicit their protagonism.[112] Moreover, Freire's paradigm lacked a fuller biblical epistemology and the support of ontological categories to make an authentic pedagogy for the oppressed.[113] D. Schipani[114] has proposed integrating it within a scripturally derived active experiential notion of knowing, - *yada*,[115] that restores the centrality of liberative obedience to Christian spirituality and ecclesial life. This is established by a

---

110 For an overview of Freire's work see Johns, *Formation, 24-61.* D.S. Schipani, *Religious Education Encounters Liberation Theology* (Birmingham, AL: Religious Education Press, 1988) 9-67.

111 P.L. Berger, 'Consciousness Raising and Vicissitudes of Policy,' *Pyramids of Sacrifice* (New York: Basic Books, 1975) 121-44; 'The False Consciousness of Consciousness Raising', Worldview 18 (1975) 33-8. Cf. C.B. Johns, *Pentecostal Formation: A Pedagogy among the Oppressed* (Sheffield: Sheffield Academic Press, 1993) 41.

112 Ibid., 43.

113 Ibid., 35. Cf., n. 1

114 See Schipani, *Education, 115-55.*

115 Johns, *Formation, 37-40.*

hermeneutical dialectic between present experience and Scriptural witness that points to a potential dynamic of authentic conscientisation. W. Wink has already proposed a hermeneutical paradigm that restores communion and genuine dialogue between the interpreter and the text that allows the historical-critical approach to be transcended by one which maintains the subject-object relationship approximate to actual Pentecostal praxis.[116]

Freirian notions of transformation lack a developed foundation in the experience, mystery and otherness of God and thus fail as an adequate basis for sanctification. A revised form of 'conscientisation' would not negate the necessary role of critical abstract reasoning but would embrace 'the affective-spiritual dimensions of human interaction.'[117] In Pentecostal ecclesiality this would call for a more radical catechesis of all members and the whole person in both cognitive and non-cognitive ways[118] that would offer 'an environment conducive to … Pentecostal conscientisation' as 'an ongoing dialectic of humanity and deity.'[119]

However Pentecostal theology can too easily deteriorate into being largely what Pentecostalism 'does',[120] which facilitates its contextuality but marginalises hermeneutical practice and this militates against a systematic and panoramic comprehension of Scripture. The predominance of rationalism in theology has deterred Pentecostal hermeneutics from developing beyond pneumatic illumination, the dialogical role of experience and narrative dependence.[121] For Pentecostals, truth cannot be philosophically abstract but must be experiential encounter[122] and this remains the fundamental impediment for Pentecostal communities in developing a systematic theology of transformation, both spiritual and social.[123] Nevertheless the hermeneutical implications and potential remains powerful: the

---

116 W. Wink, *The Bible in Human Transformation* (Philadelphia: Fortress Press, 1973). Johns, *Formation*, 86, n. 1, 2.
117 Johns, *Formation*, 44-5.
118 See Johns, *Formation*, 71-8; J. Westerhoff, 'Formation, Education, Instruction', Religious Education 82.4 (Autumn, 1987) 585.
119 Johns, *Formation*, 62.
120 W.J. Hollenweger, *Pentecostalism: Origins and Developments Worldwide* (Peabody, MA: Hendrickson, 1997) 311-12; Johns, *Formation*, 82.
121 Arrington, 'Hermeneutics', DPCM, 382-89.
122 Johns, *Formation*, 86.
123 Sepúlveda, 'Struggle', 316-17.

Bible is not seen so much as an account of God's past historical actions as 'the primary source book for life.'[124]

Many have questioned whether Pentecostal piety is a sufficiently profound domain to establish biblical notions of orthopraxis and orthopathy that might lead to comprehensive social transformation.[125] Pentecostal communities have often underestimated the social dimension of the work of the Spirit, which was more evident in early Pentecostalism where the Spirit's work was seen to transform not only personal but also social and structural evil. The Spirit has to be seen again as 'suffering power' and power for mission[126] although the far wider ranging action of the Spirit contended for by Hollenweger's notion of the 'Creator Spiritus'[127] is unlikely to find ready acceptance amongst Latin American Pentecostals whilst E. Villafañe's extension of the Pentecostal social ethic to embrace social structures may possibly do so.[128]

From Christian community should arise mission that becomes an eschatological sign of the divine purposes towards humankind. Such mission does not seek to dominate history but rather to model the life of the Kingdom. Thus a first social task in this mission is 'to be the church', whose social ethic is that of the community.[129] The very presence of Pentecostal communities amongst the most marginalized serves as a context of hope in an otherwise alienating social experience and so inherently embodies a missiological commitment to the oppressed world.[130]

---

124 Johns, *Formation*, 85
125 See Runyon, 'Wesley and the Theologies of Liberation', in T. Runyon (ed.), *Sanctification and Liberation* (Nashville: Abingdon Press, 1981) 10; Johns, *Formation*, 94. n. 4.
126 J. Sims, *Power with Purpose* (Cleveland, TN: Pathway Press, 1974) 101-2 cited in Johns, *Formation*, 95.
127 Hollenweger, 'Creator Spiritus', *Theology* 81 (1978) 32.
128 E. Villafañe, *The Liberating Spirit: Towards a Spanish American Pentecostal Social Ethic* (Lanham, MD: University Press of America, 1992) 163-68.
129 S. Hauerwas, *The Peaceable Kingdom* (Notre Dame: University of Notre Dame Press, 1983) 99.
130 Villafañe, *Liberating*, 127.

VIII Some missiological observations and ecclesial lessons

'Then what does Christianity have to offer the liberation of humanity? Not, primarily, a doctrine, a conceptualisation of life, or a world plan; but actual men and women gathered in ...Christian communities scattered across the face of the earth.'[131]

The crisis of Catholic base communities has accentuated the need for deeper foundations and a broader theological basis and need for the still unrealised Pneumatology upon which a Christian praxis and transformative pedagogy can be founded for the renewal of ecclesial mission by means of grass-roots communities in Latin America.

However as grass-roots Pentecostal communities reflect the 'utterance' of the people, who have spurned intellectualised theologising[132] because of their dissident roots in socially peripheral culture, any conceptual progression needs to be rooted in more directly accessed biblical reflection and application 'from below' and 'within' the communities themselves. A potential ecclesial approximation and relationality exists between the movements based on a mutual openness to the primacy of Biblical discourse and its foundational underpinning in the revelation of God's being and ecclesial relation to the world i.e. there is an urgent need to establish a basis for ecclesial mission that derives from a theologically biblical framework of a doctrine of the triune God that addresses the ontological, transformative and pneumatic concerns of that vision.

1. Crisis of society, crisis of church

The radical shifts and crisis over Catholic and Protestant notions of church and their perceived missions in Latin American culture[133] does not simply relate to the particular problems of clericalism, ecclesial institutionalism and functionalism but to a deeper failure of historic Protestant and Catholic ecclesiology to develop a constitutive role for pneumatology in the Trinitarian

---

131 J. Comblin, *Being Human: A Christian Anthropology* (Markyknoll: Orbis, 1990) 2.
132 Lehmann, *Struggle*, 221.
133 J. Sobrino, *La Resurrección de la Verdadera Iglesia* (Santander: Sal Terrae, 1984) 221.

coming into being of church[134] exposed during a time of profound socio-cultural changes in Latin American societies. Such changes are relentless and thus exert new ecclesial pressures which in turn call for new responses and articulations that become a narratival continuity of faith[135] and the ontological transcendent relationships that undergird it.[136]

2. Coping with a rapid passage to a postmodern society

The chronic social crisis of Latin America, the emergence of grass-roots Pentecostal and Catholic ecclesial communities have to be viewed against the background of the rapid transition of the continent from a pre modern to a postmodern society.[137] The long period for the gestation of Enlightenment thinking and the substantive and comprehensive industrialisation experienced by Europe and North America has not been replicated in Latin America. The continent's modernity has been rather 'a mix, a hybrid, that has serious problems ...a precarious modernity, subordinated or peripheral.'[138] Thus Latin America passed relatively rapidly through a limited experience of Enlightenment modernity which brought it under the influence of a sequence of Western ideologies and their promised emancipations[139] to pass on to an engagement with postmodern forms of cultural diversity for which its earlier premodern syncretic Catholicised, but diversely religious, popular subcultures seems to have well suited it.[140]

Progressive liberative ecclesiology was particularly affected by the crisis of modernity itself[141] which only belatedly began to influence Latin America Catholicism in the post-Vatican II period when the continent was already beginning to reflect postmodern

---

134 J.D. Zizioulas, *Being as Communion. Studies in Personhood and the Church* (London: Darton, Longman and Todd, 1985) 140.

135 D. Batstone (et al) in D. Batstone (et al) *Liberation Theologies, Postmodernity, and the Americas* (New York: Routledge, 1997) 14-15.

136 L. Boff, *Trinity and Society* (London: Burns & Oates, 1988) 24.

137 B. Martin, 'From pre-to postmodernity in Latin America' in P. Heelas & D. Martin (eds.), *Religion, Modernity and Postmodernity* (Oxford: Blackwell, 1998) 106.

138 Larraín, *Modernidad*, 234 (my translation).

139 Cf discussion Ibid., 17-54; Comblin, *Cristianos*, 363-73 which draws on M. Araujo de Oliveira, *A Modernidade da America Latina* (São Paulo: Loyola, 1992) 77-86.

140 The impact of the phenomenon of modernity was more superficially felt in Latin America where only a small liberal secular élite came under its direct intellectual influence and industrialization was limited. Martin, 'Postmodernity', 108-9.

141 M. Vasquez, *The Brazilian Popular Church and the Crisis of Modernity* (Cambridge: Cambridge University Press, 1998). 226-34. Cf., Batstone, Postmodernity, 15-16.

tendencies as the continent was progressively incorporated into global capitalism. Hence Latin American Catholicism is at present caught in an institutional quandary and religious ambivalence: it is acutely aware of the need for an ecclesiology that is both popular, and, therefore, under duress missiologically to engage simultaneously with pre, modern and now postmodern socio-religious currents, and yet to remain 'Catholic' in cohering with its historic dogmatic and centralist institutional convictions. After the unmanageable creative forays of the post Vatican II period it has at present officially opted to retrench, or rather encamp, along the boundaries of earlier ecclesial certainties pending some future more ordered, but as yet undefined, advance.

Meanwhile, the expansion of Pentecostal ecclesial movements, which were only incipient as modernity's impact began to affect Latin American popular culture, has increased as migratory shifts caused by urbanization brought about social transformations and the breaking of Catholicism's ecclesial and religious monopoly. Thus the renting of Latin America's colonial 'sacred canopy',[142] proceeded ever more vigorously and still continues in the present but now as 'an integral part of a dramatic transformation of the continent in a postmodern direction.'[143]

3. End of Christendom, the rise of church[144]
Nevertheless, given the non-fulfilment in postmodernity of modern Enlightenment sociology's prediction on the demise of religion,[145] the future prospects for the church in Latin America are seemingly expansive but particular ecclesial crises confront post-

---

142 As social dislocation broke up the old Catholic-popular religious relations and controls space for autonomous popular religious development increased and were made wider by indigenised Protestant movements. The analogy of P. Berger's, *Sacred Canopy* (Garden City, NY:, Doubleday, 1967) is applied by D. Martin to the Latin American context in Martin, *Tongues*, 26, n.1.

143 B. Martin, 'Postmodernity', 106. The effect of postmodernity is seen culturally in terms of the 'fragmentation, contradiction, the symbiosis of the local and the global, the contraction ...of time and space, the fusion of "high" and "low" culture, the prevalence of spectacle' that relates back to the 'new structures of global capitalism, the communicative logic of the technologically new systems of information and communication, and the pivotal role of cultural as well as other kinds of technical experts within post-industrial capitalism.' Ibid., 105 cf., discussion in Bosch, *Transforming*, 349-62. Bosch, incidentally, misreads the 'vigor' in Latin American Catholicism. Ibid., 352.

144 Acknowledgements to P. Richard, *Mort das cristiandades e nascimento da Igreja* (Sâo Paulo: 1982).

145 Cf., discussion B. Martin, 'Postmodernity', 102-6.

Christendom Catholicism, Protestantism, Pentecostalism and 'post-Pentecostalism.' In the latter the notion of what the church is in mission becomes increasingly diffused, or disputed or, as it is caught up in the stream of the eclecticism of postmodern diversity, mutationally degenerates as earlier Protestant ecclesial theological reflection diminishes.

The crisis over the notion of church within Catholicism became increasingly evident in the post-Medellín period as regards the relationship between the Vatican directed church hierarchy and the ecclesial base. In the case of Chile and Brazil the apparent initial conciliar compromise achieved over Catholic popular ecclesiology proved critically unstable, thus provoking the resort to more centralist, hierarchical controls over contextualized ecclesiality. This has especially jeopardised grassroots developments though it has been a crisis that most acutely threatens the structural-institutional authority of a eurocentric Vatican. In both symbolic and real terms, the Vatican attempt to control grass-roots developments highlights the continuance of a Catholic notion of *ecclesia* as the necessary hierarchical and cultural predominance of the few over the 'many' which under-girds traditional ecclesiastical structures and practice. This has consequent implications for the notion of God and transformative relationships as in turn a monistic theology of God has direct consequences for ecclesiology. Moreover a central tension within Catholic ecclesiology is the extent to which a centrally defined uni-model of church can be maintained under such an ecclesiastical structure in an inculturating worldwide communion. Whilst globalisation exercises powerful centralist trends it also increases the impact of postmodern trends on historic religious institutional monopolies in a culture of 'market' and 'choice'.[146]

Whilst this ecclesial issue remains institutionally and dogmatically unresolved within Catholicism, Pentecostal grass-roots communities and 'post-Pentecostal' movements continue to erode and fragment the historic Catholic ecclesial hegemony.

---

146 P.L. Berger, 'The desecularization of the World: a global overview' in P. L. Berger, (ed.), *The desecularization of the World: resurgent religion and World Politics* (Grand Rapids: Erdmanns, 1999) 5.

4. Pentecostal communities: breaking dams, widening streams

Popular religious culture provided the terrain of dissidence though not the content of the message for Pentecostal ecclesial communities: both emancipatory and religious protest against the established Catholic order as well as, paradoxically, against aspects of Protestant congregational life reflective of enlightenment values characterised Pentecostal communities.

The external emotional and spiritual expressiveness of Pentecostal experience and empowerment belies the internal order, discipline and supervisory authoritarianism of community life in a Brazilian culture impacted by modernity. This ethos that juxtaposes freedom with discipline accounts, in part, for the popular ascendancy of Pentecostal communities over the CEBs and Protestant movements. Earlier Pentecostal ecclesiology adopted a posture of rupture with Brazilian and Chilean society thus fostering a social under-realisation in relation to the world. Nevertheless, whilst there are exceptions, slowly the social and theological dualism that characterised earlier Pentecostal communities has ceased to be a fundamental barrier to pragmatic socio-political action and mission as Latin American society has increasingly opened to a wider cultural and religious pluralism.

The emergence of an autochthonous Pentecostal movement from within existent Protestant ecclesial institutions highlights the inability of the latter to bridge the gulf to the 'other' peripheral, popularly dissident culture that catalysed within the neo-colonial conditions of a Catholic hegemonic society being weakened by liberalism. The initial Pentecostal sense of rupture and of 'walk-out' from both Catholic and historic Protestant structures has only gradually eased in the process of popular expansion but simultaneously institutionalisation has embodied a vigorous independence and activism in the contextualised character of each movement. However, whilst earlier Pentecostal movements remained somewhat symbiotic-dissident with Catholicism in Latin America,[147] the later post-Pentecostal movements have become more marooned and isolated from historic orthodox theological and ontological foundations that the *IMP* in Chile possessed, for

---

147 In comparison with the more wide-ranging religious syncretism that has characterized some African Independent churches, earlier Latin American Pentecostal movements were reactive both to Catholicism but also to indigenous religious influences. See Yates, *Mission*, 130-32, nn., 8-12.

instance, through its Biblical, holiness and Methodist roots and the *AD* and *CC* possessed through the past influence of respective Baptist and Presbyterian traditions.

Increasingly neo-Pentecostal movements, such as the IURD, reflect the uncritical syncretised assumptions of consumer religion in a culture impacted by neo-liberalism. The more tenuous becomes the conceptual links with historic ecclesial patterns the greater the prevalence towards adopting merely pragmatic and eclectic notions of community. The emergence of post-Pentecostal movements points to a more diverse and paradoxical tension over religious continuity with Latin American culture. Such movements have become more notably syncretistic and mutational in terms of more traditional Catholic and Protestant ecclesiality. Post-Pentecostal movements exhibit an over-realised eschatology that has made them prone to a manipulative spirituality preoccupied with personal material provision, healing and a soteriological expectation characterised by a narrow physicality. The *IURD*, for instance, as a post-Pentecostal movement, has become increasingly opportunistic and pragmatically adaptable. At the same time these same characteristics undermine its own theological stability and leave it prone to merely functionalist notions of doctrine, leadership and congregation.

The pressures within contemporary popular ecclesiology illustrate the paradox underlying religion itself[148] and the semiotic potential inherent in Pentecostalism was arguably also latent in primitive Christianity.[149] In Biblical terms, as early Pauline ecclesial discourse exemplifies, the primitive Christian communities were clearly prone to comparable tensions[150] and the later development of 'proto-Catholic' structures sought to preserve the

---

148 According to J. Van Baal, *Symbols for Communication: An Introduction to the anthropological study of Religion* (Assen: Van Gorcum, 1971) 214-41 cited in Drooger, 'Visiones', 39. For IVRD, see p.129.

149 G. Theissen, *A Theory of Primitive Christian Religion* (London: SCM, 1999) 122-24. Theissen describes primitive Christian communities characterized by 'a sign system which the first Christians constructed on the basis of Jewish religion. They built a semiotic cathedral out of narrative, ritual and ethical materials, a world of signs *and* a world in which to live.' Ibid., 286. See N.T. Wright, *The New Testament and the People of God* (London: SPCK, 1992) 365-69.

150 There was a notable ecclesial instability in the early Christian communities which were self-consciously missionary yet imbued with a strong confidence in the Holy Spirit. D. Bosch, *Transforming,* 165-66. W.J. Larkin and J.F. Williams (eds.), *Mission in the New Testament: An Evangelical Approach* (Maryknoll: Orbis, 1998) 77-84.

stability and doctrine of the movement in the face of 'manipulative' and heterodox threats that indiscriminate inclusive ecclesiality exposed it to. Nevertheless, with the stricter more 'bureaucratic' structures and hierarchical order in the post-patristic period came the gradual assimilation of spiritual charisma into an over-formalised clerical office and institutionalised authority that became so detrimental to ecclesial life and mission[151] often only overcome before the Reformation in some of the monastic orders.[152] As the issue of authority in the church became predominant in the medieval forms of *ecclesia*, structural rigidity followed that subsequently became a recurrent source of missiological tension.[153]

6. Crumbling highways, new pathways, enduring visions

Despite the concerted efforts of those committed to restoring historic ecclesial structures and authority, the emergence of new ways of being church can only accelerate rather than diminish in the Latin America in transition to postmodernity. Thus, the critical ecclesial situation points to the need for a renewed ontological basis for the notion of church that can integrate the legitimate transformational and pneumatological concerns that the grass-roots communities have incarnated in their community *praxis* and, so, theologically undergird their distinct but not incompatible missions in Latin America.

A central ecclesial problem for Catholic mission in Latin America is the historic institutional form of *ecclesia* constituted as an 'eternal and unchangeable order'[154] that had ceased to be a credible dogma or embody a meaningful experience for many lay people in modernity.[155] It is in this context that Pentecostal ecclesial movements have continued to gain popular allegiance[156] but are made vulnerable by their limited theological discourse,[157] ministerial functionalism and

---

151 See J.D.G. Dunn, *Unity and Diversity in the New Testament: An enquiry into the Character of Earliest Christianity* (London: SCM, 1977) 112-13; See Turner's discussion of primitive ecclesial relation to the Spirit and ministry. M.M.B. Turner, *The Holy Spirit and Spiritual Gifts: Then and Now* (Carlisle: Paternoster, 1996) 279-85.

152 Bosch, *Transforming*, 201-2, 230-34.

153 Ibid., 201.

154 Ibid., 185.

155 J.L Segundo,*The Liberation of Dogma* (Maryknoll: Orbis, 1992) 183.

156 M. Volf, *After Our Likeness: The Church as the Image of the Trinity* (Grand Rapids: Eerdmans, 1998) 1-8.

157 Protestant churches lacked 'theology'. R. Padilla, cited in J. Míguez Bonino, *Rostros del Protestantismo Latinoamericano* (Buenos Aires: Nueva Creación, 1995) 109.

an institutionality heavily dependent on the primacy of dynamism and efficacy. Notwithstanding the movements' indigenous communicativeness, a legacy of social marginalisation and the absence of theological dialogue and reflection on *praxis* exposes later popular mutations to external assimilation and syncretism in postmodernity through an increasing lack of biblical consciousness of essential ontological foundations.[158]

Whilst some conceptual Pentecostal theologisation occurs as 'God is shown to be real through testimony, not through doctrine...the experience of God has absolute primacy over dogma and doctrine in Pentecostalism.'[159] Hence, attempts to formalise Pentecostal 'theology' are resisted through fear of 'mutilating its essential emphasis: the primacy of experience over doctrine, and of relationship over belief.' Nevertheless, whilst the 'freedom of the Spirit' breaks the moulds of the 'doctrinal categories' limited by modernity's rationalism,[160] the Pentecostal movements retain the Scriptures as the accessible and living Word of God and thus their oral-experiential emphasis does not constitute *per se* a rejection of doctrinal notions nor of theological reflection; rather it is the relation to doctrine and the nature and end of that reflection that is questioned.[161]

Both liberative and Pentecostal communities, in different respects, depend on a renewal of dialogue and engagement with

---

158 The Pentecostal movement points to the experience of the 'intense encounter with God' and 'not a specific doctrine' as the 'constitutive aspect of Pentecostalism.' J. Sepúlveda, 'Reflections on the Pentecostal contribution to the mission of the church in Latin America', *JPT* 1 (1992) 100.

159 Sepúlveda, 'Reflections', 101.

160 Even while Western Christianity resisted the Enlightenment it assimilated much of its thinking. D. Bosch, *Believing in the Future* (Leominster: Gracewing, 1995) 15-25. This was seen in the prevalence of certain responses to modernity. Under the dominance of reason faith was privatized, theology became a 'science' and 'Christian society' entertained secularity. Theology increasingly adopted a subject-object analysis, and direct causality supplanted purpose, whilst a distinction was made between fact and value thus gradually turning the Christian faith into one possible religious option. Christian fundamentalist reactions to all of this entered into the modern missionary movement as did the notion of the immunity of the religious domain to all investigation, the inevitability of progress and the emancipation of the autonomous individual. Bosch, *Transforming*, 269-73. The pre-modern popular world of Latin America, whilst being touched but not much changed by Modernity's passage, could eclectically opt for the features that appealed most and notions of emancipation and individual autonomy certainly did.

161 Ibid., 101-2. Cf., Shaull, R., 'From Academic Research to Spiritual Transformation: Reflections on a Study of Pentecostalism in Brasil' *PNEUMA*, Vol. 20, No. 1 (Spring, 1998) 73-80.

the ontological foundations of ecclesiology.[162] This presents distinct difficulties for both ecclesial visions due to the concern to avoid either the entrapment of instrumental abstraction on the one hand or the dependency of intellectualised theologisation on the other. There is an intuitive reluctance to enter domains where literate rationality, empiricism and deductive logic create the objective states where grass-roots subjective concerns become appendages to the dominating cultures of the intellectual, non-committed centre. Thus, this grass-roots dissent is not to be dismissed as merely inherent functionalism for it preserves the fundamental principle that Biblical discourse and contextual reflection on the ontology of being and communion needs to occur within the community of mission and not isolatedly in the detached domain of the academy.[163] Nevertheless, a tension remains, and is likely to be exacerbated in postmodernity[164] over how truth is to be ascertained and error avoided without a process of rigorous pedagogy within the Pentecostal ecclesial community. Such formation has to be fostered by ecclesia that retains the discipline of critical reflection on *praxis* but within an ontological, transformative and pneumatic faith commitment rooted in the gospel.

The base communities have received intellectual leadership and support from beyond their immediate ecclesial context in the form of pastoral agents and collaborating liberation theologians who have supplied key hermeneutical methodology and theological orientation with a heavy emphasis on biblical texts.[165] However the Pentecostal movements have had to depend on their own autochthonous personnel for their limited theological

---

162 In the case of post-Pentecostalism the paucity of theological foundation deepens the crisis over the articulation of any semblance of ecclesial ontology.

163 This is an acute problem for the church if theology is to develop but not become captive to extraneous agendas thus fomenting internal debilitation or insular dissent and reactionism. See J.A. Kirk, *Mission of Theology and Theology of Mission*, (Leominster: Gracewing, 1997) 23, Cf., fuller discussion, 7-22.

164 Whilst Enlightenment modernity brought valuable critical tools for the analysis and criticism of reality its general legacy is now perceived as producing 'fear, disenchantment, threat, a feeling of being abandoned, doubt, alienation and anxiety.' R. Guardini, cited in Bosch, *Transforming*, 274.

165 Nevertheless a more thorough-going biblical hermeneutic was called for by committed evangelical scholars. J. A. Kirk, *Liberation theology:an Evangelical view from the Third World* (London: Marshall, Morgan & Scott) 1979, 183-94.; R. Padilla, 'La teología de la liberacion:una evaluacion crítica' in *Misión* (Jul./Sep.) 1982, 16-21.

development and hence their general ability to theologically reflect on *praxis* has been limited. A *'praxis* way of knowing' as supporting the contextual commitment to grass-roots pedagogy is a methodological tool but not a curriculum.[166]

A Pentecostal hermeneutic is needed that allows Pentecostals to elevate their discourse and understanding, so that an ongoing critical lack of theological engagement and methodology is overcome to avoid confining the movements to the vagaries of erroneous or abusive secular, cultural and religious ideas. Growing Pentecostal institutionality may help address this[167] for whilst presently being very reluctant to submit to formal educative processes which imply a re-submission to external socio-cultural hegemonies that might restrict Pentecostal notions of freedom and autonomy, the maturation of Pentecostal movements will bring with it corresponding infrastructures of learning, but under the control of the movements themselves. But some models will be needed for these if they are not to become authoritarian 'catechetical' systems which allow no critical judgement.[168]

Postmodern models of institutional learning are increasingly conceding more space to religious diversity and subjectivity. Through the medium of distance and extension learning the eccesial base context, local leadership and congregational can hope for resources for development.[169] This coheres with the need for the local ecclesial community to again become the centre of biblical reflection on *praxis* utilising contemporary didactic and media resources aided by supportive partnership and collaborative networks and agencies. The dominance of the fictitious 'un-reason-able' neutrality of modernity's scholar and scientist becomes relativised itself as new paradigms of learning and engagement emerge.[170] Even so, the

---

166 Schipani, *Educación*, 118-19.
167 The socio-religious distrust of theologising and the authority of the intelligentsia is only overcome as Pentecostalism creates its own intellectual discourse and theological reflection. See Lehmann, *Struggle,* 220-22.
168 See discussion on Christian Education in D. Schipani, *El Reino de Dios y el ministerio educativo de la iglesia* (San José: Ed. Caribe, 1983) 162-195; Kirk, *Theology*, 53-61.
169 Various extension and distance learning programmes bridge the didactic gulf between, the learning institution and the members of grass-roots communities. In Chile, where the author worked, SEAN, FLET and the CTE programmes were effective but only touched a small proportion of the grass-roots ecclesial constituency.
170 M. Polanyi's *Personal Knowledge* (1958) and T. Kuhn's *The Structure of Scientific Revolutions* (1972) have helped marked shifts to new post-modern paradigms of

pace of development is critically slow in the face of the magnitude and dimension of the Latin American ecclesial movements. This only serves to exacerbate more the crisis in the notion of church in the continent.[171] There is urgent need for a renewed basis for ecclesial mission rooted in a Trinitarian vision of God[172] rooted in a restored Pneumatology that affirms the mission of the Spirit in the Christian community that is also a sign of the mission of the triune God in history and society

The neo-Christendom vision of the Roman Catholic Church,[173] with its inherent hierarchical centralised clerical power structures continues to dominate current Vatican relations and Latin American ecclesiastical policy. This has isolated influential sectors of the official church from grass-roots developments,[174] which have been undermined by Catholic restorationism, socio-cultural shifts and Pentecostal and post-Pentecostal ecclesial expansion. Official Catholicism has resisted progressive calls for the implementation of ecclesial reforms, apprehensive of the potential consequences for its present centralised institutional structures and traditional ecclesiastical relationships.

---

knowledge that combine some de-structured elements from an Enlightenment model of learning but adapted to the context and being of the subject's own commitment. Cf. Bosch, *Transforming*, 351 There is the sense that Bosch's own post-modern mission paradigm cannot encompass the greater plurality of ecclesial trends and forms that are still to emerge in these shifts.

171 The question now is not so much about the nature of the reflexive hermeneutical process that is needed to strengthen Christian formation and thinking but a relational and logistical one: how the ecclesial communities can be brought into the cycle of such reflective development.

172 This is not to argue that the doctrine of the Trinity can be directly utilized to construct an ecclesiology that details precise modes of Christian community and relationships. Rather it offers 'the critical principle against which we can measure present institutional arrangements.' It allows a refounding of ecclesial vision that can rigorously assess whether Christian movements engender communion and transformation and ' *perichoresis* among persons.' C. La Cugna, *God for Us: The Trinity and the Christian life* (New York: Harper Collins, 1991) 402-3.

173 The insistence in the Catholic 'new evangelisation' on maintaining historic western notions and structures of the institutional church with little concession to alternative conciliar ecclesial emphases, especially that of the 'people of God.' Neo-Christendom minimizes *aggiornamento* and Catholic diversity, distinguishing between the possible legitimacy of shifts in social doctrine but the inadmissibility of changes to essential Catholic dogma. See a Latin American critique in Comblin, J. *Cristianos Rumbo al Siglo XXI* (Madrid: San Pablo, 1997) 41-8; Míguez Bonino, *Rostros*, 108-9.

174 P. Hebblethwaite, 'Liberation Theology and the Roman Catholic Church' in C. Rowland (ed.), *The Cambridge Companion to Liberation Theology* (Cambridge: Cambridge University Press, 1999) 96; C. Rowland, 'Epilogue: the future of liberation theology', in Rowland, *Liberation*, 249-50.

7. Ecclesia as mission

Churches as communion possess a high vocational mission as 'the social means of incorporating all the dimensions of human life in the world in their comprehensive fulfilment by God' yet they face great obstacles to its pursuit. The church can opt to be an entirely alternative society whose mission is to raise alternative societies or be deviated by 'wrongly particularises itself' so that it differentiates itself from the world in ways other than God intends.[175] Both approaches lead to confusion. Church in the former option loses its 'doxologically-constituted vocation to embody the social form of freedom with and for the world' whilst in the other it may narrowly concentrate only on superficial 'evangelical' or 'personal' tasks that delimit its holistic and eschatological vocation. In both instances the priority of mission for the church - to 'transform the social forms of freedom'[176] and to fill up the broad meaning of evangelisation risks being diminished.[177]

A Trinitarian hermeneutic within mission which encompasses the ontological, transformative and pneumatological ecclesial concerns forms a fundamental theological basis for renewing and judging the development of grass-roots Christian communities in Latin America. It is an approach to ecclesiology that not only reconstitutes dialogue within historic Catholic and Protestant traditions but also challenges the whole Christian movement to deeper relational life and mission that diminishes the institutional insecurities about ecclesiastical status and reinforces the primacy of their task before God to internal life and external movement within Latin American society. *Ecclesia* as mission is a transformational discourse and often counter-cultural that is ontologically founded, and pneumatically revealed yet needs to be articulated more in oral and textual testimony. Anything less than this breadth of ecclesial vision fails to adequately convey to the people of God in Latin America and the wider world, the true basis for human community and personhood in the redemptive purposes of God for humanity, for in Christ the old has gone, the new has come. (2 Cor. 5.17)

---

175 D.W. Hardy, 'The Missionary Being of the Church: Missionary Ecclesiology', paper delivered at the Mission in Theology Lectures (Cambridge: Currents in World Christianity Project, 1999) 21.

176 Ibid., 22.

177 See Míguez Bonino, *Rostros,* 137-43.

PART III

SPIRITUALITY FOR MISSION: PAST AND PRESENT

CELTIC AND BENEDICTINE MONASTIC TRADITION AND THE CHURCH IN SOUTH AFRICA

Esther de Waal

I want to begin with involving you in four scenes, to set the scene of what I want to discuss with you.

The first two take place in 1989, in Johannesburg, in a South Africa which is still under apartheid, (where my name proves useful since I can pass myself off as Africaans, for what I am doing is strictly speaking illegal). Twenty five people have gathered for a week at St Benedict's house in the white suburb of Rosettenville, black, coloured, white, Anglican, Roman Catholic, Dutch Reformed, Protestant, to share our life together, to build a temporary community, based on the Benedictine rhythm of body, mind and spirit, prayer, study, work. We pray the offices together, we study monastic themes together, and, perhaps most interesting in its effects, we spend the afternoons in manual labour. It is this perhaps more than anything else which breaks down the barriers between us as we share in the work of clearing the garden, cleaning the gutters, working the kitchen, mending linen. Living, eating, working and praying together we meet and talk and listen to one another, learning from the experience of a man who brought a group of men together in the sixth century in a fragmented and torn apart world, as the collapse of the Roman Empire removed all the hitherto known certainties and landmarks of society.

At tea time Peter, a young black man from Soweto, emerges from working in the kitchen, making a birthday cake (which in itself breaks the boundaries, for it is not usual in African culture to find a man in the kitchen). Standing there in the midst of this group he suddenly exclaims: 'Why has the Church kept all these good things from us?'

Later that evening, the time when we share music or poetry, I read some of the Celtic poems, prayers, blessings. I read ones which are from the very earliest days, and ones that have come down to us from oral tradition. I end by reading St Patrick's Breastplate. And at that point Abel Molefe exclaims, 'This brings tears to my eyes. This touches my heart. You are speaking of things that we know and have always known.'

And now two more recent examples. It is the Eastern Cape and it is spring of 2001. That week of 1989 had been shared with an American Anglican Benedictine prior, and it laid the foundation of something that ultimately came to birth two years ago, the foundation of a new Benedictine community uMariya uMama weThemba, Mary Mother of Hope, outside Grahamstown. I was there on an extended visit, and taking my part in the community's life I was teaching the young African novice. The brothers had given him a history of the order to read which simply left him bewildered and bored. I began rather differently - I took the Dialogues, the life of St Benedict written a hundred years after his death by St Gregory who relied on the memories of monks of successive generations of that monastery - in fact on oral tradition. We followed this life - some of it was quite close to the bone! Dropping the billhook into the lake was very close to the reality of what we had been doing that afternoon, clearing bush above the water tank. Suddenly Emmanuel exclaimed -jumping in the air as he said it, as he did in moments of joyous excitement: 'This is a man of God, he is a man of prayer, he is my friend.'

And now, as my final example, picture a Presbyterian parish, deep in the mountains, a place originally settled by the Settlers sent out from Scotland in the 1820's to be a block between the whites and the Xhosa. Narrow, conventional Presbyterians, with a proud heritage to maintain, I had been asked by their minister to introduce them to the fullness of the Celtic tradition. We are sitting round in the churchyard, and a local hunter (who is too large to fit into a chair, but has to be given a tree stump) exclaims: 'But this is how I have always prayed, but I felt guilty about it, and I told no one. And now I find that this is natural, and part of the Christian tradition.'

I have taken two Benedictine and two Celtic examples and they are very different in their settings. What are the implications for us here today, in Cardiff, and how do we take them on board in a way that is practically useful in what we are interested in and engaged upon?

My question is quite simple: do we have here TOOLS for mission? Do we even begin to recognise this? Do we handle this responsibly? Are we surprised? Should be we surprised?

It is vital to clear away any possible misconceptions before going any further: I am talking about the *monastic tradition* and not about monasticism. By monasticism I mean the contemporary lived out life of monastic communities of men and women, founded in Africa, most often by an existing monastic order in Europe or America. Many of them do amazing work but they also raise many problems [1]

But my concern is with a living tradition, expressed in a text, in the case of the Benedictine tradition, written in the early 6th century, the Rule of St Benedict, which I would characterise as the work of a man who shows an extraordinary grasp of the human psyche, knows about the human condition, about the difficulties of living together, of earning a living and still putting God the centre of one's existence. I am talking about the Celtic tradition as I understand it and, not about the Celtic church or Celtic spirituality as it is often embroidered by Celtic enthusiasts and romantics today.

1   On this I refer you to an article by L.L. Ngewu, now the principal of the College of the Transfiguration in Grahamstown   "Religious Communities and African Culture. Has Anglican Religious Life Any Future in the diocese of St John's Transkei?" *Journal of Theology for Southern Africa*

My concern is with their understanding of Christianity, as coming from a deeply rural people, brought to us in a series of early texts, (comparable in date with the Rule of St Benedict) but in this case also with a continuing life through the oral tradition by which it was expressed in its household or family form, was discovered and translated for us in the 19th century in Scotland and Ireland, and now easily available.

I think that it is most important that we take the Benedictine *and* the Celtic traditions together. The popular juxtaposition of the two makes a travesty of what I believe is infinitely more important - what they hold in common, and how we need them both. We need to hold them together so that they enrich one another and to deepen and strengthen what each can give.

What they have in common is, for a start, that both show us the Christian faith and practice as it comes down to us from the 6th century. So this is early, or the word that I prefer to use is *primal*. We are taken behind all the divides and instead we are dealing with something that we can all share in common. We are taken behind the tragic party divisions and labels which were so powerful a part of the Victorian missionary impulse; behind the divides of the Reformation which parcelled us up as Catholic or Protestant; behind the schism of 1054 and the split of East and West – and in dealing with Africa I think this is an extremely important issue but one which time precludes me dealing with today.

Because it is primal it touches something which is basic, fundamental, foundational in all of us personally and corporately. It is these values which I now wish to examine. 'It touches the heart' said Abel Molefe. Here we have heart-knowledge, heart-learning. When I came to introduce St Benedict to Emmanuel I told him the story of St Benedict's life, as one would any story-telling in oral tradition. So when we came to the part when St Benedict leaves his academic studies at the University of Rome, running away 'with the old nurse' I suddenly realised that here was the Old Wise Woman of oral tradition – that he was exchanging learning for wisdom... It is, I believe, because both these traditions deal not in creeds, and credal, cerebral declarations of faith, but in words that touch the heart, in images of poetry, and above all are soaked in the biblical allusions of the Scriptures, that they have resonance with people in a way that no amount of vision statements and declarations and new popular jargon, ever can.

It may well be a legend, but it will illustrate the point that I am making here. St Patrick and his holy way of life made such a profound impression on two pagan princesses that they came to him and asked him: Who is this God of yours? How can he be known and served and loved? And St Patrick does not reply by giving them the tenets of the creed, even the Nicene rather than the Athanasian creed. Instead he replies in a way that would strike a chord in them because he tells them of what they already know. He gives them a great creation celebration, speaking of God the creator and maker of the universe, the craftsman, the builder. Using terms which are at once specific and concrete and immediate but which are also full of poetry...

> He has his dwelling around heaven and earth and sea
> And all that is in them.
> He inspires all,
> He quickens all
> He lights the light of the sun.
> He furnishes the light of the night.
> He has set start to minister to the great lights[2]

Both are essentially monastic and that means corporate. It is true that the expression of that life is very different indeed between the neat and orderly Benedictine community and the Celtic monastic city - that there is one Rule in the case of Benedict, and in the Celtic world almost as many rules are there are monasteries. Nevertheless this is the starting point: This is corporate, shared life. It is a household, an extended family. In the case of the Celtic world it was extended to include both monastics and lay men and women. Children were found in both, and as to animals I guess they were as much part and parcel of the Benedictines as they undoubtedly were of the Celtic - it is just that there they have crept into the legends and the carvings and the illuminated manuscripts rather more clearly. So there is kinship, a common life, and a set of values which springs from that.

'A person is a person in relation to another person' That familiar African saying expresses exactly what I am talking about.

Both are close to the earth. This is generally the first thing associated with the Celtic tradition. They saw the universe as a

---

2   See *Threshold of Light, Prayers and Praises from the Celtic Tradition* ed A.M. Allchin and Esther de Waal, Darton, Longman & Todd, 1989. p 4

gift from God to be respected and reverenced, and therefore that meant a concern for cultivation, for the responsible handling of the soil, for making land fruitful so that it will he handed down to the next generation and beyond. The whole liturgical life of St Benedict's monastery is adjusted to pay attention to the changing seasons for men who work the fields, as do their hired labourers. They make use of the latest technology - a mill, newly invented, is mentioned. Here is corporate, shared land usage, and it speaks to the reality of African life today as most people know it.

But any bland religion which presents a creation-centred spirituality does less than justice to the fullness of the Celtic tradition. Here what we have is a creation-filled, but not a creation-centred tradition. For the cross lies at the centre, and the Celtic tradition puts the crucified Christ at its heart, just as the paschal mystery is the pivot of the Rule of St Benedict. Any "Christian teaching" in Africa, (or elsewhere), which does not look at fear, suffering, evil, dark forces is simply going to patronise a people who have known suffering in all its forms, social, economic, political. The forces of the dark have to be faced. St Benedict is very clear about conflict and battle. He addresses us all in the Prologue as soldiers who are called upon to fight in Christ's army. In the high cross at Monasterboice there is a carving of Christ and his followers, and they are armed, each carrying a breastplate. Christ himself is here the conquering hero, the warrior who has taken on the forces of the dark and has overcome them in order to set his people free. He is the hero, who risks his own life, even choosing death, in order to set his people free. At mass in Zimbabwe the Shona people at the moment of consecration clap slowly, as they would to welcome a returning tribal hero.

Such an emphasis is not something that is very popular in the west today where we shy away from such a vocabulary and such images. But it holds an immediacy in the African situation. There is suffering, disaster, tragedy, the threat of AIDS-and there is also *fear.* 'Fear is the first reality in the African heart' I once heard someone say. A witch doctor had just moved into one of the streets of the small town in which my Celtic week-end was taking place, and already there were ugly rumours about uncomfortable things that were happening. There is undoubtedly much that is good in the role of the witch doctor, but there is much that is not. A recent political study on the African situation observes quite clearly 'Belief in witchcraft is unlikely to diminish, particularly in urban areas....'[3]

This is an extremely complex situation, and undoubtedly one which the churches must continue to address. But in the *caim*, the Celtic prayer of making a circle around yourself in times of need and calling upon the aid of the victorious Christ, there is a practical help, close at hand in times of need. Unless we have a Christianity which is willing to speak of these things in practical terms we cannot expect to present a Christian experience that will touch the African experience.

So any emphasis on creation must be balanced by an emphasis on redemption. On some of the later Celtic high crosses the crucified Christ holds out huge hands to bless the world which he has both created and redeemed. In some of the later crosses the crucified Christ is wearing the long white robe of the risen Christ. Here are Good Friday and Easter held together.

The Celtic tradition has always felt at home in the crossing of the divides between this world and the next. The saints and the angels are close at hand. These are the same terms in which the Africans see their world:

> African traditional world views acknowledge three actively interrelated worlds: the world of the living, the world of the departed, the spirit world. All these worlds make one unit under God's direct control and influence each other's activities.[4]

The twentieth century Welsh poet Gwenallt Jones writes of the lack of any barrier between this world and the next. It seems so natural, and so simple. Would that this had been more clearly in mind when the Victorian missionaries castigated 'ancestor worship', for here we see St David entirely fulfilling what makes up the African understanding of the living dead:

> There is no barrier between two worlds in the Church,
> The Church militant on earth
> Is one with the Church triumphant in heaven,
> And the saints are in this Church which is two in one.

---

3   There is an interesting discussion of the constantly evolving effects of the irrational upon the contemporary political practices in Africa in Patrick Chabel and Jean-Pascal Doloz, *Africa Works, Disorder as Political Instrument*, James Curry, 1999. See especially pp 74-76 from which this quotation is taken.

4   Wilson Sitshebo, 'How African Anglicans deal with death, funerals and bereavement'.

They come to worship with us, our small congregation,
The saints our oldest ancestors.[5]

The divides go down – God is at work making his world whole. This is a wholistic spirituality. This is, in sum, what it was in the Benedictine and the Celtic traditions which evoked an immediate response to those very differing situations in Africa.

* * * * * * *

I remember with gratitude African hospitality. It was pouring with rain, making a noise on the corrugated iron roof, when we arrived unannounced in this township home. At once somebody went rushing off for cold drinks, and while still holding my bottle of Coca Cola the host asked a blessing. This was a profoundly simple and significant moment. The Celtic tradition recalls us to the fullness of the role of blessing in our lives - both its theological significance, and also, in practical terms, the many forms that it can take in daily life. Blessing is a reciprocal act: we are blessed by God, and we bless God in return. We are not asking for blessings, as so much of the rewriting of Celtic prayers today tends to suggest.

When we bless we extend God's blessing to each other and to the whole world of Creation. When we bless God we acknowledge God as the source of our life and welfare and the origin of all goodness and gifts. To bless is thus an act of giving thanks and praise ... and therefore, I would add, not one of asking for yet more blessings and more good things to be showered down upon us, as our consumer and feel-good society so often seems to encourage us to do.[6]

* * * * * *

Any monastic tradition is built on the concept of unity and diversity. It is spelt out, as it were, on so many different levels. Most obviously St Benedict brought together men from a falling-apart world at the end of the Roman Empire, Goths and Vandals, invaders, patrician Romans, men with degrees, illiterate men, landowners and slaves. He wanted to build them all into one

---

5   *Threshold of Light*, op. cit., p. 39.
6   See especially chapter 7 'The Blessing and the Curse,' 'in Richard J Woods, *The Spirituality of the Celtic Saints*, Orbis Books, Maryknoll, New York, 2000, pp. 146ff.

family which respected individual differences of gifts and grace while yet seeing each one as equal in Christ. As his monastic communities of men and women grew and spread, they all followed his rule but they did so in very different terms, dictated by the land, itself and by their situations of economic, cultural and geographical differences. A Celtic monastic community respected the many different callings which yet united men and women in one common goal; monastics, artisans and artists, teachers and farmers.

When the Celtic missionary saints, the *peregrini*, set out to bring the message of Christ to other countries and St Columbanus had to face the envy and rivalry of the bishop in Gaul, he applied this same approach to the wider situation. 'Let Gaul contain us side by side as the Kingdom of Heaven shall contain'. Such openness - they loved Rome, dreamt of seeing it, longed to make the pilgrimage to the place that spoke of the catholicity of the church. There is no doubt of a theology of the unity of Christ's body in all its members (in heaven and on earth) and yet they are only too happy with liturgical diversity.[7]

* * * * * * *

I go to Africa to receive and to learn. That only happens when we can have a conversation. A conversation is only possible when the words I use have resonance with those to whom I am talking. All I have been saying is simply that I believe that in the Benedictine and Celtic monastic traditions we have a common language which enables us to be in touch with one another at a level which is illuminating and enriching on both sides.

---

7   The stational system in Rome at this time - the moving daily round different churches - made the city a microcosm of a church which accepted diversity of language and usage, and which allowed Celtic spirituality to flourish with all its peculiar cultural variants.
This very important theme - which is unpalatable to those who want to find a Celtic church which they can set against all that Rome stands for - is explored by Eamonn O'Corrigan in his Jarrow lecture, for 1994, *The City of Rome and the World of Bede.*

CELTIC SPIRITUALITY:
a re-invented tradition
for 21st century Mission

John Burgess

The Development of Tradition

Tradition is an important part of religion and the Christian faith early on developed its traditions. Frances Young[1] understands that the development of the Christian tradition derived from a need to articulate a faith which had been one primarily based on experience. She acknowledges that the creeds of the Church embody and articulate a tradition of faith that in the past has been understood to simply be the retelling of "facts",[2] but that this is a partial understanding. They also represent the formulation and interpretation of experience for different contexts. Tradition then, is something that is dynamic and changing, and not static. Parratt[3] expresses the need for tradition to be dynamic and understands that it is reformulated regularly to meet the changing needs of a context. Consequently the concept of tradition as something that is fixed from the past and unchanging is no longer considered to be an acceptable definition.

Tradition is normally considered to be a body of experience, wisdom, ritual and truth, that is related to a particular context and culture. It is an expression of the belief system or worldview of a particular group of people, which could be a social group or a religious group, and is generally considered to be derived from antiquity. So Parratt[4] will say that the purpose of tradition is to contextualise belief so that it makes the worldview of the social group appropriate for a new or changing context. When a tradition

---

1   Young F. *The Making of the Creeds,* London, SCM, 1991
2   *ibid,* p ix
3   Parratt J. *Reinventing Christianity: African Theology Today,* Michigan, Eerdmans, 1995
4   *ibid.* Parratt is exploring the need to contextualise theology into African contexts and so understands that the traditions of the church that have been imported to Africa need to be reinterpreted to bring about a new tradition or contextual theology that will provide an appropriate articulation of Christianity in the African context. Consequently he considers that the Christian tradition is "reinvented" for each new context

is unable to deal with the issues that arise from a changing society and culture, and when it is no longer a stabilising process, then the tradition itself is seen to be irrelevant and a new tradition needs to be developed.

The periodic rise in interest in the Celtic tradition is an example of this re-invention of tradition in the face of a rapid change in society. The Celtic tradition has been called upon, plundered and manipulated to help give a foundation and stability to a society that is involved in a paradigm shift and questions the relevance of its institutions to deal with the needs of the contemporary society.

The Development of the Celtic Tradition in Gildas and Bede

Gildas was living through the era of disruption and crisis of the "Saxon invasion" of Britain in the mid 6th Century, that was moving Britain from the Roman era into the early medieval period bringing with it new worldviews, concepts and ideologies. Consequently it could be described as a period of paradigm shift.

What is clear to Gildas is that the Church was unable to deal with this period of crisis and needed to find new ways and methods. His work "The Ruin of Britain" is a contribution to the development of a new tradition for Christianity in an attempt to be relevant to the new era. He builds his new Christianity from the Bible and from the past, claiming that the Roman period was a golden era of politics, social structure and Christianity[5]. Central to this new tradition is the concept that Christian ethics and *praxis* is more important than doctrine.

Gildas builds a tradition from the past that he feels will address the needs of his day and uses the tradition to rebuild the church with a structure that centres around a reformed clergy and responsible and pious political leadership. This will give a firm foundation for the people so that the church can be an effective spiritual instrument for the people, becoming a popular faith. It is the beginnings of a Celtic tradition as it engages with the era that has become known as the Celtic Christian era of British history, and it conforms to, and perhaps originates the model, which is clearly part of the Celtic tradition.

---

5   Winterbottom M. (ed & tr) *Gildas: The Ruin of Britain and Other works* - The Ruin of Britain 8

Bede[6] continues the work of Gildas, and is able to develop the tradition focusing on the practice of the Celtic saints as the model. The crisis for Bede is the Church in the new political era of the establishment and consolidation of Saxon political rule in England. He sees the church in England of the eighth century as having succumbed to the temptations of wealth and ease that have been brought about through the stabilising of the political situation[7].

Bede re-invents the Celtic tradition as a model for his time. The tradition that he presents is one of a golden age of spirituality, where the Christian is judged not simply by his conformity to doctrine, but the way his faith is lived out. Bede is concerned about orthopraxis as well as orthodoxy. The Celtic tradition is presented as one that is a model for asceticism, piety, humility, love, prayer and evangelism. The lives of the saints, particularly Aidan and Cuthbert, are the examples of this. While Bede is ready to dismiss the British Church as heretical, he has a great love for the northern saints. He only devotes part of one chapter to Columba[8], because his book is primarily concerned with England and not Scotland, but recognises the important influence of Iona on the kings and saints who produced the Golden Age of Christianity in Northumbria. Bede seems almost consciously to be building a tradition, for he is selective in his approach to the historic material, and he puts his own interpretation upon it, so that his mission and use of the tradition is to encourage a new practise of faith in England.

The Continuing Use of the Tradition

Bede, and to a lesser extent Gildas, have given us a model of the re-invention of the Celtic tradition as a useful tool to address the needs of a society or church in crisis. Evidence for the use of this Celtic Tradition can also be found throughout the history of Britain and particularly of England.

The development of the "lives of the saints" at a time when Church and State became increasingly powerful under the Norman

---

6   Bede wrote many works but chiefly we refer to his *History of the English Church and People*. Modern translations - Shirley-Price L. (ed & tr) *Bede: A History of the English Church and People*, Harmondsworth, Penguin, 1968; McClure J. and Collins R. (ed & tr) *Bede: The Ecclesiastical History of the English People*, Oxford, Oxford, 1994

7   Bede 3: 5, Shirley-Price L. *op cit.* p 148

8   *ibid.* 3: 4 p46-7

overlords is another example of the re-invention of tradition. Hagiography is particularly a medieval literary skill[9], and the Celtic tradition was in the forefront of this movement. It is from the 11th - 13th century that the majority of the lives of the saints arose, either as new documents or the rewriting of older written or oral material[10]. These lives become a means of providing a spirituality for the people that will allow them to become part of the new political and religious order, subject to it and yet at the same time religiously fulfilled. We see, then, the use of the Celtic tradition to develop an "alternative" Christianity in the face of a growing institutionalisation, power and uniformity of the European Church.

The era of the Protestant Reformation[11] brought with it a general distrust of tradition which led the Reformers to develop a very strongly based Biblical tradition of Puritanism. The basis of this tradition was the re-invention of the early church found in the interpretation of the New Testament material. England had moved on to a literary era where the oral traditions of the past were suspect and so one cannot expect much reference to the Celtic tradition. However Foxe does make reference to the Church in Britain before the coming of Augustine as living an uncorrupt faith when the word of Christ was truly preached.[12]

Later Protestantism does however make use of the Celtic tradition when it is used as propaganda against the Roman Catholic Church. This seems to re-emerge again in the late 19th century[13] and early 20th century, when Roman Catholicism achieved significant growth and increasing influence in England and Wales.

9   Delehage H. *The Legends of the Saints,* London, Longmans, 1907 (tr. V.M. Crawford), p 16
10 Doble G. H. *Lives of the Welsh Saints* (ed Evans D.S.) Cardiff, University of Wales, 1971, p 10, 12
11 Bosch, D. J., *Transforming Mission,* New York, Orbis, 1991, p 239
12 Pratt J. (ed). *The Acts and Monuments of John Foxe,* London, Religious Tract Society, undated, vol 1, preface p xx
13 The 19th century was also important for the development of the Celtic tradition as it was the period that saw the flowering of romanticism and consequently the re-discovery of the Celtic period of British history. It is from this period that the present interest in Celtic studies is ultimately derived. While the defence of Protestantism in the face of the growing Roman Catholic Church was one development of the tradition, the other development that took place was in relation to the growing interest in foreign mission.

This was perceived as a great threat to Protestantism in England and gave rise to the publishing of material which was anti-Catholic in nature. Some authors made use of the Celtic tradition in their attacks on the Roman Catholic Church. The main development of their argument centred on two aspects. The first was to re-develop the tradition of an apostolic foundation of the Church in Britain,[14] through the retelling of the various traditions of Caractocus and Paul, Joseph of Arimathea, and King Lucius, thus establishing a tradition of an independent church in Britain derived from Paul and other apostles but unrelated to Rome and the apostle Peter. The second strand of the argument centred on the Celtic Church itself, as a separate development, that was related to the Church in Gaul, but not of Rome.[15]

Another use of the Celtic Tradition that is particularly seen to develop in the late nineteenth century and continued into the mid twentieth century is in support of foreign missions. For example, Thomas[16] attempted to gain some authenticity and antiquity for the Church in Wales, possibly in the face of the growth of non-conformity, by claiming a missionary power for the diocese which is related back to Kentigen. Thomas is interpreting the events of the past in the light of contemporary practises and so understands

---

14 For example Morgan, R.W. *St. Paul in Britain*, London, Covenant Publishing Company, 1860. In the preface he writes: that the early Christian history of Britain "is sufficient to demonstrate the untenableness of the supposition that Britain is indebted to Germany - a country which has never itself been free - for its free institutions, or to Italy for its Gospel faith. The leading principles of her laws and liberties are of pure indigenous growth; and her evangelical faith was received by her directly from Jerusalem and the East, from the lips of the first disciples of Christ". also: Jones, D.D. *The Early Cymry and their Church,* Carmarthen, W. Spurrell & Sons, 1910; Lewis, Lionel Smithett *St Joseph of Arimathea at Glastonbury or The Apostolic Church of Britain* London, A.R. Mowbray, first published in 1922.

15 Davies D. *The Ancient Celtic Church and the See of Rome,* Cardiff, William Lewis, 1924

16 Thomas, D.R. *A History of the Diocese of St. Asaph,* London, 1870 p 5. He writes: "The Institution founded by Kentigen soon attained a high repute. Partaking of the nature of a missionary colony, something like the Universities Mission to Central Africa, and combining in its scheme not only the offices of Religion, but also the several duties of education, husbandry, and handicrafts, it drew together a large number of members ...

Besides this they would follow the common practice of the church at the time, and extend their missionary labours over the surrounding district, either setting up a cross to mark their stations, or else taking advantage of the periodical gatherings of the people at the wells, which they gradually appropriated to Christian uses; until the liberality of the individuals or the increasing wealth of the Church, enabled them to erect capaellae near the spots, the prototypes in character and purpose of the chapels of ease, and of the school and mission churches of our own day."

the tradition to be a missionary tradition. In his case he relates it to the work of the Universities Mission to Central Africa, and so both authenticates his claims for the Church and the methods that the missionary society was using in the second half of the nineteenth century. Some authors of the time consider that mission is undertaken both at home and overseas.[17] Yet others understand the Celtic tradition to be a model for imperialistic mission.

The use of the Celtic tradition for the encouragement of missionary endeavours continues into the 1960's where many of the "popular" writings about the Celtic Christian period focus on the saints as primarily missionary in nature. By then, however, there was a growing embarrassment about the connection between British imperialism and mission and so the Celtic saints are contrasted with Augustine, who as the imperialist is out of favour. In its stead the Celtic saints become a model for what might be considered an incarnational and contextual style of mission. Foster designs his model for mission from the Celtic saints as a fivefold concept.[18] The saints built a base for mission in their monasteries, used the method of public preaching for evangelism, trained "native" clergy, were an example of the Christian life and preached the simple gospel. It is also interesting to note that in referring to Bede, he makes his own translation, so that what other contemporary authors translate as "Bishop", he translates as "missionary".[19]

But by the middle of the 20th century there was the beginning of the move away from the Celtic Tradition being a model for mission to being a model for a personal spirituality.[20] In the post-

---

17 Charles (Charles R. *Early Christian Missions of Ireland, Scotland and England,* London, SPCK, 1893) surveys the lives and work of a number of saints, mostly Celtic in an attempt to encourage her readers to return to a faith in Christ that is deeper than the divisions of the Church of her day. She considers this faith to be inherently missionary and relates the saints of the eighth century to the missionaries of her day.

18 Foster J., *They Converted Our Ancestors,* London, SCM, 1965, p 118
John Finney's recent book (Finney J. *Recovering the Past: Celtic and Roman Mission,* London, DLT, 1996) also makes this contrast.

19 Foster *op cit.* p 97. for example translating Bede 3:3, Foster (p99) writes "the missionary preaching the gospel" and Shirley-Price reads "while the Bishop preached the gospel", and where Foster writes "From then on many Scots missionaries began to come and to preach with great devotion.." Shirley-Price writes "Henceforth many Scots arrived day by day ... preaching the Word of God". McClure and Collins translation agrees with Shirley-Price.

20 e.g. Leatham D *They Built on Rock,* Glasgow, The Celtic Art Society, 1948 and *Celtic Sunrise: An Outline of Celtic Christianity,* London, Hodder & Stoughton, 1951 and Duckett E. *The Wandering Saints,* London, Catholic Book Club, 1960

war period overtly Christian mission gave way to an emphasis on the social Gospel; there was a general uncertainty of the Christian faith in the face of the forces of science and secularism, and a growing awareness of the religious plurality of society. These together influenced the move to the privatisation of religion and the concern for individual spirituality in Britain.

The Contemporary Expression of the Celtic Tradition

Our very brief survey of the material relating to the rediscovery of the Celtic tradition throughout the last 1500 years of British history has shown that the rise in interest of the subject coincides with certain times of crisis in the life of the Church. These crises represent the struggle of the Church in dealing with new cultural situations that some scholars would understand as paradigm shifts. The present is understood by some missiologists[21] and many sociologists as such a moment of paradigm shift and is given the title of the post-modern era.

The post-modern culture is characterised as being a consumerist culture, which is "eclectic",[22] "pick and mix",[23] "recyclic"[24] and "wallowing in change".[25] It involves the rejection of metanarratives replacing them with an emphasis on experience over above received knowledge and cognitive faith, and a focus on individuality rather than community, particularly in terms of relationships. It is the celebration of multiplicity, diversity, difference and choice. The metanarratives, history and all academic systems become resources that are plundered for entertainment and experience, and the images and concepts plucked out are removed from any context and reduced to a commodity to be used. The post-modern paradigm, then, is very appropriate for a re-invention of traditions, and provides the process for the development of tradition.

---

21 Bosch *op cit.*
22 So: Sarup M. *An Introduction to Post-structuralism and Post-modernism;* 2nd ed. Hemel Hempstead, Harvester, 1993; Harvey D. *The Condition of Postmodernity: an enquiry into the origins of cultural change,* Oxford, Blackwell, 1990; Featherstone M. *In Pursuit of the Postmodern; An introduction in Theology Culture and Society* (Special issue on Postmodernism) Vol 5 number 2-3, June 1988; Gellner E. *Postmodernism, Reason and Religion,* London, Routledge, 1992; Connor S. *Postmodernist Culture: An introduction to theories of the contemporary,* Oxford, Blackwell, 1989
23 McRobbie A. *Postmodernism and Popular Culture,* London, Routledge, 1994
24 McRobbie *op. cit.,* Connor *op. cit*
25 Harvey *op. cit.* p 44

Recent research and surveys, such as those undertaken by David Hay,[26] the Soul of Britain Survey and my own on-going research indicate that there has been an increasing importance put on experience and particularly religious or spiritual experience in the late 20th and early 21st centuries. A survey undertaken by Hay in 1982 among students in Nottingham, suggested that 48% of the general public admitted to having had spiritual experiences. The study undertaken in 1999, which was presented at the last BIAMS conference[27] shows that figure to have increased to 76%. This may indicate that for the general public, experience is central to spirituality. However, my own on-going survey among church-goers, who could be said to represent the traditional and more institutional form of Christianity and spirituality, indicates that only 50% will admit to having had spiritual experiences. For them, then, experience is less central to spirituality.

The contemporary re-invention of the Celtic tradition, drawing together the strands of romanticism, eclecticism, awareness of the sensory, experiential and individualism in spiritual searching, is very much a method for the post-modern era. It is presented as a "popular" spirituality in which all people can participate because it does not draw hard boundaries around acceptable ways in which faith can be experienced or expressed. The individual is allowed a greater freedom than the institution of the Church or its creeds will permit. It meets the people "where they are."

The proliferation of books and pamphlets about Celtic Christianity, Celtic Spirituality and the Celtic Church indicate the great interest that has arisen in the subject. Different authors focus on different aspects of the Celtic tradition, selecting what addresses their concerns or the perceived needs of society but most agree that contextualisation is central to Celtic Spirituality. The writings of de Waal,[28] Davies,[29] Van der Weyer[30] and many others attempt to

---

26 Hay D. & Hunt K. *Understanding the Spirituality of People who don't go to Church*, University of Nottingham, 2000
27 Hay D. *The Spirituality of the Unchurched,* a paper presented to the BIAMS conference, 13th September 2000, Selly Oak, Birmingham (Supra, pp. 13 – 27)
28 De Waal E. *A World Made Whole: Rediscovering the Celtic Tradition,* London, Fount, 1991; *The Celtic Vision: Prayers and Blessings form the Outer Hebrides,* London, DLT, 1988
29 Davies O. and Bowie F. *Celtic Christian Spirituality: an Anthology of Medieval and Modern Sources,* London, SPCK, 1995
30 Van Der Weyer R. *Celtic Fire: An anthology of Celtic Christian Literature,* London, DLT, 1990

present the Celtic tradition as a type of Christianity derived from and related to the rural experience producing a personalised faith that focuses on experience and the immanence of God in all things.[31] The Iona Community has understood the Celtic tradition to emphasise the immanence of God in all places, such that its beginnings were in the inner city of Glasgow, attempting to bring the professional clergy and the laity closer together. David Adam[32] also developed his neo-Celtic tradition in the mission situation of the inner, industrialised city. For Simpson[33] and Mitton[34] the Celtic tradition is presented as an alternative to Church which is historic, institutionalised and controlled by dogma and creeds and a professionally dominated religion. Toulson[35] and Sheldrake[36] want to emphasise the importance of the revival of respect for sacred places and times, which can be linked historically to the spiritual roots of the people.[37] For Woods,[38] Lack,[39] Hume[40] and others, the retelling of the lives of the Celtic saints encourages contemporary spiritual seekers to experience "God's all pervading presence"[41] within the whole of life and creation.

31 Much of the evidence for this is drawn from the work of Alexander Carmichael in the compilation known as the "Carmina Gadelica" Carmichael A. *Carmina Gadelica: Hymns and incantations collected in the Highlands and Islands of Scotland in the last century,* Edinburgh, Floris, 1994

32 David Adam has written many books of Celtic Poetry in which he includes some ancient material, but mostly writes his own compositions "in the Celtic style", e.g. *The Edge of Glory,* London, SPCK, 1985; *Tides and Seasons,* London, SPCK, 1989; *Power Lines,* London, SPCK, 1992; *The Open Gate,* London, SPCK, 1994

33 Simpson R. *Exploring Celtic Spirituality: Historic Roots for our Future,* London, Hodder and Stoughton, 1995

34 Mitton M. *Restoring the Woven Cord: Strands of Christianity for the Church Today,* London, DLT, 1995

35 Toulson S. *The Celtic Alternative,* London, Century, 1987; *The Celtic Year,* Shaftesbury, Element, 1993

36 Sheldrake P. *Living Between Worlds: Place and Journey in Celtic Spirituality,* London, DLT, 1995

37 Such holy spaces and spiritual roots are experienced in places like Lindisfarne, Bardsey Island and Iona, which many would accept as traditional holy places long before the advent of Christianity into Britain.

38 Woods R. J. *The Spirituality of the Celtic Saints,* New York, Orbis, 2000

39 Lack K. *The Eagle and the Dove: The spirituality of the Celtic Saint Columbanus,* London, Triangle SPCK, 2000

40 Hume B. *Footprints of the Northern Saints,* London, Darton, Longman and Todd, 1996

41 Woods, *op. cit,* p. 178

Above all the re-invention of the Celtic tradition provides an important new method for mission. Being centred on experience rather than doctrine, it affirms the spirituality of the people by allowing it to be interpreted and reinterpreted with both the changing culture and the developing spirituality of the people. It has a built-in flexibility because the concept of the Celtic tradition is little more than an umbrella term within which there can be a great deal of variety and selectivity. It is also able to hold together the paradox of tradition, that it is both a human invention and inspired by God. This dual approach to tradition enables it to be a process for the development of the relationship between the human and the divine, that is expressed and understood in "everyday" terms, and not ecclesiastical formulations. It becomes a means of incarnating the Gospel into different contexts, by the reworking of the material and the tradition. It is a contextualised spirituality.

Therefore Celtic spirituality is a new way of doing theology. Being eclectic by nature it is a new approach that by definition cannot be systematised, for once it is systematised then it loses its very nature. It has to be the expression of spirituality that cannot be held down by definitions and systems, and therefore it cannot be a theology,[42] which implies a system. Understood in this way, the re-invention of the Celtic tradition in the late 1980's and the 1990's has to be an invention for the post-modern era, to help to provide a model and process for a developing, contextualised, spirituality for the crisis of the changing paradigm.

---

42 Theology is defined by the *Oxford Dictionary of the Christian Church* (ed. F.L. Cross, Oxford, Oxford Univeristy Press, 1974) as "Its purpose is the investigation of the contents of belief by means of reason enlightened by faith and the promotion of its deeper understanding." Macquarrie (Macquarrie J. *Principles of Christian Theology,* Revised edition, London, SCM 1978 p 1) says "Theology may be defined as the study which, through participation in and reflection upon a religious faith, seeks to express the content of this faith in the clearest and most coherent language available."

KEEPING THE HOME FIRES BURNING:

Mission, Spirituality and a New Monasticism.

Craig Gardiner

'As fire exists by burning so the Church exists by mission,' said Emil Brunner. If he was correct, then to keep the flames burning in the West, where the fire of the Church is being gradually extinguished, we might need to re-examine the missionary character of the Church. At the same time we would need to search for a spirituality, a pattern of living, that would help keep the fires alive. Such a re-examination of mission together with a search for a supporting pattern of living forms the purpose of this paper. Christian mission and spirituality, properly understood, will be shown to be mutually dependent and co-supporting disciplines that are rooted in the concrete and communal imaging of the immanent and economic lives of the Trinitarian God. It will be argued that the fires of the Church in the West might yet be fanned to life through a new type of monasticism, one rooted in Trinitarian living wherein mission and spirituality mutually inform such a communal discipleship. This monasticism, unlike its antecedents, will not seek to separate from the world or a worldly Church but will engage with both, hoping to renew the latter and redeem the former.

In his 1991 book, *Transforming Mission,* David Bosch attempted a theological synopsis of the term 'mission' noting how it had been variously paraphrased as '(a) propagation of the faith, (b) expansion of the reign of God, (c) conversion of the heathen, and (d) the founding of new churches.'[1] However, from the outset of the book, Bosch notes that such definitions are relatively recent in origin and often associated with the expansion of the Western World. He notes that until the 16th century mission was not

---

1   David Bosch. *Transforming Mission Paradigm: Shifts in Theology of Mission.* Orbis.1991 p1.

understood in its populist contemporary sense but exclusively referred to the doctrine of the Trinity. Mission was the sending of the Son by the Father and the sending of the Holy Spirit by the Father and the Son.[2] However, from the sixteenth century onwards, beginning with the Jesuits, the term 'mission' was used to describe outward journeys by Christians, near and far, to bring people into the faith and under the authority of Church. From then on, with Protestants playing catch up, the Church wholeheartedly approved of mission as being its outward journey into the world.

Earlier, the fifteenth century witnessed the birth of a renewed awareness of inner journeys of the soul; what is now often but erroneously referred to as spirituality. Philip Sheldrake traces the development of this distinct discipline to the end of the middle ages, when God-talk moved from reflection to proposition with an accompanying relocation from the monastery to the university.[3] Later, during the scientific rationalism of the Enlightenment, religion was privatised and spirituality became a mystical 'other worldly' term, notoriously slippery in its evasion of definition, seemingly removed from every day reality and apparently at odds with the hard practicalities of the outward campaigns of mission.

During the age of European colonial exploration, mission, especially Protestant mission, developed into a child of its time. As Bosch notes, 'it was after all the new expansionist worldview which pushed Europe's horizons beyond the Mediterranean and the Atlantic Ocean and thus paved the way for a world wide Christian missionary outreach.'[4]

But as Lesslie Newbigin has pointed out, for most of this time 'missions were enterprises that belonged to the exterior of church life. Missions were carried on somewhere else, in Asia, Africa, in the slums of the city or among the gypsies, the vagrants and the marginalised. The mission church was the second-class institution, the missionary diocese had not yet graduated to the status of

---

2   Bosch. Ibid. p1. Barth retrieved the concept for modern theology in a paper read at the 1932 Brandenburg Missionary Conference.
3   Philip Sheldrake. *Spirituality and Theology*. DLT 1998. See Chapter 2 generally. Here he traces the great divorce between the two disciplines until in the words of one fifteenth century Carthusian, 'they were no more related than painting and shoemaking' Ibid. p42. Although Sheldrake is primarily concerned with theology and spirituality in this context the separation of spirituality as an inward and individual discipline had consequences for its relationship with mission.
4   David Bosch. ibid. p274 and Chapter 9 generally.

diocese without qualification.' Newbigin summarises it thus; 'The church approved of missions but was not itself the mission.'[5]

This growing externalisation of mission along with a simultaneous internalisation of spirituality allowed both to lose the essential interaction that is needed if both are to remain truly Christian. As the way the Church at home lived and worshipped was allowed to divorce from its outer experiences of missionary journey, the image of the Trinity, in which the Father who sends remains in co-equal communion with the Son who is sent, broke down. The community life of the Church, as expressed between those who sent and those who went, was no longer one of co-equal communion. In allowing this to happen the institutional Church condemned itself to an internal cooling. From then on, despite the valiant efforts of missionary movements, especially the often unacknowledged work of women, the home fires began to go out, the institutional Church became less the chosen ones and more the frozen ones; 'God's frozen people.'

Thus ironically, while for the moment Christianity continues to burn brightly where Western missions once exported it, the fires have gone out all over the sending nations. New Zealand theologian Mike Riddell is convinced that such freezing is due to western Christians continually perceiving mission as happening somewhere else. The churches were and remain structured for preservation and continuity not mission. He writes that 'in order to survive in difficult times a church will adopt practices which are conservative, exclusive, orthodox, static, careful and scrupulous because that is how institutions survive.' 'Unfortunately' he laments, 'it is also how movements die.'[6] If the church is to move beyond thoughts of survival and regain the imperative of preserving the gospel so as to burn brightly again in the west then it must return to it's calling as a movement in which both the inner and the outer journey are travelled simultaneously.[7] In this way spirituality and mission will be properly understood as communal and concrete images of the Trinity.

---

5   Lesslie Newbigin. *The Open Secret.* SPCK 1995 p2
6   Michael Riddell. *Threshold of the Future.* SPCK 1998 p12-13
7   Andrew Walker has noted that in times such as those before the Church in the west today, 'the primary missionary imperative is not to survive but to preserve the gospel.' Walker. *Telling the Story* SPCK 1996 p190

Such a movement church, a church which exists for and by mission, will no longer have the crusading mind of past ecclesiological paradigms it but must be replaced with what Koyama might call a 'Crucified Church,'[8] what Moltmann calls the 'Open Church,'[9] and what Bonhoeffer called 'the church for others.'[10]   Such an open, crucified church, existing for others, needs to be engaged, reflective, flexible, experimental, participatory and acquainted with grief. It should in the words of Riddell 'be open at the edges while committed at the core.'[11] Above all such a church will be culturally aware of the others who do not regard themselves as church and it will live to serve such others. In doing so, it will participate and experience the *zeitgeist* of its culture, understanding its song, its art, the habits of its leisure and spending, and the cry of its heart. If it is to be effective in re-igniting the fires of mission the church must be counter-cultural rather than anti-cultural; unafraid to welcome and affirm what is good in the world but also willing and able to present a living critique of the surrounding culture when it prevents people encountering God.[12]   It will live with and for others, it will seek peace and justice not just peace and quiet.[13]   In doing so it will be inherently missiological.

Meanwhile, in the popular culture of such others, spirituality is 'the new black.' It is the 'in-thing', the trendy word on people's lips from churches to wine bars and even into corporate business. In James Redfield's international best seller, *The Celestine Prophecy,* the nine insights discovered in an ancient Peruvian manuscript are said to lead each of us on a personal journey toward the cosmic energy that begets a new image of human life, and a positive vision of how we will save the planet, its creatures and its beauty.[14] These insights are entirely fictional but Redfield displays such a keen awareness of the condition of western humanity that

---

8   Kosuke Koyama. *Water Buffalo Theology.* p158-9
9   Jürgen Moltmann. *The Open Church.* SCM 1978
10   D. Bonhoeffer. *Letters and Papers from Prison.* SCM 1956. *Outline for a Book.* p166
11   Riddell. Ibid p151 The phrase is that of Riddell's own congregation and is quoted by him with approval.
12   Such a church would of course present an equally strict critique of itself.
13   This comparison was related during personal conversation with Norman Shanks, leader of the Iona Community, and originates with a volunteer working on Iona in 1999.
14   James Redfield. *The Celestine Prophecy.* Bantam. 1994.- inside front cover.

his books sell millions and workshops on their spirituality have now sprung up across the USA and beyond. As John Drane has commented on this approach to spirituality, 'what used to be the preserve of idealists who patronised wholefood shops, burned joss sticks and read eastern mystics – has now become big business.'[15]

But in the post-Christian, post-modern world, self-constructed personal paradigms of belief and life-style choices are the norm. In this world, hard theology may produce doctoral theses, mission may be approved (if not fully practiced), but it is spirituality that sells out print-runs in the bookshops. While such events have a undoubted missionary dimension (after all people are buying the books, going to the seminars etc) unfortunately, as Mark McIntosh notes, a quick tour of the spirituality section of any such bookshop will likely display 'all the proclivities for individualistic quests for something inner – inner self, inner child and even the inner wolf.' But he continues, 'in the consumerist consciousness of much of the northern hemisphere such shopping for a private inner world says little about the hard work of talking and living together and seems to correspond all too well with the enormous growth of private security firms.'[16] To follow down this popular but escapist path would generate a church of atomised 'inner-worlders.' Such people might comfortably gather around them a psuedo-community of like-minded individuals but it remains questionable if it will keep alive the fires of the missiological imperative which seeks to welcome and embrace those who are distinctly other than themselves, communally and concretely reflecting the love of God who embraced fallen humanity into communion with the Trinity. Leonardo Boff argues that, 'The Trinity avoids solitude, overcomes separation and surpasses exclusion. The Trinity allows identity, the Father – difference of identity, the Son – and the difference of difference, the Holy Spirit. The Trinity prevents face-to-face confrontation between Father and Son in a 'narcissistic' contemplation. The third figure is the difference, the openness, the communion.'[17] Such an exemplar of identity and community rejects an individualised spirituality that seeks either escape or self-fulfilment and embraces a missionary purpose that is public and costly.

---

15 John Drane. *Evangelism for a New Age.* Marshall Pickering. 1994. p15
16 Mark McIntosh. *Mystical Theology.* Blackwells. 1999. p5.
17 Leonardo Boff. *Trinity and Society.* Burns and Oates 1992. p3

Yet at the BIAMS conference in 2000, David Hay commented specifically on the growth of such atomised experiences. He noted that while church attendance had dropped 20% in ten years, the numbers of those interviewed who claimed to have a spiritual experience had increased almost 60%. As Hay noted, the dramatic increase in spiritual experience was probably little to do with more occurrences and more to do with the degree of social permission now granted for such events. But in Colin Greene's response he noted how contemporary western culture had inherited the secular division between the private and the public. Greene claimed that religion was out because it no longer provided a public vision of truth, meaning and human flourishing and so was identified with an increasingly marginalized, hierarchical, outmoded and now largely discredited institution called the church. On the other hand claimed Greene, 'spirituality is in because it pertains to the individual and hence private quest for some meaning and purpose to life.' [18] I suggest that such 'spirituality' is doomed to disappoint because it lacks the essential communal dimension that is longed for by humanity made in the image of a God who is a Community of Love. The Church, if it is to remain on fire, must have a mission spirituality that challenges such privatised inner quests and addresses the hard work of the world learning to live in harmony with God and others who are different to ourselves. Such a church might best begin by asking questions of its surrounding culture, not least. 'Why is the West turning spiritual?' or perhaps more accurately. 'Why is the West seeking to transcend itself?'

I offer one possible answer to that question. As Zygmunt Bauman has convincingly argued, science is no longer held in awe as the societal panacea.[19] Many people have lost faith in the hard empiricisms of modernity, the brave new world which Bonhoeffer famously declared had 'come of age' now finds itself deep in 'mid life crisis', anxiously wondering about the meaning of it all.[20] It is

---

18 See David Hay. *Spirituality of the un-churched.* and Colin Greene *Understanding People who Don't go to Church.* Both BIAMS 2000 Conference Papers
19 Zygmunt Bauman. *Mortality, Immortality and Other Life Strategies.* Polity 1992
20 If any need a indicator of these cultural shifts Richard Burridge has illustrated it well by contrasting the various 'generations' of Star Trek, which have moved from boldly going to the edges of outer space, to the need for the exploration of inner space and counselling in the next generation. In Deep Space Nine, we find a parable of our time as the spiritual world of the prophets of Bajor is contrasted with the rampant consumerism of the Ferangi Quark and the militarism of the Cardassians. The final generation, Voyager no longer explores the worlds beyond

almost clichéd to remark that people are now suspicious of the meta-narratives of scientific rationalism and institutionalised religion. In the west, as Drane notes, 'people are, for the most part 'post-modern' in a sociological sense rather than ideologically 'postmodern'. The end of our cultural love affair with modernity has come about more on pragmatic grounds than as a result of philosophical principle'[21] But such people *do* perceive themselves as fragmented and unconnected, separated from centres of power, from others, from creation and indeed, such de-centred individuals feel separated from their very selves.

People often feel that they no longer belong to anyone or anywhere in western society. Particularly in the underclass of society, fiscally marginalized from the opportunity of pseudo-transcendence through consumerism but reeling from the individualism that has broken former community solidarity, this can result in feelings of isolation, depression and suicide. Alternatively it may generate passionate and even violent tribalism.[22] Such people are unlikely to refer to this in terms of their 'spirituality' although I believe the term is still appropriate as it contains their essential pattern of living. Those for whom the term spirituality *has* become a common vocabulary are primarily the more affluent who address their fragmentation through the mystical. They embrace with enthusiasm the plethora of books, tapes, retreats and gurus on offer in the mushrooming market of things spiritual. Not all of this is Christian, but there is certainly an increased interest in spirituality within the church. However, as we have noted, running through much of this growth is a virulent consumer mentality that often displays escapist themes and a rampant individualism that favours therapy over theology.

But such private quests are a pseudo-spirituality that often deals only in escape or personal fulfilment. They assiduously avoid any encounter with the reality of otherness. They fail to realise that true spirituality is ultimately derived from the Trinity and hence can never be practised alone. Such escapism is then clearly not a

---

but having been flung to a distant quandrant of the universe they are desperately trying to return home. This journey is personalised by the attempts of an Emergency Medical Hologram and a former Borg machine to develop their human selves. Burridge. *Faith Odyssey. 2001.* Bible Reading Fellowship 2001.

21 John Drane. *Cultural Change and Biblical Faith* Paternoster. 2000 p94
22 As this was being written (July 2001) territorial / race riots were erupting in the North of England.

true Christian spirituality, it lacks both concreteness and communality and thus cannot do other but fail to rekindle the fires of a missionary movement. Kenneth Leech condemns it as 'a dangerous diversion from the living God, from the demands of justice, from engagement with reality.'[23] He laments how individualism has distorted Christian faith and discipleship so that, 'today spirituality is marketed as a product ... belonging only to ... the private life.' In contrast he asserts that 'At its very heart the Christian life and identity is a process of incorporation into a new social organism, a new community.' For Leech, any spirituality which does not incorporate social involvement is to some extent false,[24] for true 'spirituality cannot exist apart from this social context.'[25] Thus the Church needs to be both communal and socially engaged; a concrete reflection of the interior and exterior life of the Trinity.

Expanding on this theme McIntosh is concerned with, 'developing an understanding of spirituality as a discovery of the self precisely in encountering the divine and human other – who allow one neither to rest in a reassuring self image nor to languish in the prison of a false social construction of oneself.'[26] Thus spirituality is the transformation and discovery of the self through encounter. It is not about cultivating interior experiences but deals with a new network of communal relationships and perceptions that God makes possible.

How far away is McIntosh's definition of spirituality from an insightful description of mission? Surely mission is at its heart, the transformation and discovery of the self through encounter with God and others, establishing a new network of communal relationships and perceptions that God alone can make possible? In mistakenly assuming that mission was simply what the church did, particularly what the church did somewhere else, it lost much of the original meaning from its ancient Trinitarian understanding in which spirituality and mission are intertwined; the sending of the Son by the Father, the sending of the Holy Spirit by the Father and the Son and the paradigmatic internal relationship of self giving and receiving.

23 Kenneth Leech. *The Eye of the Storm*. DLT 1993. p3.
24 Leech ibid. p.15. Quoting with approval Robert Lambourne. *Contact* Spring 1974
25 Leech ibid. p. 3-5.
26 M. McIntosh. ibid. p6.

As Saunders Davies shows us elsewhere,[27] such a Trinitarian understanding is vital if the church is to live in life-affirming relationship with the Triune God and in God's image to embrace those who are other than ourselves in the world. Others such as Jürgen Moltmann, Miroslav Volf, and Paul Fiddes echo this theme.[28] Moltmann writes in *The Church in the Power of the Spirit*, 'It is not the church that has a mission to fulfil to the world; it is the mission of the Son and the Spirit through the Father that includes the church, creating church as it goes on its way.'[29] John Zizioulas adds that such a Trinitarian spirituality would involve, 'the emergence of an identity through a new set of relationships, those provided by the church as the communion of the spirit.'[30] If spirituality is to avoid private introspection and remain a shared experience committed to participating in the Missio Dei, transforming both church and its social context, then we must find a new identity through the relationships provided by the church as the communion of the spirit. But how will this be accomplished?

I want to suggest that the fires of spirituality and mission might be kept alight through a new monasticism that has at its core, relationships that concretely reflect the characteristics of both the immanent and economic lives of the Trinity. Accordingly it will not see equality with God, other individuals or communities as something to be grasped but rather will give itself in service to God and those other than itself. Furthermore, while this new monasticism might share with the old a celebration of the above values that stand in contradistinction to those of the world, this will also be a new way of living clearly distinguishable from traditional monasticism. The traditional monastic life, in all its many and various forms, eremitic and coenobitic alike, has historically sought to exist removed from the world and even apart from the institutional Church. The new monasticism will be one wherein communities seek to redeem the world and renew the Church by

---

27 Saunders Davies. *Mission and Spirituality for Life*. (Supra pp.29 – 42).
28 Jürgen Moltmann *Church in the Power of the Spirit*. SCM. 1975.
    Miroslav Volf *After Our Likeness; The church as the image of the Trinity* . Eerdmanns. 1998.
    Paul Fiddes, *Participating in God; A Pastoral Doctrine of the Trinity*. Westminster. John Knox Press. 2001.
29 Moltmann. Ibid. p64.
30 John D. Zizioulas. *The Early Christian Community in Christian Spirituality in World Spirituality An Encyclopaedic History of the Religious Quest Vol. 16* Crossroad. 1987. Quoted in McIntosh. ibid p7.

choosing to live within them both as 'colonies of heaven.'[31] Hauerwas and Willimon helpfully remind us that 'a colony is a beachhead, an outpost, an island of one culture in the middle of another, a place where the values of home are reiterated and passed on to the young, a place where the distinctive language and lifestyle of the resident aliens are lovingly nurtured and reinforced.'[32] Through living in this way the new monasticism would maintain a proper interaction of spirituality and mission that remains contextually engaged, creatively expressed, communally experienced within the usual complexities of everyday life.[33] Thus, in being fully engaged with the plural realities of Church and World, a new monasticism might keep the home fires of God's people burning in the 21st century.

Such a project will require sensitive and capable guides, guides who might gather our fragmented epiphanies into new communities and make sense of what is being said, spiritually and missiologically, to the church today. I propose two such guides. Both have advocated the need for a 'new monasticism.' One is the German pastor and theologian Dietrich Bonhoeffer.[34] It was Bonhoeffer who saw the home fires of German Lutheranism going out in the face of Nazism. He critiqued the church of his day for failing to be truly missionary in nature and so failing to be of any use to the world around it. In May 1944 he identified the same malady of structures predicated on survival as we have already noted above. Bonhoeffer wrote; 'Our Church, which has been fighting in these years only for its self preservation, as though it were an end in itself, is incapable of taking the word of reconciliation and redemption to mankind and the world. Our earlier words are therefore bound to lose their force.'[35] Bonhoeffer added prophetically that future Christians would be limited to two things, 'prayer and action on behalf of others.' It is in such a

---

31 Stanley Hauerwas and William Willimon note how Moffat translates *politeuma* in Phil.3:20 as 'we are a *colony* of heaven.' These would not be religious retreats from the world but like Jesus would be a presence in the midst of the world. This image has also been helpfully adopted also by Ian Bradley see below, footnote 59. Hauerwas/ Willimon. *Resident Aliens.* Abingdon. 1989. p11.

32 Hauerwas and Willimon. Ibid. p12.

33 These are many of the qualities Riddell regards as vital for a spirituality for mission today. See Michael Riddell Ibid. p131ff.

34 David Ford has recently said that D. Bonhoeffer might well be the 20th century theologian who is most fruitful for the 21st century. *Bonhoeffer Holiness and Ethics.* Durham Lecture 18th May 2000

35 Bonhoeffer. *Letters and Papers from Prison.* Thoughts on Baptism. p160.

fashion, within a new monasticism, that spirituality and mission are re-united.

Our second guide is less well-known, but his legacy is perhaps as vital as that of Bonhoeffer if we are to examine how spirituality and mission might interact for the renewal of the church and the furtherance of the Missio Dei. This guide is George MacLeod, founder of the Iona Community.

Both Bonhoeffer and MacLeod came from privileged social backgrounds but became champions of the poor and powerless. Both men rejected the privatised pietism condemned by Leech and McIntosh and sought a public and private interaction of spirituality and mission. Both guides advocated doing so through a new experiment in communal living; a new monasticism.

In 1937 Bonhoeffer established a seminary in which to train pastors for the German Confessing Church. Such work was banned by the Nazi regime and faced imminent destruction at their hands. Yet Bonhoeffer did not predicate his seminary on modes of survival but the Trinitarian characteristics of openness to others and action on their behalf. Prior to opening the seminary he wrote, 'the renewal of the church will come from a new form of monasticism which has in common with the old only an uncompromising allegiance to the sermon the mount.'[36]

When Bonhoeffer spoke of a 'new monasticism' he was not arguing for a return to separatist, cloistered life, indeed he proposed the opposite; new monasticism was to be the locus for a discipleship that brought mission and spirituality together so that Christians might be fully engaged with the world, 'drinking the earthly life to the dregs.'[37]

In the two years before it was closed by the Gestapo, Finken- walde seminary became the laboratory for Bonhoeffer's thinking on this new monasticism.[38] Although Bonhoeffer rejected any

---

36 Bonhoeffer. Letter dated 14/1/1935. *Gesammelte Schriften* Vol III. Munich 1974 p25. See also Letter to Erwin Sutz dated 11th September 1934. In G. Kelly and F. Burton Nelson *Testament to Freedom*. Harper Collins 1995 p412.
37 Bonhoeffer. *Letters and Papers from Prison June 27th 1944*. In doing this Bonhoeffer may well have been guilty of stereotyping the 'old monasticism,' paying too little regard to its many and various historical manifestations. The author welcomes comments on this aspect of the paper.
38 This is written up in the books, *Life Together*, (*Cost of*) *Discipleship* and *Spiritual Care*.

suggestion of the students taking formal vows, during the six months each group lived in Finkenwalde, it became for them, not only a place of theological teaching, but also a community of prayer, meditation, discipleship and confession as well as a home for recreation and relaxation. In short it became a colony of heaven, where Bonhoeffer's theological maxim of 'the church existing as Christ in community'[39] could become a reality. It was a community in which a section of humanity was being remade and redeemed through being in relationship with God and with one another. Community life was summed up in the phrase 'being-with-each-other and being-for-each other.'[40] After each group of students had left and later when the seminary was finally closed, Bonhoeffer and others continued to maintain this being-with-and-for-others by writing letters of encouragement, hints on sermons and relaying prayer requests. Unfortunately, the execution of Bonhoeffer in 1945 effectively brought this specific aspect of the experiment in new monasticism to an end. However, the spirit of this new monasticism continued in the lives of the Finkenwalde students who survived the war and, through the books Bonhoeffer wrote about this period, particularly *Life Together*, its spirit has continued to challenge and inspire other similar communities.[41]

Indeed in his *Letters from Prison* Bonhoeffer himself hinted at how others might continue to practice such a new monasticism. He thought that in the future 'our being Christians will be limited to two things: prayer and action for justice;' his claim that 'All Christian thinking, speaking and organising must be born anew out of this prayer and action,'[42] was predicated on a communal spirituality that sought to be and act for others. The midwife of the church rebirth would be a new monasticism.

A similar experiment was begun by George MacLeod in the 1930's and is flourishing today; this is the Iona Community. Like Bonhoeffer, MacLeod 'definitely barred the cloistered life'[43] but

---

39 Bonhoeffer *Sanctorum Communio* DBWE. Vol 1. p121 Fortress Press 1998.

40 The maxim has its origins in Bonhoeffer's Habilitationsschrift where he conceived freedom as being free for the other because one is bound to the other. See *Creation and Fall* DBWE Vol 3. Fortress Press 1997. p62-3.

41 In the early days of the Iona Community Bonhoeffer's *Life Together* was almost mandatory reading. In the UK alone, Bonhoeffer's comments on a new monasticism have been influential in the more recently formed Northumbria Community and the Community of Aidan and Hilda.

42 Bonhoeffer. *Letters and Papers From Prison.* Ibid. Baptismal Letter. p160.

43 George MacLeod. *The Coracle* October 1938 p 12.

hoped that "without anyone taking "permanent vows" without withdrawing from the world, we want to see if an industrial undertaking – however small - can be launched in which we are still "in the world" but a little less "of it.""[44]   Although not consciously drawing on Bonhoeffer, the new monasticism of the Iona Community places a high value on his combination of prayer and action for justice. The Community has its roots in ministry among the inner city poverty of the 1930's. It began in a similar way to Finkenwalde, as an experimental community for the training of ministers who would renew both Church and World. [45] Originally it was intended to have a rolling membership, each new member would remain in the community for a few years until they had completed a curacy of team ministry in an inner city housing scheme. It has now become a community of around 240 members, laity and clergy, whose ambition is 'to seek new ways to touch the hearts of all.'[46]

The new monasticisms of Finkenwalde and Iona were originally conceived as temporary periods of preparation for an engaged discipleship of integrated spirituality and mission. While both groups were geographically specific for a short and intense period they were always intended to become a dispersed community of members fully involved in the life of Church and World. In this both groups were at odds with the traditional perception of monasticism as people under vows living in seclusion for the world. Yet, despite the intended temporary nature of the community, what Iona soon discovered was that their dispersed members continued to belong to one another even after the completion of their curacy. A community whose values and relationships were formed in the image of the Trinity would not dissolve so easily. Many longed to continue and deepen their experience of belonging in a more permanent community, albeit

---

44 George MacLeod. *The Coracle* May 1939 p 20. Indeed regarding allegations that the community were playing at being monks MacLeod wrote, that they were 'an exceedingly calculated movement within the normal purpose of the Church. Poverty is not our aim, far less is the principle of celibacy involved. Those who come here claim no sacrifice; we only claim a privilege to make perhaps the sacrifice of those who work in really difficult places a little less acute.' Ibid. p18.

45 Although this is true to MacLeod's vision, right from its inception the community also included the lay craftsmen as full members. These men stayed on to build through out the year after the ministers departed for inner city ministry at the end of the summer. They would still be working there when the next year of divinity graduates arrived the following spring.

46 Miles Christi. Rule of the Iona Community.

one that remained geographically dispersed. Members wanted to be-with-and-for-others who, like themselves, were seeking to bring together mission and spirituality in their local situations. There was a need to know others and to be known by such others. The new monasticism in which Bonhoeffer had placed his hope for the future church began to grow in the Iona Community because it offered people a place in which they might belong, a place where new ways of integrating mission and spirituality could be risked and new fires set alight. In effect, despite the initial temporary purposes for such communities, once those within them had glimpsed something of the reality of relationships that sought to concretely image the life of the Trinity, they could not stop belonging.

As former paradigms of belonging collapse, as the family, the street, the parish etc fragment and disperse, the self-constructed and individualistic attempts at transcendence referred to above as pseudo-spirituality have not satisfied the human longing to belong. An indication of our malaise can be found at Amazon dot com. There, one of the most popular books is John O'Donohue's *Eternal Echoes*. It is subtitled *Exploring our Hunger To Belong*. It is dedicated to 'those who inhabit lives where belonging is torn and longing is numbed.'[47] Its popularity indicates how deeply many feel that they no longer have a place where they belong and how their longings have been anaesthetised by consumerism and triviality. Mary Grey suggests that such people long to be engaged in the task of soul making. Soul making involves gathering the widely scattered elements of ourselves on personal, communal and socio-political levels into caring community.[48] Gathering such fragments is the beginning of belonging and is the remaking of our souls. In the fragmented and increasingly mobile lives of contemporary church and culture, a new monasticism involved in such soul making may offer an alternative and more workable interpretation of the traditional monastic vow of stability.

Bonhoeffer recognised the need for the stabilising influence of such soul making and noted the need for it to take place within new communities.[49] In the isolation of his prison cell he lamented

---

47 John O'Donohue. *Eternal Echoes*. Bantam Press 1998

48 Mary Grey. *Beyond the dark Night*. Mowbray. 1997. p15

49 For Bonhoeffer, the image of God in which humanity is created was not some property inherent to the individual, but the relationship between people. This relationship was established in the unbroken community relationship of creation.

how his life had been fragmented by political history and wrote 'The important thing today, however, is that people should be able to discern from the fragment of our life how the whole was arranged and planned.'[50]

Central to the practice of fragment gathering and of living in the image of the Trinity is Bonhoeffer's theme of the polyphonic life. Drawing on musical theory Bonhoeffer suggests that the *cantus firmus* of our lives is found in loving God. It is around this root theme that the fragmented counterpoints of living and loving in our particular contexts are then arranged.[51] Bonhoeffer says this *cantus firmus* 'is to be sought both *in thought and practical living* in an integrated attitude to life. The person who allows themselves to be torn into fragments by events and problems has not passed the test for the present and the future.'[52] If the church is to pass the test for the present and the future, the common denominator must surely be its combining of 'thought and practical living', its integration of spirituality and mission. Both Bonhoeffer and MacLeod recognised the need for this to take place in new monasticisms, communities of soul making. Only when living stably, rooted in a Trinitarian reflection of belonging- with-and-for others, would people be sufficiently empowered and free to take risks of thinking and practical living that were needed for the renewal of themselves, the Church and World.[53] Such risks began to be taken in the new monasticism of the Iona Community.

However after the Fall, such relationship could only be rediscovered through being in community with Christ, being in the redeemed community of the church. See *Creation and Fall.* Ibid. Generally.

50 Bonhoeffer *Letter and Papers From Prison.* Ibid Letter dated *23/2/1944. p75.*

51 *Letters and Papers From Prison. 20/5/1944.* See a recent discussion of this theme by David Ford *Self and Salvation* Cambridge 1999 Chapter 10 and for its relationship to Trinitarian thinking see David S. Cunningham. *These Three Are One. The Practice of Trinitarian Theology.* Blackwell 1998 p130 ff

52 Bonhoeffer. *Letters and Papers from Prison.* Letter dated, *29&30/1/44.* Here he actually refers to 'the common denominator is to be sought...' but the idea remains essentially that expressed elsewhere in the prison thinking as a 'cantus firmus.'

53 Despite Bonhoeffer's claims that 'new monasticism' would be unlike that of traditional monastic practice, parallels with the traditional vow of 'conversio morum' are apparent both in Bonhoeffer's own work at Finkenwalde and in the Iona Community. This is perhaps inevitable and welcome, given that Bonhoeffer, MacLeod and the early monastics all share a deep love of the Sermon on the Mount. Where the new monasticism remains novel is its commitment to remain as part of the Church and World and in its primarily dispersed membership with concomitant devolved accountability.

Iona Community members were soon joined by a network of financial supporters and a branch of Associates who met for prayer and discussion. Youth and women associates soon followed. The new monasticism of thought and practical living began to flourish. These developments arose not because the Community planned them but because in the words of a former community leader, 'hungry people were looking for bread.'[54] People wanted, needed, to belong. As members from different occupations and denominations sought to remain in community while living at distance from one another, they discussed what it was that placed them in a relationship of being-with-and-for-each-other. The answer was, as with early monastics, a Common Rule by which they agreed to live. This Common Rule was not the lifelong vows of traditional monasticism but it did enable mutual support and accountability for a disciplined Christian life. As with Bonhoeffer's students at Finkenwalde, the Iona Rule consists of a commitment to daily prayer and Bible study including a monthly cycle of prayer for members, the world and areas of community concern. Belonging is enabled by new members sharing in a two-year induction programme, together with regular monthly meetings as local family groups and quarterly plenary gatherings one of which is a week on Iona itself. Members also commit to account to one another for the use of their money, as well as how they have planned and accounted for their use of time. The Rule also includes a commitment to work for peace, justice and the integrity of creation.[55] Each year members have to consider whether they wish to renew these commitments.

Support for such variations on the theme of new monasticism has been steadily growing. Andrew Walker, who has argued that the current broad church is bereft of plausibility in the post-modern world, advocates a return to structures akin to the monastery, the religious community and even the sect, albeit without becoming sectarian.[56] This is what Hauerwas and Willimon have in mind

---

54 Ron Ferguson. *Chasing the Wild Goose. The Story of the Iona Community*. Wild Goose Publications. 1998. p62.
55 One important difference with the Iona Community is its reversal of the usual pattern of monastic life in that few of those working 'on site' on Iona are members of the Community. Most members remain scattered throughout the UK and beyond.
56 Andrew Walker. *Telling the Story*. 1996. p190. Walker rightly notes that a Church organised on sectarian lines need not be theologically deviant or cultish (p191) but stresses the need for gathered communities of committed believers to be properly initiated into a body dedicated to living gospel values. (p193-4).

when they talk of Christians living as 'resident aliens and as colonies of heaven.'[57] Ian Bradley, adopting the title 'Colonies of Heaven' similarly argues that the renewal of the church might well lie in such new monasticisms. Drawing on Celtic models of Christian monasticism Bradley specifically notes the growing numbers of dispersed communities like Iona who live by a common rule[58] and argues that 'in the post modern pick and mix spiritual supermarket people are actually craving commitment, discipline and obedience.'[59] Norman Shanks, leader of the Iona Community agrees that the demanding five fold rule of the Community is one of its strongest 'selling points' offering the possibility of discipline, within increasingly highly pressured lives.[60] Indeed R.J. Foster has even argued that the traditional monastic disciplines of poverty, chastity, and obedience might be successfully reworked by the laity in lives committed to simplicity, fidelity and service. These would form strongly counter-cultural alternatives to a world based upon money, sex and power.[61] Thus, while the call to traditional monastic living is in decline (as indeed are numbers attending the institutional churches) there is an increasing appeal exercised by dispersed communities incorporating some form of disciplined and counter cultural life.[62] While Walker is correct to add that commitment to such a disciplined life

---

57 S. Hauerwas and W. Willimon. Ibid. p11-12.

58 Others might include The Living Way, Epsom, The Community of Aidan and Hilda, The Northumbria Community and the Corrymeela Community. It is accepted that the simple fact of their growth does not in itself validate their legitimacy but their continued expansion does raise questions as to the future *loci* of Christian spirituality and mission.

59 Ian Bradley. *Colonies of Heaven*. DLT 2000. p55. See also Ray Simpson, in *Exploring Celtic Spirituality* Hodder and Stoughton 1995. p41ff. Hauerwas and Willimon helpfully note that 'a colony is a beachhead, an outpost, an island of one culture in the middle of another, a place where the values of home are reiterated and passed on to the young, a place where the distinctive language and lifestyle of the resident aliens are lovingly nurtured and reinforced. *Resident Aliens*. Abingdon Press.1989. p12.

60 Norman Shanks *Iona God's Energy*. Hodder and Stoughton. 1999. p65.

61 R.J. Foster. *Money Sex & Power; The Challenge to the Disciplined Life*. Hodder and Stoughton. 1985. An original view on how this might be implemented within the Church may be found in Matt Rees, *Changing our Habits* an unpublished M Litt. dissertation for St Andrews University written under the supervision of Ian Bradley, 2000.

62 Bradley notes an increasing number and appeal of places of particular spiritual attraction, Iona, Lindisfarne, St Deiniol's Library etc where people visit for varying periods of time to develop their faith and argues that such centres may now be more appropriate and appealing than the existing model of church as building and institution. Ibid p53.

needs 'constant social reinforcement,' by which may be understood communal affirmation and accountability, this dimension should be acknowledged not simply for its pragmatism, but because communities in which individuals are affirmed and released to become fully themselves correctly images the life of a God who is Three Person in One and One God in Three Persons. Thus, what makes Christian communities such as Iona different from other gatherings of people is their constant concrete reaffirmation, through word and deed, that the life of the community is rooted in the life of the Trinity. Such new monastic communities become icons of the Trinity, ambassadors of spirituality and mission, calling the Church to renewal and presenting a concrete expression of God to the World.

Neither Bonhoeffer nor MacLeod advocated a 'new monasticism' for the sake of warm fuzzy moments shared between friends. Nor was it to validate a 'siege mentality church', desperate to separate from the world. Their mission looked outwards to the world, not inwards to itself. For Bonhoeffer, 'the church only existed when she existed for others, not when fighting for its preservation.[63] Mission and spirituality in the new monasticism would be concrete and incarnational, there could be no escapist 'flight to the invisible'.[64] He would have approved of MacLeod's story of the church window in which a vandal's stone had changed the stained glass message from 'Glory to God in the Highest' to reveal the truth of 'Glory to God in the High St.' He would have blessed a new monasticism dedicated to finding 'new ways to touch the hearts of all.' He would have been in accord with a community which acknowledges that commitment to social transformation is no more than 'a pious hope and a false witness unless they as individuals and together seek to put it into practice.'[65]

If space permitted, we might have explored how the hearts of all are being touched by the Iona Community and how closely they correlate with Bonhoeffer's theology. This would include ecumenism and especially its role in the renewal of worship. It would also include pacifism, as well as a commitment to what Bonhoeffer called 'the view from below'; poverty, racism, human

---

63 Bonhoeffer. *Letters and Papers from Prison.* Ibid Baptism Letter. p160.
64 Bonhoeffer. *Cost of Discipleship.* SCM 1959 p106.
65 Miles Christe. p22

rights etc.[66] It would also include a discussion of ecological concerns and finally the vital issue of personal holiness.

We will never know how the new monasticism proposed by Bonhoeffer might have developed had he lived. However his prediction for its importance to church and society in our time, not least its role in reuniting spirituality and mission, seems uncannily accurate. The Iona community is certainly an example of what it *might* have looked like. It is not the only example we might have chosen and indeed in 1939 MacLeod himself recognised that Iona 'was not a model that must at once be applied to all industry but as a symbol of the essential principle to which somehow we must all get back.'[67] I believe it well illustrates the value of a dispersed community of Christians engaged in bringing together mission and spirituality for the renewal of church and society. In 1988, the Golden Jubilee of the Iona Community, its then leader commented, 'The need for a supportive network of people committed to radical spirituality and radical politics will grow and will require to operate both within and outwith the institutional church ... God has provided resources for us beyond our limited imaginings. The resources are there for a purpose – building and rebuilding the common life.'[68]

New monasticisms such as Iona are leading the way in helping people build and belong to a common life rooted in God. In such a common life, spirituality and mission come together in the image of the Trinity for the renewal of the church and the salvation of the world. It is perhaps not too optimistic to believe that such new monasticisms may contain the relationships and places in which the church in the west could once again exist by mission; that its home fires would again be burning.

---

66 See particularly Bonhoeffer comments on the view from below in *Letters and Papers from Prison*. After Ten Years. Ibid. p134ff

66 Norman Shanks. Ibid. p38

67 George MacLeod. *The Coracle*. May 1939 p20.

68 Shanks. Ibid. p38.

SELECT BIBLIOGRAPHY

A M Allchin & E de Waal (eds.): *Threshold of Light: prayers and praises from the Celtic tradition* (DLT, 1986)

D Barrett: *World Christian Encyclopaedia* (OUP, 1982)

S Barrow & G Smith (eds): *Christian Mission in Western Society* (CTBI, 2001)

Zigmunt Bauman: *Liquid Modernity* (Blackwell, 2000)

D Bebbington: *Evangelicalism in Modern Britain* (Allen & Unwin, 1989)

B Beit-Hallahmi & M Argyle: *The Psychology of Religious Behaviour, Belief and Experience* (Routledge, 1997)

L Boff: *Trinity & Society* (Burns & Oates, 1992)

D Bonhoeffer: *Life Together* (SCM, 1954)
    Letters and Papers from Prison (SCM, 1956)
    Cost of Discipleship (SCM, 1959)

D Bosch: *Transforming Mission: paradigm shifts in the theology of mission* (Orbis, 1991)

C Braaten: *A Flaming Centre: a theology of the Christian mission* (Fortress, 1977)

I Bradley: *Colonies of Heaven* (DLT, 2000)

P Brierley (ed): *Religious Trends No 2: 1999-2000* (Christian Research, 2000)

W Bühlman: *The Coming of the Third Church* (Orbis, 1978)

W R Burrows: *New Ministries: the global context* (Orbis, 1980)

S Coleman: *The Globalisation of Charismatic Christianity* (CUP, 2000)

G Cook (ed): *New Face of the Church in Latin America* (Orbis, 1994)

D S Cunningham: *These three are one: the practice of Trinitarian theology* (Blackwell, 1998)

D W Dayton: *Theological Roots of Pentecostalism* (Scarecrow Press, NJ, 1987)

J Drane: *Evangelism for a New Age* (Marshall Pickering, 1994)
    Cultural Change and the Biblical Faith (Paternoster, 2000)

J D G Dunn: *Jesus and the Spirit* (Eerdman's, 1997)

R Ferguson: *Chasing the Wild Goose: the story of the Iona community* (Wild Goose Publications, 1998)

P Fiddes: *Participating in God: a pastoral doctrine of the Trinity* (John Knox Press, 2001)

J Finney: *Recovering the Past: Celtic and Roman Mission* (DLT, 1996)

A Giddens: *The Consequences of Modernity* (Polity Press, 1990)

Mary Grey: *Beyond the Dark Night: a way forward for the Church* (Cassell, 1997)

C Gunton: *The Promise of Trinitarian theology* (T & T Clark, 1991)
    The Outrageous Pursuit of Hope (DLT, 2000)

Alister Hardy: *The Divine Flame: an essay towards a natural history of religion* (Collins, 1966)

D Hay: '"The Biology of God": what is the current status of Hardy's hypothesis?' *International Journal of the Psychology of Religion,* vol 4, no 1 (1994) pp 1-23

D Hay & G Heald: 'Religion is good for you' *New Society* (17 April 1987)

D Hay & G Nye: *The Spirit of the Child* (Harper Collins, 1998)

D Hay & K Hunt: *Understanding the Spirituality of people who don't go to church* (University of Nottingham, 2000)

J A Kirk: *Liberation Theology: an evangelical view from the Third World* (MMS, 1979)

P Lakeland: *Postmodernity: Christian Identity in a fragmented age* (Fortress, 1997)

K Leech: *The Eye of the Storm* (DLT, 1993)

D Lehman: *Struggle for the Spirit: religious transformation and popular culture in Brazil and Latin America* (Polity Press, 1996)

L Luzbetak: *The Church and Cultures: new perspectives in missiological anthropology* (Orbis, 1998)

C L Mariz: *Copy their poverty: Pentecostals and Christian communities in Brazil* (Temple UP, 1994)

David Martin: *Tongues of Fire* (Blackwell, 1990)

J McClure & R Collins: *Bede: the Ecclesiastical History of the English People* (OUP, 1994)

M McIntosh: *Mystical Theology* (Blackwell, 1999)

A McRobbie: *Postmodernism and popular culture* (Routledge, 1994)

John Milbank: *Theology and Social Theory* (Blackwell, 1993)

J Moltmann: *The Spirit of Life* (SCM, 1992)

Parker Palmer: *The Courage to Teach* (Jossey Bass, 1998)

J Parratt: *Reinventing Christianity: African theology today* (Eerdman's, 1995)

P Richter & L Francis: *Gone but not Forgotten* (Richter & Francis, 1998)

M Riddell: *Threshold of the Future* (SPCK, 1998)

W C Roof: *Spiritual Marketplace* (Princeton UP, 1999)

A Ross: *A Vision Betrayed: the Jesuits in Japan and China 1542-1742* (Edinburgh UP, 1994)

W Saayman & K Kritzinger: *Mission in bold humility: David Bosch's work considered* (Orbis, 1996)

N Shanks: *Iona: God's Energy* (Hodder, 1999)

P Sheldrake: *Living between worlds; place and journey in Celtic spirituality* (DLT, 1995)

Spirituality and Theology (DLT, 1998)

A Shorter & Joseph Njiru: *New Religious Movements in Africa* (Pauline Publications, Nairobi, 2001)

R Simpson: *Exploring Celtic Spirituality* (Hodder, 1995)

Brian Stanley: *History of the Baptist Missionary Society 1792-1992* (T & T Clark, 1992)

D Stoll: *Is Latin America turning Protestant?* (University of California, 1990)

J V Taylor: *The Go-between God: the Holy Spirit and the Christian Mission* (SCM, 1972)

M Vasquez: *The Brazilian Popular Church and the Crisis of Modernity* (CUP, 1998)

Miroslav Volf: *After our likeness: the Church as the Image of the Trinity* (Eerdman's, 1998)

E de Waal: *A life-giving way: a commentary on the rule of St Benedict* (Liturgical Press, 1995)

The Celtic way of Prayer (Doubleday, 1999)

A world made whole: rediscovering the Celtic tradition (Fount, 1991)

Kallistos Ware: *The Orthodox Way* (St Vladimir's Seminary Press, 1995)

P Ward: *God at the Mall* (Hendrickson, 1999)

R J Woods: *The Spirituality of the Celtic Saints* (Orbis, 2000)

Timothy Yates: *Christian Mission in the Twentieth Century* (CUP, 1994)

(ed) *Mission - an Invitation to God's future* (Cliff College, 2000)

J D Zizioulas: *Being as Communion: studies in personhood and the Church* (DLT, 1985)

MISSION
- AN INVITATION TO GOD'S FUTURE
Edited by
Timothy Yates

Papers by Jürgen Moltmann, Theo Sundermeier, Christopher
Rowland and Anton Wessels

What is the shape of the Christian mission to be in
the 21st century?

This is an especially pressing question in Europe,
which appears to be increasingly de-Christianised. In
this collection of papers, some of the leading thinkers
on mission in Europe address such issues as the
theological foundation for mission, the place of
dialogue with other faiths, the use of the arts in the
cause of mission and questions of post-modernity.

"Exactly the kind of theological writing which can inspire
the ministerial practitioner" *Expository Times*

"Essential" *Missiology*

"Addresses issues of real concern to ministers and
churches" *Regent's Review*

"Good food for a new century" *Theology*

CLIFF COLLEGE
PUBLISHING
2000

ISBN 1 898362 25 4
Price £9.95

A companion volume to

MISSION and SPIRITUALITY
CREATIVE WAYS OF BEING CHURCH